A Revolution of Their Own

A Revolution of Their Own

Voices of Women in Soviet History

edited by
Barbara Alpern Engel and
Anastasia Posadskaya-Vanderbeck

translated by
Sona Hoisington

WestviewPress
A Division of HarperCollinsPublishers

Copyright © 1998 by Westview Press, A Division of HarperCollins Publishers, Inc.

Published in 1998 in the United States of America by Westview Press, 5500 Central Avenue, Boulder, Colorado 80301-2877, and in the United Kingdom by Westview Press, 12 Hid's Copse Road, Cumnor Hill, Oxford OX2 9JJ

Library of Congress Cataloging-in-Publication Data
A revolution of their own : voices of women in Soviet history / edited
   by Barbara Alpern Engel and Anastasia Posadskaya-Vanderbeck :
   translated by Sona Hoisington.
      p.   cm.
   Includes bibliographical references and index.
   ISBN 0-8133-3365-2. — ISBN 0-8133-3366-0 (pbk.)
      1. Women—Soviet Union—Social conditions—Case studies.   2. Women
and communism—Soviet Union—Case studies.   3. Women—Soviet Union—
Biography.   I. Engel, Barbara Alpern.   II. Posadskaya, Anastasia.
HQ1662.R43   1998
305.42'092'247—dc21   97-26662
                                                                              CIP

The paper used in this publication meets the requirements of the American National Standard for Permanence of Paper for Printed Library Materials Z39.48-1984.

10   9   8   7   6   5   4   3   2   1

Contents

Acknowledgments

This book never would have come into being without the help of an international feminist network—the network that brought the two of us into contact in the first place, initially at a Berkshire Conference on Women's History and then a conference on "Women and Russia," held in Helsinki, Finland, where we first explored the possibility of this shared endeavor. In the project's initial stages, Colette Shulman and Katrina VandenHeuvel provided inspiration, encouragement, and invaluable advice, while Anastasia Posadskaya's colleagues at the Center for Gender Studies and the Institute for Socioeconomic Studies of Population in Moscow offered institutional and intellectual support. Russia's nascent feminist network proved vital to Posadskaya as she sought to locate narrators and arrange interviews. She is deeply grateful for the invaluable assistance of Tatiana Frolova of Tomsk, Lidiia Fleisher and Margarita Karpechko of the Zarechnyi-Sverdlovsk region, Rimma Menadzhieva and Ella Vorobeva of Ekaterinburg, Eleonora Ivanova and Natella Zinchenko of Moscow, and Nina Voevodina of Novozybkov. The recommendations of these women gained Posadskaya entry into people's homes, where the women waited patiently through the interviews, and afterward provided Posadskaya with their best accommodations for the night. We also thank Joan Wallach Scott for a perceptive and helpful reading of an earlier version of the introduction and the afterword. Sona Hoisington immediately caught the spirit of this project and has served as an able and genial translator from the first. Her insights have contributed in many ways to the book.

A grant from the John D. and Catherine T. MacArthur Foundation funded most of the work, including the interviewing, the transcription of interviews, and the translation. During the months when the interviews were being edited and annotated, Barbara Engel received support from the Rutgers Center for Historical Analysis and Anastasia Posadskaya was supported by the Institute for Advanced Study (Princeton) and the Institute for Research on Women (Rutgers). Posadskaya is grateful to Joan Wallach Scott and Cora Kaplan for their warm welcome. Our thanks as well to Volodia Konovalov, who served as a most able transcriber, and to Larisa Fedorova, Tania Troinova, and Mark Rosenberg, who assisted Posadskaya with the mechanics of transcription, copying, and in particular, printing with a printer that refused to do its job. Tania Troinova also helped Posadskaya to communicate with our narrators by telephone, fax, and post. In the last stages of preparing the book for publication, Posadskaya received assistance from Kevin, Paul, Don, Laura, and Michael of C. J. Vanderbeck and Son, Inc., while Engel relied on Patricia Murphy of the University of Colorado history department, who prepared the manuscript for publication, and on Betty Jo Thorson, who kept the office going so that Engel had time to complete the work.

Anastasia Posadskaya also thanks her "feminist mother," British researcher Cynthia Cockburn, who first interested her in feminist methods of sociological analysis; and Ronald Greele, of Columbia University, and Paul Thompson, of Oxford, both of whom encouraged her interest in oral history and provided advice on the techniques and methodology of interviewing. Her deepest gratitude goes to those closest to her—her mother, Tamara Albertovna, her husband, Michael, and her daughters, Genia and Dorothy—for always loving, understanding, and supporting her. Barbara Engel warmly thanks LeRoy Moore, who cheerfully accompanied her on the various excursions that this work required and listened with genuine interest to countless conversations about Russian women and the Soviet experience.

Finally, the two of us are grateful for the serendipity that brought us together. Creating this book has been a joy from start to finish. Our collaboration has provoked much laughter as well as many stimulating conversations. It has prompted us to rethink what we believed we knew, deepening our understanding of the lives and circumstances of the women whose stories unfold in these pages. The work has given us the gift of friendship.

All royalties from the sale of this book will be directed to projects assisting Russian women, with the generous support of the Global Fund for Women, 2480 Sand Hill Road, Suite 100, Menlo Park, California 94025–6941.

Barbara Alpern Engel
Anastasia Posadskaya-Vanderbeck

Glossary

Bolshevik(s): The party that took power in Russia in October 1917, founding a socialist state that later would become the Soviet Union.

Central Committee: The central decision-making body of the Communist Party of the Soviet Union.

ChON: Acronym for Extraordinary Units on Special Assignment, which were military formations composed of party members, Komsomol members, and sympathizers.

commissar: A party worker who served in the Soviet army and was responsible for ideological work among officers and soldiers.

Council of People's Deputies: A popularly elected governing body of the Soviet Union.

CPSU: Communist Party of the Soviet Union

detskii dom/detdom: Children's shelter.

FZU/fabzavuch: A Soviet factory school for workers and peasants that combined education with vocational training.

gorispolkom: The executive committee of a city council of people's deputies, a popularly elected body.

guberniia: Province in tsarist Russia.

gymnasium: An eight-year high school that provided a traditional education, generally including the study of classical languages (Greek or Latin), before the revolution.

intelligentsia: In the tsarist era, socially concerned members of the educated elite.

International Department (of the CPSU Central Committee): A division of the Communist party that dealt with foreign communists and Communist parties.

KB: Construction design office.

kolkhoz: A collective farm.

Komsomol: Short for the League of Young Communists, which in the 1920s accepted members between the ages of fourteen and twenty-three. In Russian, a male member of the Komsomol was called a *komsomolets,* and a female, a *komsomolka.*

kulak: A supposedly prosperous peasant.

KUNZ: Communist University for Workers from the West.

KUTV: Communist University for Workers from the East.

NEP: The New Economic Policy was inaugurated by Bolshevik leader V. I. Lenin in 1921. Under this new policy, some aspects of the free market were reintroduced into Russia's command economy, which had been devastated by war, in order to restore economic well-being and win the loyalty of the peasantry.

NKVD: Beginning in 1934, this acronym referred to the political police.

obkom: A regional committee of the Communist party.

oblast: A province during the Soviet period.

OGPU: From 1928–1932, this acronym was used in referring to the political police.

orgfakultet: A managing committee.

Pioneers: The communist youth organization for ten- to fourteen-year-olds.

pood: A Russian measure equal to about 36 pounds.

rabfak: A school that was intended to prepare workers and peasants for university entrance.

raiispolkom: A regional executive committee of the Council of People's Deputies.

raikom: A regional committee of the Communist party, at a lower level than the obkom.

realnoe uchilishche: A six-year high school that provided a modern education, with an emphasis on mathematics and the natural sciences, before the revolution.

Reds: The Bolsheviks (subsequently communists) and their supporters.

RSFSR: The Russian Soviet Federative Socialist Republic.

sovkhoz: A state farm.

USSR: Union of Soviet Socialist Republics, commonly referred to as the Soviet Union.

village soviet: An elected council in charge of village affairs.

Whites: The forces that opposed the Reds during the civil war that followed the October 1917 revolution.

ZAGS: Acronym for Otdel Zapisi Aktov Grazhdanskogo Sostoianiia. These were local statistical bureaus for the registration of marriage, divorce, birth, and death.

Zhenotdel: The Women's Bureau of the Communist party, established in 1919 and abolished in 1930.

A Revolution of Their Own

◙ Introduction

This book contains the stories of eight Russian women whose lives have spanned the twentieth century—an era of tremendous social and political turmoil and change. Russians who were born in the early years of the century and survived to see the collapse of the Soviet Union experienced three revolutions, two world wars, a civil war, and the world's first thoroughgoing attempt to create a socialist society. Millions lost their lives in conflicts and upheavals; millions more suffered persecution and repression at the hands of their own government. Yet other millions, especially women and men from lower-class backgrounds, gained educational and employment opportunities beyond the dreams of their parents and grandparents. Women found work outside the home and gained access to education and professional training, taking pride in these accomplishments.

We know relatively little about how ordinary Russians experienced the traumas and opportunities of the revolutionary and Stalinist eras of Soviet history (1917–1953) and virtually nothing about what these events meant to Russian women. Yet the emancipation of women was one of the goals of the revolution. Although never a top priority, efforts to achieve women's emancipation were far-reaching and substantial; but they took place in the context of a traditional, patriarchal, peasant culture and in the midst of massive social turmoil that tore families apart. In the end, women did not achieve equality but merely an expansion of their social roles to include participation in the labor force and economic responsibility for the family, in addition to the work they had always done at home—what scholars call women's "double burden."

The possibility of gathering oral histories in Russia is itself the product of profound change. Until a few years ago, the stories that the state-controlled media told Soviet citizens about themselves and their past consisted only of triumphs and achievements. To speak of failures, of losses, even of one's own personal suffering was dangerous, especially between 1929 and 1953, when people were imprisoned not only for criticizing leader Josef Stalin but even for expressing doubt about the ability of the Soviet Union to achieve its goals. People kept silent about their negative thoughts and experiences or shared them only with others whom they completely trusted. Even personal details that seem perfectly ordinary might become dangerous in certain contexts. Anastasia Posadskaya, coeditor of this book, remembers how her Jewish grandmother would respond when she was asked about her pre-revolutionary past: "I don't remember my mother's name, or my father's name, or my brother's name. . . . I've forgotten what language we spoke at home. I don't know why we always hid in the cellar when the cossacks came to town," she would say, although she had been a teenager during these events and had no trouble remembering other occurrences in her past. People's silence gave an illusory unity to collective memory: Everyone's experience was made to seem the same. In recent years, this illusion of commonality has vanished as alternative versions of the Soviet and prerevolutionary past have become known.

This book is the outgrowth of our shared curiosity concerning what the Bolshevik revolution really meant to women. Barbara Engel is a historian of Russia who has devoted her scholarly career to chronicling the lives of Russian women; Anastasia Posadskaya, an economist by training, has long been active in the Russian women's movement and was a founder and director of the Center for Gender Studies in Moscow. We recognized in the new openness of today's Russia an extraordinary opportunity to ask questions that would have been unthinkable just a short while ago. The Bolshevik revolution was the first in history to try to emancipate women; after the 1930s, official rhetoric trumpeted the complete equality of the sexes. We wanted to learn more about the reality behind the rhetoric and about how women actually experienced efforts to transform their social roles. As feminists we were also convinced that the lives of "ordinary Soviet women" would reveal much about other aspects of the Soviet past—most importantly, its impact on the family and personal life, about which very little has been written. We decided to interview women born before 1917 because they belonged to the first generation to fully experience the new order brought into being by the revolution of 1917, yet they also retained memories of the ways of life that preceded it.

In order to uncover the relationship between women's experiences and political change, we developed questions that encouraged women to speak about family and sexual relations, childbirth and childrearing, and the division of labor in the home, in addition to matters commonly discussed in history books. We adopted the "life history approach," a method that is just starting to be used in the former Soviet Union. We made this choice for political reasons: The life history approach encourages the narrator to shape her own story as well as to tell it in her own words, and thus puts her at the forefront of the historical stage. Not only does this add a human dimension to the statistics and generalizations that history books routinely offer; we also found that it enabled us to set private experiences alongside public accomplishments and to appreciate more fully the key role that women played in sustaining everyday life even in the most difficult of times, under the conditions of revolution and war.

The vast majority of Soviet citizens began their lives as peasants, untouched by the sweeping changes that the industrial revolution had brought to the West. Russian peasants farmed much as their ancestors had, turning up the soil with wooden plows and harvesting their grain with a scythe or a sickle. At the turn of the century, most peasants (and about 86 percent of peasant women) were illiterate, unable even to sign their names. According to custom, the survival of the peasant community as a whole took precedence over the material interests of individuals: Most communities held land collectively rather than individually, allocating it to peasant households according to the number of male workers (or sometimes, the number of mouths to feed) in each and periodically reapportioning it to reflect changes in household composition and need. Strong patriarchal traditions emphasized the importance of family ties and granted the male head of the household near absolute power over other family members. Women promised unconditional obedience to their husbands in the marriage ceremony, and divorce was virtually impossible. Marriage brought ceaseless childbearing: Peasant women bore nine children on average, about half of whom survived to adulthood.

At the close of the nineteenth century, rapid industrialization began to undermine the peasants' natural economy and traditional way of life. Peasants experienced an increasing need for cash, and the development of industry, mines, and railroads enabled them to earn it by leaving home. While most remained on the farm and maintained their customary way of life, hundreds of thousands went off to seek work. In cities, factory towns, and mining settlements, they encountered low pay and demoralizing working and living conditions. Many became responsive to the message of Russia's radical intellectuals, who for decades had criticized the social and political systems and provided visions of revolution by and for the lower classes. Simmering social and political tensions erupted in revolution in 1905, as industrial workers, intellectuals and students, and even industrialists and liberal members of the nobility briefly combined forces to wrest modest political concessions from Tsar Nicholas II, who until then had enjoyed absolute power. Reform only temporarily postponed revolution. Russia's poor performance in World War I intensified the nation's social and political conflicts. In February 1917, the tsar was overthrown in a popular uprising and replaced by the liberal Provisional Government, which itself lasted only eight months. In October 1917, Vladimir Ilich Lenin led the Bolsheviks to power in the name of Russia's tiny industrial working class, ushering in a new era in Russian history.

The Bolsheviks brought with them an agenda for far-reaching social and economic change, drawn from their readings of Karl Marx and other socialist thinkers. They viewed the Russian revolution as the first socialist revolution in the world. The proletariat had triumphed over the bourgeoisie, as Marx had predicted, and the Bolsheviks were certain their example would inspire others. Led by the Bolshevik party, which claimed to represent the class-conscious worker's vision and will, the proletariat was to rule and to create a socialist society.

The Bolsheviks' vision of social transformation also included the emancipation of women. They proposed to equalize the sexes by socializing domestic labor—that is, by entrusting household tasks and childcare to paid workers, bringing women out of the home to become full and equal participants in socially useful, paid labor. Party leader V. I. Lenin shared with his fellow revolutionaries a view of housework as "barbarously unproductive, petty, nervewracking, stultifying, and crushing drudgery." Once women were freed of the need to exchange domestic and sexual services for men's financial support, they would relate to men as equals. Eventually the family itself would wither away, and women and men would unite their lives solely for love. In 1918, the Bolshevik government promulgated a family code that was aimed at paving the way toward women's emancipation. It equalized women's status with men's, removed marriage from the hands of the church, and made divorce easily obtainable by either spouse. In 1920, abortion became legal if performed by a physician.

However, the circumstances that followed the revolution were not propitious for anyone's emancipation. Within a matter of months, the nation was embroiled in bitter civil war, which continued until the end of 1920. Men either went off to war voluntarily or were conscripted by the Reds (the Bolsheviks) or their opponents, the Whites. Among those opposed to the Bolsheviks were groups who had formerly enjoyed privileges, like the nobility and military elite. Armed challenges to the Bolsheviks were supported by money and troops from Russia's former wartime allies, Great Britain, the United States, and France. The famous Admiral Kolchak led the White campaign in Siberia, where Anastasia Posadskaya conducted many of our interviews, but the White forces also had many other leaders, and the war was fought on many fronts. Everywhere it brought devastation. During the civil war, about a million men perished in battle. The economy disintegrated almost completely, and the food situation became catastrophic, especially in the cities. In a policy known as "war communism," the Bolsheviks abolished private trade and requisitioned grain from the peasants by force. They nationalized factories, shops, and banks, paying the workers in kind. They also attempted to feed the urban population collectively, in public dining halls and canteens, and they established shelters to care for homeless and abandoned children. These public services were grim and ineffective, crippled by terrible material scarcities. Instead of serving as shining examples of the socialist future, they left a negative impression, as several of our narrators indicated. Hardship and hunger took their toll: Epidemics killed millions, typhus alone taking the lives of 1.5 million people between 1918 and 1919.

Substantial numbers of urban dwellers fled the cities. At least in the short run, the revolution worsened most women's and children's lots. Most of our interviews offer a dark picture of this period because our narrators were children at the time, and the upheavals hit children hardest of all. The deaths of millions of men deprived wives of husbands and children of fathers and destroyed fragile family economies. After the civil war ended, a famine broke out along the Volga river, taking the lives of tens of thousands. Millions of homeless children wandered the streets, their parents dead or unable to care for them. Desperate parents sometimes placed their children in a children's home, as did the mother of one of our narrators, *Antonina Berezhnaia*. Because Berezhnaia belonged to the nobility, a group that was persecuted after the revolution, her placement in a children's home may have saved her life. It certainly helped her overcome the social handicaps that resulted from her "incorrect birth." In the children's home, Berezhnaia learned to adapt to the requirements of Soviet life.

In an effort to rebuild the economy, Lenin changed Communist policy in March 1921, restoring the market, which had been abolished during the civil war, and permitting peasants once again to buy and sell. Private production resumed on a small scale. This policy, which lasted until the late 1920s, became known as the New Economic Policy (NEP). A prosperous period followed for most peasant villages: The NEP brought improved technology and a better standard of living. *Irina Kniazeva*'s family acquired its first iron plow; *Anna Dubova*'s father opened a small shop in their village. However, industry recovered too slowly to absorb the tens of thousands of unemployed workers and migrant peasants seeking jobs. If they were fortunate enough to be registered as "unemployed," uprooted peasants like *Elena Ponomarenko* could subsist on the portion of food they received at labor exchanges as they stood waiting for a job.

Life remained difficult for many lower-class women, too. While younger women, like *Sofia Pavlova,* might have enjoyed the free sexual unions based on love and unsanctioned by law that flourished in the 1920s among "advanced" youth, women with children suffered from the family instability that resulted from the war and postrevolutionary upheavals. In the early 1920s, 14 percent of Soviet marriages ended in divorce, a stunning figure when one considers that before 1917 divorce was virtually nonexistent. The high unemployment rate of the 1920s made it hard for single and divorced women to support their children, and the child support that fathers were required by law to pay was nearly impossible to collect.

Although the NEP left the peasant culture and way of life largely untouched and failed to alleviate the burden on mothers, the NEP years nonetheless brought changes in many other realms. The Bolsheviks regarded certain groups as "class enemies" and had begun accordingly to act against them. Among the disfavored were the clergy, as proponents of religion, "the opiate of the masses" in Marx's famous phrase; the nobility; and kulaks, supposedly wealthy peasants who were viewed as "exploiters." Churches were shut down. Class enemies lost property and voting rights. Their children were forbidden access to higher education, or were required to put in time on the factory floor before they could obtain it. Some of these "former" people—as the government called members of the "former exploiting classes"—were persecuted, as was *Vera Fleisher's* father, a Russian Orthodox priest. In contrast, for individuals from working-class or poor peasant backgrounds, the future seemed promising. Many workers' schools (*rabfaks*) were opened to prepare workers and poor peasants for university entrance, and the customary qualifying examinations for university admission were eliminated. Working-class supporters of the revolution enjoyed many opportunities for upward mobility: They received the chance to study in special schools and to move off the factory floor into managerial positions, and they were encouraged to join the Bolshevik (later the Communist) party. The revolution also brought new opportunities for lower-class women to speak on their own behalf. In 1919, the Central Committee of the Communist Party of the RSFSR had granted permission for the formation of a Women's Bureau (Zhenotdel) to coordinate the party's work among women. In the 1920s, thousands of factory women selected as delegates temporarily left their workplace to gain the political experience that would enable them to become more active. They attended literacy classes and learned skills of political organization. The impact of such new opportunities can be seen in the life of Sofia Pavlova: Bolshevik efforts to advance women, working-class women in particular, encouraged her to become a political activist, drew her into the party, and assured her and a female friend places in a special party school.

Then, in the late 1920s, another wave of change broke over the Soviet Union, accompanied by a struggle against yet another enemy. This change was initiated by Josef Stalin, who had become the party leader after Lenin's death in 1924 and following intensive intraparty struggles. Its immediate cause was an unexpectedly low level of state grain procurements following the 1927 harvest. This time, the target was the kulak, the so-called wealthy peasant, a category in fact almost impossible to identify with precision. "Kulaks" were allegedly withholding grain from the market in order to sabotage the revolution by starving the cities. Signaling the start of the anti-peasant campaign, the number of "prosperous" peasants deprived of the vote increased and their taxes rose. Peasants who failed to pay faced prison. Then came a frontal assault: In late 1929, Stalin declared as his goal the liquidation of kulaks as a class. Party activists recruited from the cities confiscated kulak property and drove the peasants from their houses. Some kulaks were sent to Siberia to begin farming again without implements or resources, forced to build their own houses in the dead of winter; others were sentenced to involuntary labor. As the interviews of Anna Dubova and *Elena Dolgikh* make clear, members of kulak households sometimes suffered different fates. While fathers and husbands sat in prison or suffered exile to distant places, their wives and children found themselves homeless and without any means of support. Expropriation usually took place in the winter, which meant that people were unable to find the berries, nuts, and mushrooms that they might have been able to gather in the forest during the warmer months. Children's homes refused to admit the offspring of kulaks; if relatives took them in, they risked being labeled kulaks and suffering the terrible consequences—which is what happened to Elena Dolgikh, who lost her job as a teacher for sheltering her own mother and siblings. Long after kulaks left the village, the label remained affixed to them, even to the younger members of the household. Such a label became an enormous obstacle to obtaining an education and finding a decent job. Kulak children who managed to establish themselves remained vulnerable to denunciation. As a result, people sometimes went to desperate lengths in order to escape their background: Some signed statements renouncing their kulak kin, as did Elena Dolgikh and Anna Dubova, or took advantage of marriage laws that enabled women to conceal their origins behind the surname of a socially acceptable husband, as did Dubova.

Even peasants who were not expropriated as kulaks nonetheless suffered a dismal fate: Their animals and implements were seized and they were herded onto collective farms, where they lost control of the products of their labor. According to Soviet policy, government requisitions and the struggle to build up heavy industry had priority over the well-being of peasant farmers. Receiving almost no return on their labor for the collective, peasants grew what they could on their tiny private plots, went hungry, and in desperation, sometimes pilfered grain, risking execution by firing squad and confiscation of all their possessions—according to a law that went into effect in summer 1932. That same year, a terrible famine broke out in parts of the countryside, especially in Ukraine. In response, the government issued a new internal passport law that greatly restricted peasants' ability to leave their villages: Urban residents and wage earners of sixteen years and older received a passport, but not peasant villagers. To live in the city, a person now needed a special permit. It thus became much more difficult for peasants to establish residence in a city, although it was still possible because of the voracious demand of industry for workers. The 1930s witnessed the continuation of the prerevolutionary pattern of young peasant girls migrating to the city to become domestic servants. For a peasant girl too young or a woman too old to join the industrial labor force, or with an "incorrect" (kulak, religious, or political) background who wanted to escape the village at any price, permission to live in town and to have a roof over her head was more than adequate compensation for the miserable wages she inevitably earned as a servant, especially as service provided a chance for the young to move on to better things. There were 50,000 domestic servants registered in Moscow in the early 1930s according to urban censuses, which undoubtedly underestimated their numbers, given that peasant women fleeing the campaign against kulaks would have had good reason to hide when a Soviet official came to the door.

Other dramatic changes also occurred during this period. The first Five-Year Plan, announced in 1929, was declared "fulfilled" only three and a half years later. The Five-Year Plan was the Soviet Union's effort to raise itself by its own bootstraps and to build the bases of a modern industrial economy. New factories, mines, and plants provided work for millions, ending unemployment and creating an insatiable demand for laborers. Evening classes and special training courses opened, offering technical training and advancement into management to capable and ambitious young workers who proved themselves on the factory floor. Doors swung open for women in a position to take advantage of the opportunities. Antonina Berezhnaia's devotion to production and eager participation in political life caught the eye of her superiors in an armaments plant. She succeeded in entering and graduating from a technical institute, became an engineer after the war, and was later promoted to a supervisory position. Sofia Pavlova obtained a position teaching at an institute of higher education. With only seven years of schooling, Elena Ponomarenko, the child of a peasant gardener, was appointed to an editorial position at a local newspaper and trained on the spot. Caught up by a campaign encouraging women to fly airplanes and drive automobiles, Anna Dubova left her job decorating cakes in a confectionary factory and learned to drive and maintain an automobile, and although she quickly lost interest in the work, other women enjoyed working as pilots and chauffeurs. Even Elena Dolgikh, who in her own words had lived her entire life under a "sword of Damocles" on account of her kulak origins, managed to obtain an education and went on to become a superintendent of schools.

Most of our narrators were among the first generation of Russian women to be trained for occupations outside the home, and for some, this was an exhilarating time. In the words of *Vera Malakhova*'s mother, "Whoever wants to study can, wherever they like, for free, so long as they are not lazy." Malakhova's mother had implored her own father to allow her to study, but instead he had sent her to work as a nanny in a physician's family. Her daughter, Vera, the child of a poor, working-class family, received a stipend to finish high school and another to attend medical school in the late 1930s. For others, however, change brought no improvements. One of the women who enjoyed neither occupational mobility nor the benefits of industrialization was Irina Kniazeva. Illiterate and struggling to support her children in the impoverished countryside on her miserable wages, like millions of other peasant women, she was in no position to take advantage of the new opportunities in the cities.

Despite the increased opportunities and efforts to overcome the unequal relations between women and men, inequality persisted in public life and women rarely obtained the same rewards as men. There was widespread social prejudice against women fulfilling the work roles traditionally designated for men, as Antonina Berezhnaia learned when she became chief administrator of five large metalworking plants in the Urals in the late 1940s. Sexual harassment was commonplace. Vera Malakhova, who served as a physician in World War II, often encountered it at the front, where some officers and party officials abused their authority to gain access to "intimacy," in Malakhova's words. Some women preferred "women's work," as did Anna Dubova, who regretted abandoning the "clean" trade of cake decorator for the "dirty" work of maintaining automobiles. In any case, state policy ensured that the labor market remained sexually segregated. The majority of women stayed in the lowest paid positions, despite 1930s campaigns to bring women into previously male professions and the successful breakthroughs of women such as Berezhnaia. Medicine became a predominantly female profession, as did teaching. Except for the highest supervisory positions, which men usually occupied, both medicine and teaching were poorly paid. After Elena Dolgikh's husband abandoned her and her children, the family often went hungry on her teacher's wages. In precisely the same position, Vera Fleisher enjoyed a higher standard of living only because *her* husband, who was a military physician and an officer, continued to send her money. Men dominated in the party, the military, and the state hierarchies.

The revolution also transformed women's family lives. The social upheavals and policy shifts that accompanied collectivization and rapid industrialization made housekeeping more difficult. Peasants flooded the cities, about 23 million of them between 1929 and 1940. Housing failed to keep pace and the food supply remained uncertain, resulting in severe overcrowding and widespread hunger and undernourishment. Government leaders invested in heavy industry rather than in the consumer sector, exacerbating the shortages. It became almost impossible to find clothing or basic household items. Wages were so low that one wage earner could barely support a family with children, especially when that wage earner worked outside of industry or was female. Day-care centers, communal laundries, and other facilities that were supposed to socialize domestic labor remained very scarce. Equally important for women's lives, having abolished the Zhenotdel in 1930, in 1936 the government adopted an explicitly pronatalist position, outlawing abortion, attributing to all women "natural" maternal instincts, and defining motherhood as a responsibility to society that must not be shirked. While a kind of militarized masculinity was celebrated in images of muscular workers storming the industrial "front," women were supposed to be womanly, that is, sweetly naive and modest, and to take responsibility for the home as well as to work outside it. In an effort to stabilize the family, the government made divorce both complicated and expensive. Divorced fathers were obligated to pay a quarter of their wages to maintain one child, one-third for two children, and two-thirds for three. In reality, however, it was difficult to enforce child support payments. Illegitimate children were distinguished from others by having a blank space left on their birth certificates where the father's name would have been written. As it began to trumpet the virtues of the socialist family, the government also grew less tolerant of casual liaisons and began to penalize couples who failed to register their marriages. Sofia Pavlova, a Communist party member, had not bothered to register her marriage with her first husband in the 1920s, but a decade later she felt the need to register her second.

The demands on women as workers and as mothers sometimes conflicted because of the failure of the government to socialize domestic labor as it had promised to do. Raising her sister's three children in a small provincial town and working as a journalist, Elena Ponomarenko did the laundry by hand after she put the children to bed, and grew accustomed to going without sleep. Because there was no childcare in her village, Irina Kniazeva had to leave her children alone when she went to work, and she lived in constant fear that they would accidentally burn down the house in her absence. But even where day-care centers existed, most of our narrators preferred not to send their children to them, at least not full time. Anna Dubova explains that most women considered it shameful to place a child in a day-care center because of their association of such centers with the miserable children's shelters of the postrevolutionary period. So what did mothers do? Unable or unwilling to quit their jobs, many turned to their own mothers for childcare. Their mothers also did much of the rest of "women's work," standing in lines at the shops, hauling water from the pump and boiling it to wash clothes, and providing whatever modest level of domestic comfort the family enjoyed. In some cases, female servants did this work. These were women too old or girls too young to take advantage of new work opportunities, or peasant women in desperate flight from their villages. As Dubova put it: "At the time [the late 1930s], it was very easy to hire someone because so many people were needy. People were glad to get work as nannies or domestic servants." Even workers' families employed servants in the 1930s and 1940s. Like mothers, servants were a crucial factor in enabling urban wives and mothers to work outside the home and yet raise children.

The multiple demands on women, the overcrowded conditions, and the lack of social support made it imperative for women such as our narrators to limit the number of their children. Despite the pronatalist policies of the government and the absence of reliable contraception or trustworthy sources of information about controlling fertility, family size did not increase in the 1930s; it rose only briefly after the abolition of abortion and then continued to decline. These interviews tell us the fearsome price that women paid to control their fertility after 1936, when abortion became illegal. They resorted to back-alley abortions, learning of abortionists from their female friends, extended family members, and colleagues. It is chilling to read of the methods used—infusions of laundry soap into the uterus administered by an abortionist or by the woman herself, or self-induced hemorrhage to gain medical assistance and legal evacuation of the womb. Women who became infected during these procedures or who sought assistance for heavy bleeding were often interrogated at the hospital before they were treated, as the authorities attempted to learn the names of underground abortionists. Abortionists were punished with one or two years' imprisonment if they were physicians and at least three if they were not. The woman herself received a reprimand for her first offense and a fine if caught again. Although there is no way of knowing how many women resorted to illegal abortions or how often, the relatively stable birthrate suggests that the experiences of our respondents were probably typical and quite common. Despite the terrible price women had to pay, they resisted the coercive power of the state in the realm of reproduction.

None of the legal changes aimed at shoring up the family were successful, at least in part because the social and political upheavals of the 1930s often tore it apart. The industrialization and collectivization drives of the early 1930s had uprooted millions. Then, starting in 1934 and gaining momentum between 1936 and 1938, the government launched a campaign of repression against alleged "enemies of the people." Millions, mostly men, were arrested, imprisoned, and sentenced to forced labor or execution. Those who came from the "wrong" background, such as the nobility or clergy, were particularly vulnerable, as was Fleisher's father, who died at hard labor in a camp in Siberia. Intellectuals were vulnerable too. Vera Malakhova recalled: "My school friends were all from families of the intelligentsia, and all their fathers had been put in prison. Their fathers were all shot." Members of the Communist party were most vulnerable of all; but no one was exempt. As a result, people became frightened of each other and far less willing to speak openly: Even a relative might repeat a person's careless words or denounce that person to the authorities. Historians in Russia and the West continue to dispute the precise number of people who were imprisoned or executed during this period, but recent studies have estimated the number of victims at about four million. The lives of several of our subjects were disrupted by these events: Sofia Pavlova lost her beloved second husband; Elena Dolgikh believed that the man she loved lost his life because of his connection to her, a "kulak daughter."

Soviet culture also contributed to family instability. With great fanfare, the government celebrated events that furthered its ideological or political agenda, such as triumphs of production, diplomatic victories, and the like, but denigrated personal life. It separated even the families of its ardent supporters—for example, by assigning a husband and wife to different cities, as happened with Sofia Pavlova and her first husband. "You are a communist," her supervisor told Elena Ponomarenko when she resisted going off on a mission and leaving her seriously ailing mother alone. "And for a communist, the political takes precedence over the personal."

Moreover, the revolution seems to have had a negative impact on the attitudes of many men toward their family roles and responsibilities. Only by interviewing this generation of men could one fully determine what prompted them to behave as they did. Nevertheless, if the stories of these eight women are at all typical, they point to a dramatic shift. Most of our narrators were born to large patriarchal families, in which the father was the indisputable head of the household; and if he died, the grandfather took his place. Their daughters speak of them as responsible men, "severe but just." These were men who took seriously the obligations that came with their authority over women and children. None of the fathers ever abandoned his wife and children; instead, the men continued to support them as long as they were able, even in times of repression. By contrast, husbands walked out of the lives of several of our narrators with remarkable ease. Undeterred by restrictive divorce laws, the men abandoned the women, often in the most difficult of circumstances—for example, right after the birth of a child. With only one exception, these husbands failed to provide support for their abandoned families, despite laws mandating that they do so.

In men's absence, and with no social resources to assist them, it was these women who shouldered the responsibility for sustaining the family. The majority of our narrators headed their own households during one or another period of their lives. But although all of them worked for wages, most did not earn enough to support themselves and their children. Because the government provided no financial assistance until 1944 and then provided it only in particular circumstances and only to a very limited degree, the loss of a husband's wages brought utter destitution. The experiences of Dolgikh, Dubova, Fleisher, and Kniazeva, each an abandoned wife, underscores the enormous importance of having two wage earners in a family with children, in the absence of government assistance. In that regard, it is instructive to compare the narrative of Dolgikh with that of Fleisher, both of them teachers. When Dolgikh's husband ran off with another woman, she struggled desperately to feed her children on her wages. In contrast, Fleisher, whose husband was an army officer, earned decent money, and continued to provide for her even after he left her, enjoyed relative comfort and security. In the lives of five of our narrators, the "new Soviet family" essentially consisted of a mother who "saved the children," in Fleisher's words, raising one or two by herself, often with the help of her own mother or a nurse but with no evident support, financial or otherwise, from the government.

The outbreak of World War II dramatically slowed repression and forged new unity in a divided society, but it also wreaked extraordinary destruction, divided families, and left women once again to fend for themselves. In August 1939, the Soviet Union signed a nonaggression pact with Nazi Germany, which allowed the two countries to divide Poland between them and to invade the Baltic states. The Nazi invasion of the Soviet Union on June 22, 1941, took the world and most Russians by surprise. In the first months of the war, the Germans scored spectacular victories that allowed their forces to lay siege to the city of Leningrad and brought them to the outskirts of Moscow. Further south and east, the Germans set their sights on the rich oil fields of the Caucasus. Those Russians who came under Nazi control were subjected to unmitigated horrors. Utterly contemptuous of the Slavs, whom they regarded as racially inferior, the Nazis treated the Slavic populations in captured areas with unrelenting brutality. Soviet citizens mobilized themselves in an extraordinary effort at self-defense. During the four years of warfare, able-bodied men between the ages of eighteen and forty were rarely seen away from the front. Women also volunteered: About 800,000 women went to the front, a fraction of those who wanted to, and they constituted about 8 percent of military personnel by 1943. Women served as soldiers, fighter pilots, tank drivers, and in partisan units. Women also occupied non-military positions that put them in the direct line of attack—in medical battalions, as telegraph operators, and as laundresses for fighting units, for example. One of these women was Vera Malakhova, who spent four years as a frontline physician. Focusing on her wartime experiences, Malakhova's narrative shows what life was like for a woman at the front. Others tell us, more briefly, about life behind the lines, where women bore the burden of work in collective farms and on the factory floor, laboring twelve hours a day, seven days a week, on half-empty stomachs. The war actually improved the economic position of Elena Dolgikh because she obtained a position in a factory producing for the front and received much higher rations than she had as a teacher. For others, the chaos and extremity of war eased some of the tight ideological and social discipline that the Communist party exerted. During the war years, however, the vast majority experienced nothing but suffering: Close to 6 million people were captured by the Germans and turned into slave laborers; some 25 million more had been evacuated or fled as refugees. At the war's end, most of these were left homeless, as their houses and villages had been razed by fire. In 1990, Mikhail Gorbachev announced that the number of wartime dead was 27 million, not 20 million, as people had previously believed. In 1946, Soviet women outnumbered men by nearly 26 million.

Despite the central role women played in the war effort both on the front lines and behind them, war did not transform the unequal relations between the sexes. Wartime propaganda drew on gender distinctions and reinforced them, representing women as the embodiments of home and family for which men risked their lives. Even women who served as soldiers were depicted as girlish, by contrast with brave and manly men. In the military and medical hierarchies, men usually were in positions superior to women's. Men who survived the terrible toll of war were virtually guaranteed upward social mobility, especially if they joined the Communist party, while women, with few exceptions, remained stationary. Most painful of all, in the immediate aftermath of the war it was male heroes who were celebrated, with only a few female exceptions, such as partisan Zoia Kosmodemianskaia, who was glorified as a martyr. Not only were women's military contributions largely effaced, but as Malakhova tells us, sexual promiscuity was often imputed to those who served at the front. Civilians sometimes referred to such women as "field campaign wives" and "whores." After the war was over, women who had served at the front were supposed to forget the experience, take off their uniforms and boots, put on dresses and high heels, and marry and have children. Many concealed their wartime experience in the hope of finding a husband, although the wartime devastation made this very difficult.

The armistice did not end the suffering. The Germans had destroyed towns and villages, blown up bridges and railroad tracks, and bombed major cities. The country lay in ruins, and new tensions with the West were making reconstruction difficult. Once again, people's well-being took second place to public priorities. Wartime rationing of food and manufactured goods continued until 1947, and prices rose dramatically. People went hungry and patched their old clothes. The housing that had been destroyed during the war was not rebuilt, and as apartment buildings became ever more crowded, newcomers to the city had to seek shelter in hostels resembling barracks. Political controls, which had been loosened to some extent in the course of the war, were again tightened and remained so until Stalin's death. In response to wartime losses, the cult of motherhood intensified: Women continued to work outside the home, but the state also encouraged women, even unmarried women, to reproduce. It increased maternity leave to 35 days before childbirth and 42 days afterward, and provided a small allowance to help mothers rear children born after the war. Dubova's interview suggests that a stigma on single motherhood nevertheless remained. At the same time, family legislation grew more conservative. Women could no longer bring paternity suits, the cost of divorce rose, and a tax was levied on the income of people with fewer than three children. This tax was particularly unfair to single or widowed women, who were not responsible for their childless state.

The death of Stalin in March 1953 brought an end to the most severe repression. In the mid-1950s, millions of people were released from the camps. In 1956, Nikita Khrushchev, the new Soviet leader, accused Stalin of creating a "cult of personality" and of terrorizing his fellow communists, in a secret speech before a meeting of the top Communist party leadership. The following years saw a general easing of censorship and increasing public criticism, not only of Stalin's rule but also of other aspects of the Soviet past. Then, after the fall of Khrushchev in 1964 and the rise to power of Leonid Brezhnev, ideological and political controls were reimposed, although never again as severely as in the years of Stalin's rule. The political events of these decades seem to have left little impression on the memories of our narrators.

On the other hand, the events that took place after 1985 have profoundly affected the shape of the life stories that are related in this book. In March 1985, Mikhail Gorbachev assumed leadership of the Soviet Union and slowly began the processes of transformation known as glasnost (or openness) and perestroika (rebuilding), processes that gradually gained momentum and led to his own downfall and the disintegration of the Soviet Union itself in 1991. In the late 1980s, long-standing historical and ideological verities were opened to public debate, and people were deluged by revelations about ugly aspects of their country's past that contradicted decades of government propaganda. Not a week went by without the appearance of a new film, book, article, or television program challenging the accepted interpretations of history. Members of formerly persecuted classes, such as the nobility, began to express pride in their social heritage. Churches reopened and people attended services in numbers greater than at any time since the 1920s. Monarchists spoke openly of their loyalty to the Romanov dynasty, calling Tsar Nicholas II a martyr and seeking some scion of the Romanovs to assume Russia's throne. Soviet penal camp survivors came forward to tell their stories, and an organization, Memorial, was founded to preserve information about their experiences. Members of repressed nationalities became organized and demanded the restoration of their rights and autonomy. Books long suppressed by censorship were published. An eager public viewed films formerly consigned to studio closets. Dissidents who had been forced to emigrate in the 1970s and 1980s returned to visit and to stay. No event in Soviet history remained exempt from criticism—not the character of V. I. Lenin, the traditionally revered leader of the October revolution, nor Soviet conduct during World War II, hitherto regarded as flawless. Glasnost brought a gender backlash, too. The communists were accused of destroying the family and undermining women's "natural role" as wives and mothers and guardians of the family hearth. Many Russians began to feel that it was imperative to stop "driving" women into the labor force and allow them to return to their proper sphere, the home.

By ending political repression and allowing people to speak publicly and for the first time of the unspeakable, glasnost legitimized some people's memories and made it possible for them to tell their stories relatively openly. Even as this openness destroyed the authorized version of the past, however, it provided no satisfactory replacement for it, no new collective memory through which people could understand their lives and find meaning in them. It became hard for people to make sense of the past. Widespread attacks on the version of history to which many Soviet citizens had devoted their lives has aroused understandable anger and resentment in many, as well as a terrible feeling of loss. The sense of crisis and shock is intensified by another loss, that of a key element that once united the population—pride in being citizens of a superpower, the Soviet Union. This pride has been replaced by national membership (in Russia, Uzbekistan, Ukraine, and so on), which has erected borders and barriers between states that were once part of a unified and powerful nation. To many Russian citizens of the former Soviet Union, the feeling is akin to what U.S. citizens might feel if they suddenly needed a passport and visas and special currencies to travel around their country. In addition, the last few years have severely eroded the system of social supports that ensured hardworking and upstanding Soviet citizens some medical care and security in their old age. Inflation of over 1,000 percent has destroyed people's life savings and reduced the buying power of pensions. Unable to afford the new goods that are now available, many older people subsist mainly on bread and worry about surviving from one pension check to the next or dying of hunger. Although the effect of such stark changes, both positive and negative, varies according to the individual, they have profoundly affected the ways that our narrators speak about their lives.

Our narrators conclude their stories in the early 1950s, with a brief coda in which they react to current changes. Most were nearing the age of retirement by then (age 55 for women); their youth and childbearing and childrearing years had come to an end. These women's lives coincided with the most turbulent events of their era. Their stories reveal the personal price that was paid for the public achievements of the Soviet period and the genuine pride that many people still take in what was accomplished, despite the price—or perhaps because of it.

We have used a modified form of the Library of Congress system of transliteration, except in the case of well-known names and institutions, and have eliminated the soft signs. Commonly used acronyms and frequently mentioned groups and institutions are identified in the glossary.

◈ Living Someone Else's Life

ANNA AKIMOVNA DUBOVA

Anastasia Posadskaya interviewed Anna Dubova at her one-room wooden dacha near Moscow on a sunny day in May 1994. Dubova lived in an apartment during the winter months, but moved for the warm months of the year to the countryside, where like countless other retired women she spent her time preparing for the next winter. She would plant a garden, and in late summer, she would harvest and preserve vegetables as well as fruits, nuts, and mushrooms. This was hard and time-consuming work, but home gardening and canning were absolutely essential for her survival during the winter—as they were for many others'—and Dubova said she loved to do it.

Posadskaya and Dubova talked on the porch. In order to speak with Posadskaya for a few hours, Dubova had to tear herself away from preparing a meal for her two grandchildren—a boy and a girl of ten and twelve years, respectively, who had come to stay at their grandmother's dacha for the holidays. During breaks in the conversation, Dubova fed the children stewed fruit, offering some to Posadskaya as well. People recommended Dubova as a narrator primarily because she belonged to an important dissident sect of the Russian Orthodox faith—Old Belief. At the end of the seventeenth century, Old Believers rebelled against the Russian Orthodox church in the conviction that reforms then taking place in the dominant church were destroying the very foundations of faith. The tsarist government reacted by persecuting them. Rather than submit to the new practices or to the authority of the Antichrist, whom they believed to have taken power in the person of the tsar, whole families and villages fled to inaccessible forest regions, where they lived according to their own customs. In subsequent years, the persecution occasionally eased, and in the nineteenth century some Old Believers enjoyed considerable economic success as merchants and traders. But most remained very strict in their beliefs, which continued to differ in important respects from those of the dominant Rus-

Dubova in 1997

sian Orthodox church. As it turned out, however, Dubova's Old Believer
origins had left little trace on her adult life, and her narrative went far beyond the subject that had led us to select her for an interview. She even
looked more worldly than Posadskaya had anticipated, with close-cropped
hair and wearing a light summer dress and little apron. She was eager to
talk about her life, as if she had waited years for this opportunity.

Anna Dubova grew up in a large, patriarchal, peasant family in a village
near Smolensk, in western Russia. Her parents' religious faith may have
been reflected in the great severity with which her father treated his wife
and children and in the literacy of her mother, as literate women were far
more common among Old Believers than among the Russian Orthodox.
However, in most respects the childhood that Dubova described differed little from that of millions of other children raised in hard-working, modestly
successful peasant families. In order to subsist in an environment where the
weather was unreliable and the land unyielding, Russia's peasants had to
engage in intense, virtually endless toil. Dubova recounted her family's way
of life in detail: "Father slept with his hat on—that is, he labored day and
night." Everyone's work was essential to the family's survival: "Our people,
the family, worked the land all by themselves. Even the small children

worked." From her family's perspective, poverty was the consequence of a failure to work and of sitting around gossiping for hours on end, not of misfortune or social injustice.

Dubova's father was wary of the Bolshevik revolution from the first. Her grandmother, interpreting it through the prism of Old Belief, even regarded it as the coming of the Antichrist. But in the 1920s her family was doing well. Lenin's New Economic Policy (NEP), initiated in 1921, permitted private trade in manufactured goods and allowed peasants to market their produce. The farm became prosperous, and her father even acquired a small shop, where he traded goods that he bought in the city. Then, in 1929 the government launched a drive to collectivize agriculture and liquidate the kulaks (supposedly wealthy peasants) as a class. Because of his shop, her father was branded a kulak. Threatened with exile to the far north, the family managed to escape, as we learned at the very end of Dubova's interview, only because her parents promised to give her in marriage to the local Communist party secretary, on whom their fate depended. Dubova was thirteen years old at the time. Despite the promise (which remained unfulfilled), the family lost their farm and began a period of wandering from place to place. In the 1930s, anyone with "kulak ties" was believed to be an enemy of the revolution. In order to retain the rights to work, vote, and move about freely, someone with a background such as Dubova's might have to sever her ties with her relatives. Before she could go off to Moscow to join her older sister, who already lived in the city with her husband, Dubova had to sign a paper renouncing her parents.

In Moscow, Dubova joined millions of other peasant women and men who had left their villages during these years to participate in the Soviet Union's great industrialization drive. She completed a factory apprenticeship school, which provided her with a rudimentary education and training in a trade, and became a cake decorator in a confectionary factory. Then, in the mid-1930s, a state-sponsored campaign aimed at bringing women into trades that had hitherto been dominated by men convinced her to train as a chauffeur, a change she subsequently regretted.

Dubova's personal life reflected the chaotic conditions of her time and the ineffectiveness of state policies aimed at strengthening the family. Still fearful that her kulak origins would catch up with her, soon after coming to Moscow she married a minor party activist whom she did not love in order to change her surname and "find refuge," as she openly acknowledged to Posadskaya. She bore him a child, and then, after World War II began and he left for the front, she became involved with another man and bore a second child. The second man soon abandoned her, leaving her in desperate need, a single mother with two children. "There was never enough to eat," she remembered. "You'd go to the kitchen and think, Maybe I should just hang myself."

From her perspective, the opportunities offered by the revolution provided little compensation for the way of life she lost. Deeply religious, she had to conceal her faith even from the men with whom she was intimate during the decades when religion was persecuted. Much of what she encountered as an adult violated the values of cleanliness, sobriety, and hard work that her father had instilled in her as a child. At least in retrospect, she preferred the life of a peasant to the life of a worker, and the years of her childhood would always be the "golden age." That is why, as she said, "I lived someone else's life." If the socialist revolution had not occurred, she was sure that life would have been better: "I would have lived on the fruits of my labor. Our level of civilization would have been higher, and everyone would have been better off materially, too."

◈   ◈   ◈

Anna Akimovna Dubova: I don't even know where to start. Well, let's see, I come from a peasant family tree, so to speak. At first they were extremely poor. But somehow Grandmother, although she herself was uneducated, longed to see my father advance in the world—as they used to say. So she sent him to study in a theological seminary, to learn to sing and to read, and in general to acquire a proper church education. He studied in Kaluga. Then he came back, married, and began to till the soil. The family had been so poor that when the household property was divided up between Grandmother and her two brothers, it turned out there really was nothing to divide—no money to build with.[1] And so Grandmother left her two children—a son (my father) and a daughter—and went to Leningrad to earn money so they could build themselves a hut.[2]

Anastasia Posadskaya-Vanderbeck: You must mean to Petersburg.

Yes, of course. At that time it was still Petersburg. I don't know how long she stayed there, but she earned the money, came back, and they built a small wooden hut. It was very primitive, but they lived in it.

When did all this happen?

All this happened before I was born. I'm talking about my grandmother.

Oh, I see, and you were born—

I was born in 1916, in that very hut.

---

1. Dubova's grandmother was evidently a widow who returned with her children to her father's house after her husband's death. That is why she was included in the division of household property, from which women, and in particular married daughters, were normally excluded.

2. It was not uncommon for a peasant widow to leave her children in the village while she went off to earn money elsewhere.

Where was it located?

In Smolensk oblast, in the village of Gavrilovo, which was in the Sychevka district. Since my father was better educated than anyone else in the village, they treated him with greater [respect].

Was he a priest?

No, he wasn't a priest; he was the choirmaster and directed the church choir. But he was highly respected in the village. Then he began to till the soil. He had a lot of children to feed. Mother had a baby every year. She gave birth to fourteen children in all. Seven survived and seven died. And all of us who survived lived in the village until collectivization was imminent.

And was your mama also of peasant stock?

Yes, she was. She was ten years younger than Father. Then in 1928, we were all deprived of the right to vote—that is, all of us who were adults at the time.

But why?

Because we were considered wealthy in comparison to the other, poor peasants.

Anna Akimovna, tell me, please, what sort of house you had, what sort of farm.

Our house, as I've said, was no better than anyone else's, even worse.

How many rooms did it have?

Actually, there were two huts separated by a passage. Then there was a barnyard. By this time we had a lot of farm animals. Father began to prosper, but of course this was all relative.

What kind of animals did you have?

Well, we had an Orlov stallion, a trotter, to pull our carriage, because at that time it was considered a sign of respectability to have such a stallion. Father always said, "Since I have a lot of girls, I must make a good name for my family, so that I can marry off my daughters well, so that people will recognize that they come from a fine family."

And how many daughters were there?

There were five girls and two boys in our family. And five boys and two girls had died. Literally the same number. Then we had a work horse, two cows—the third was a heifer—a bull, and that's it. That's all the livestock we had.

What about poultry?

We kept a lot of poultry—geese, ducks, turkeys; and I, of course, tended them all, and that was a lot of work. In general, we never stopped working.

Father "slept in his cap"—which is to say that he worked day and night. He kept bees and had an apiary. Yes. Just imagine, mama had a baby every single year, and there were so many farm animals to take care of, and we didn't have any hired help. We did it all on our own, with our own people, our own family. Everyone worked, even the small children. What's more, Grandmother was still alive. There were so many people, and everybody had to be provided for.

The deaths of the babies must have been upsetting. What did they die of? Do you remember?

I think they died from lack of care. They were fine, healthy babies when they were born. But then they died when they were a year old, or two years old, or three, because our parents were always busy working.[3] There was no understanding of the importance of medicine, no medical services. We lived thirty kilometers from the main city in the district, no one sought or received medical treatment, Mother didn't have any of her babies in a hospital.

She had her babies at home?

All of them.

Did a midwife come to help, or did she give birth all by herself?

There was a midwife. Babies were so poorly cared for from the moment they were born. People had such primitive notions. Just to think about the way newborn babies were treated back then is horrible. They were immediately given a homemade pacifier to suck,[4] bread to suck. When those of us who survived got a little older, Father immediately taught us the alphabet and how to write our letters—even before we started school. In general many children who lived in the village never attended school, but we all went to school.

You mean to say there was a school in the village?

No, the school was quite a distance from the village. We went there on foot. But when it was bitterly cold, we were taken in a sleigh.

And who took you?

Parents took turns: One day it would be my parents, then the next day the parents of some other child. That's when it was bitterly cold, because we had such severe winter weather. Sometimes you'd be walking to school and you'd see birds that had literally frozen to death, lying alongside the road.

---

3. Infant mortality was high throughout peasant Russia at the time. In 1900, 275 of every 1,000 newborns died in the first year of life.

4. This homemade pacifier, known as a *soska,* consisted of grain or other foods that had been chewed by a member of the family, then put inside a cloth and placed in the infant's mouth.

And your mama and papa—how did they get along?

Very well, very well. Although Mama sometimes recalled his strictness. Father was extremely strict. He wasn't a sadist, you couldn't say that, but he was very strict. We were very careful to mind our manners at the table, yet even there Father was always keeping close watch on us—not Mama, mind you, but Father. He was in complete charge of our upbringing. Mother was always having babies; she didn't have time for anything else. Of course, she had to cook and bake, and feed the farm animals and milk the cows—all of that had to be done. But everyone in the family had specific chores, and everyone knew what their chores were. We had a creamer, a device that separated the milk from the cream—I was responsible for that—and I had to wash it. Then there were lots of plates, and I had to wash them too. There was always a large group of us at the table, and, believe me, we sat up straight and were extremely well-behaved. If the older children were sitting at the table, Father was apt to say: "Why are you slurping your food? Is that polite?" Or, let's say, one of us sat down and spread her legs awkwardly. Then Father would say: "Why are you sitting like that? Girls sit with their legs together. Don't you dare let me catch you sitting like that again!" Yes, Father was extremely strict, and he treated Mama strictly and he treated us strictly—just about the same.

What makes you say that?

Well, if he demanded something from us, let's say, and Mama, God forbid, came to our defense, chances are he would shout at her and give her a real dressing-down. That's one thing. And then, Mama wasn't really in charge: She didn't make the decisions about what to buy or how to dress the children. When my older sisters got big, Father even went to Moscow just to buy them outfits. The younger kids ran around barefoot in tattered clothing, but the older ones had to be dressed up so they could make a good impression.

And he didn't consult with your mother?

Yes, he did consult with her. He really loved my mother, he really did. Mother would go to fetch water, and he would say: "Girls, what's wrong with you! Didn't you see that your mother has taken the pail and gone off to get water. Go help her. Make it snappy!" That shows how much he cared about her. When Mama was pregnant, she had to carry those heavy tubs on her big stomach to water the farm animals, and nobody thought anything of it. Father, of course, felt sorry for her. He would get up early so she could get more rest, bring in the wood, milk the cows, and drive them to pasture—even though all this was considered woman's work. She only had to get the stove going and feed the family, when she got up.

And did your mama ever have any time to herself?

No, she never did, because there was so much work to be done. What's more, Father wouldn't let her go and gossip with the other women; he considered that inappropriate for a man of his standing in the village. He forbade her to sit with the womenfolk and chatter idly, and Mama obeyed him.

Anna Akimovna, what other kinds of farm work did you do?

Well, we raised farm animals, and, let's say, some survived that we didn't need. We would take them to town and sell them and use the money to buy some manufactured goods. And we would do the same thing with honey. And thanks to this we lived well—by village standards, we lived well. Now take my father's cousin who lived right next door to us. He and his family often sat around and gossiped. They had time for that. And this cousin was always in debt to us; he was forever coming over to borrow something. First, they didn't have enough bread; then it would be something else, and then something else, and all because they would just sit around for hours on end. But our family lived better than others, thanks to Father. He was industrious himself and forced his whole family to be industrious, too, and not idle away the time. Consequently we had things to sell, something was always left over. Now, in order for something to be left over, you had to grow something. But the soil in Smolensk oblast was poor. However, since we had a good number of farm animals, there was lots of manure, and we would spread it on the fields. So our yield was a little better. Moreover, Father was a good planner and he rotated the crops: One year he would plant wheat, then another year something else.

And did you sell any needlework? Did your mama sew?

No, Mama didn't do any needlework; Father excused her from that because she simply had no time. She was always busy with her babies. Just imagine: I had a brother who was born in 1920, a sister who was born in 1922, another brother in 1923; these three I remember being born. There were others, but these three were the ones who survived. When was there time to do everything? She couldn't keep the house as clean as it should have been. She couldn't care for the babies the way she should have, and consequently, of course, some of them died.

Do you remember, when a baby brother or sister died, did people grieve?

Well, I remember how one of my little sisters died. It was summer, and nobody had time to care for her. Most likely she had pneumonia. And so they would leave her with me—I was quite small at the time—and say: "Baby Olga is sick. You'll have to take care of her. Watch her and keep giving her water to drink." But I wanted to go and play, so I would thrust a mug at her and run outside. No one really took it seriously. You understand? And so she died. My father took these deaths very hard—that's what my sister said. Usually he would make a little coffin, and he always cried. My mama was more restrained. In general, she was somehow calmer than Father because everything was on Father's shoulders, understand, everything.

Was your mama literate?

Well, she knew how to read and write. When I was growing up, she never had any time. But later she read a great many books. She read all the classics; she also read a great many religious books. She absolutely loved to read.

Anna Akimovna, do you remember the 1920s? I realize you were small then.

Yes, of course I do. I remember the famine of 1922. I remember we had a very good horse and sold her for one hundred poods of salt. And I remember my father brought home three sacks of millet, and that millet had already gone bad, understand?

Why did you need so much salt?

Because we used salt as a preservative. There was absolutely nothing available, and so we had to preserve meat, we had to preserve cabbage. We simply had to have supplies in reserve or else we would have died of hunger. At that time there was a typhus epidemic. And our father even went into the woods and broke off juniper branches. And he kept fresh juniper tacked up everywhere in the house, and he was constantly replenishing it. Consequently, none of us got typhus. That's how he saved the family. Many people died from typhus. Then, in 1922, they made Father chairman of the village soviet because he was better educated than any of the others.

And what's your feeling, do you think your father accepted the revolution?

You know, I'm not absolutely sure, but it seems to me that he wasn't happy about the revolution.

Even though they made him chairman of the village soviet?

No, that didn't make any difference. Somehow he could see down the road, and he sensed that something would . . . And my grandmother—you know how villagers used to say that a new tsar had come to power and that he was the Antichrist. People said that—that the forces of the Antichrist had come to power. I remember it very well.

You mean, they said that about the Bolsheviks?

Yes, Grandmother said that. She was uneducated, she lived in the backwoods, and yet she knew that the forces of the Antichrist had come to power. I remember that very well. She said: "We have a new tsar; the forces of the Antichrist have triumphed." That was when Lenin came to power.

And do you remember when Lenin died?

When Lenin died? Yes, I remember that too. Then people said, The new tsar has died. The new tsar has died, they said, but the power of the Antichrist persists. That's what they said, The power of the Antichrist persists.

Was your village quite prosperous?

Our village wasn't poor. People lived reasonably well; they were able to provide for themselves. And that's the way it was until NEP. And then during NEP, everyone began to live very well—or at least the majority did. A great many people became prosperous. There was a lot of building going on. The village was thriving, and not just our village. All the villages around were thriving, and it remained like that until the drive for collectivization began. On the whole, collectivization was terrible.

Can you talk about it?

Well, first of all, everyone was opposed to joining the kolkhoz, but people were forced to join. If someone resisted, he was punished and everything was taken from him—his land, his animals, everything he had. People were literally herded onto the kolkhoz. Then, too, the so-called wealthy peasants were singled out, although in fact there really were no wealthy peasants. Almost everybody had the same standard of living. I've already described our farm and how we lived. Were we rich? But during NEP our father—I don't know what to call this—but he would go into town, where there were large stores that were privately owned, and since we lived thirty kilometers away, they would give him some goods, and he would bring them home to the village where we had a little shop. We all suffered on account of this shop, because father would bring things home and sell them. And they would give him a percentage of the sales. And because of this we suffered.

How did you suffer?

Well, we were all branded kulaks and dispossessed.

Can you talk about it?

Of course. This I remember very well. First of all, we were deprived of the right to vote.

When was that?

That was 1928. They took away our vote because we had this shop and engaged in trade. That was the main reason. They took away my father's right to vote, my mother's right to vote, and my sister's (she was eighteen at the time). But we didn't know what that meant. So they began to explain: You won't be admitted to meetings, you won't be able to vote on anything. Well, okay, was that really so bad? That didn't seem bad at all. But then in 1929, forced requisitioning of grain began, and they started imposing taxes

*The family of Anna Dubova in 1929. Anna is standing in
the last row, far right.*

in kind, procurement quotas, and who did they impose them on? On
lishentsy,[5] of course—that is, on those deprived of the right to vote. And we
weren't the only ones affected. Other families, who were even more prosperous, were affected too. The first quota we met, the second quota we
met, and the third; but the fourth time we didn't deliver the grain, and so
my father was put in prison for not meeting . . . [6]

For not meeting the quota?

Yes, that's right. Father went to prison, and seven of us were left, Mother was
left alone. You can well imagine the trauma we suffered. All our lives we had
been protected by such a strong father and suddenly to be deprived of him.
Of course, we shed tears. Everything happened at once. Not only did they
put Father in prison, but they began confiscating our livestock because we
had failed to meet the quota. Then after about six months, Father was released from prison. He came home and everyone rejoiced, thinking that that
was the end of it. Nothing could have been farther from the truth. A short
time later, procurement quotas were again imposed, again those taxes in

---

5. In Russian, *lishentsy* means deprived ones. Peasants accused of being kulaks were deprived of the vote between 1918 and 1936. They were also liable to extra taxes and discrimi-
nated against in educational admissions and in other areas.

6. See also Elena Dolgikh's comments beginning on p. 155.

kind. And again they put Father in prison, and they literally took everything away from us. They wanted to deport us—a mother and her children—to Solovki [short for Solovetskie ostrova, islands in the far north that were a place of exile, internment, and forced labor]. But then I guess some chairman must have taken pity on us, because, after all, we were his people.[7] Now the poor peasants, or *bednota,* immediately went after our possessions. They were filled with such hatred: "Why should they have lived so well?"

You mean they snatched up all your possessions?

Yes. But others were deported to Solovki in our place.[8] There were three brothers who had a creamery but no hired help; they made the butter themselves. And all three of them, with their families, were deported to Solovki. We were told quietly not to be home the night they were seized. My older sister and two brothers went into the woods and hid there for three days, while my mama took the younger kids and went off to stay with relatives. It was, of course, a terrible time for us all. Then when everybody had returned home—for they did return—and those other families had been deported, the campaign ended. And we were told that we could settle wherever we wanted, to get going; and everything was taken from us, everything.[9] I remember so well how Mama sat and cried when they took away the cow. Then they took away the horse from the yard, and then . . . I remember we had an iron bed and a very large mirror. By village standards, we lived reasonably well. They took down the mirror, took away the bed, took away absolutely everything, and then said: "Get out of here." Yes. Then Father was released, and he immediately left for Podolsk, which is near Moscow, to work on a construction site. And he tried to get me to join him. As a matter of fact, my sister had married and was already here in Moscow. And so I left to join my sister. Then everyone gradually went to Podolsk, and Mother, too. She had a hard time in the country, even among relatives. No one would take us in any longer. Everybody was afraid that they would be accused of harboring kulaks, that people would say: "Aha, so you're sympathetic to kulaks. That's it for you; you'll be deported too." Understand? You couldn't stop to rest anywhere because people were forbidden to show sympathy for those who were suffering. I remember how Mother went to her brother, to her own father and mother, to the very spot where she had been married, and even they couldn't keep her because . . . But it made no difference: Later, they, too, were branded kulaks and dispossessed. And there was absolutely no reason for it; they suffered simply because they had relatives

---

7. At the end of the interview, Dubova gave a different version of this story.
8. Regions were assigned quotas for the dispossession of kulaks, or *dekulakizatsiia,* which party cadres had to meet.
9. Essentially, they were told to go find themselves a place to live, without any of the things they would need to set up housekeeping or to start farming.

who . . . They were asked if they had relatives who were kulaks. And so they too were dispossessed, and all our kinfolk around were dispossessed. And the worst of it was that when we arrived in Moscow,[10] of course, there was terrible famine there. Everything was being rationed, and we didn't have ration cards; we didn't have anything. It was extremely hard, and there were so many mouths to feed. Mama got work in a place where they raised rabbits for food and fur, and what remained from the rabbits she would give to the smallest child, so he would have at least something to eat. Well, okay, somehow we managed to scrape by. I was already an adolescent and had finished the factory apprenticeship school, or FZU, and was in line for work at the labor exchange. And there I got a bowl of soup.

You mean those who were registered at the labor exchange were fed for nothing?

That's right; they had a soup kitchen there. And just when it seemed we had almost gotten on our feet—one sister had gotten married, then another sister got married, and I was registered at the labor exchange—and were close to becoming "normal" people again, my older sister made friends with a girl who was a member of the Komsomol. And my sister . . . You can imagine the rest. They were on good terms, and most likely my sister told her what had happened to us, that we had been driven out of our village. Now, the internal passport system had just been introduced, which meant that everyone received passports, and it seemed like everything was okay. We thanked our lucky stars that we had survived the introduction of passports.[11] Then, suddenly, our family was again driven out. This time we were stripped of absolutely everything. We left Moscow with no money and only the clothes on our backs. What's more, we were deprived of our residence permits.[12]

That means somebody . . .

Yes, we think that this Komsomol girl reported us. And we were all thrown out, told to go wherever we pleased. We were at the end of our rope. Father

---

10. She referred to Podolsk and Moscow as if they were one and the same place, when in fact the city of Moscow and the town of Podolsk were about fifty miles apart.

11. Internal passports were introduced in December 1932. The decree required that all citizens over the age of sixteen and living in cities have passports issued by the local police. "Hidden kulaks" were not supposed to receive passports. People living outside of urban areas were not supposed to receive them either, which made it difficult (although not impossible) for peasants to leave their villages.

12. Residents in a large city were required to have a permit stamped on their passport. Without it they could not live in the city. In the interview, Dubova continued to use the words "we" and "us," as if she suffered along with her family, when in fact she remained in Moscow, as she herself made clear. Only much later in the interview did she reveal the painful fact that in order to get to Moscow in the first place, she had to write a letter repudiating her family. This action protected her in many instances, including the one she mentioned here.

... it was very hard on him. After this he got sick and began to waste away. Just imagine, he began to waste away! Where could we go with no money, with nothing . . .

But you had all been given passports?

That's right, we all had passports already. But we were deprived of our residence permits and told to get out. "Go wherever you want," they said. "Take your passports and go wherever you please." And so Father set out again to find a place to live, and he went to Rzhev, where we also had roots. There he rented some kind of shed. I stayed in Moscow. Since I was not registered with them, I "slipped through the cracks" and remained there, while he left with Mother and the four remaining children. They had a very hard time of it and suffered terrible hunger, worse even than when all this was just beginning. And in Rzhev things were also very hard for them, and the children went hungry. They started school with empty stomachs. And they continued to go hungry until the war began. And then at some point, my brother came to Moscow to take the entrance exams for an industrial college, and he spent the night under a car just so he could take the exams. He had to have somewhere to spend the night. Then another brother came to Moscow and got accepted into a factory apprenticeship school. And in 1940, just before the war, Father died.

Anna Akimovna, so you remained in Moscow with your sister?

Yes, my sister was married. Her husband's family had also been branded kulaks and dispossessed. She lived with her husband in Moscow.

Did they have a room?

Yes, they had a room, which they rented. The size of that room . . . The bed had to be so short that her husband's legs hung over the edge. It was a makeshift bed, which they put together from planks. Then they had a baby, and guess what they did for a cradle? My sister made one out of canvas, and it hung from the ceiling, and I slept under it on the floor. And they slept on this makeshift bed. That's how cramped things were. And there was a little table attached to the wall. When we slept, we would put the table up like this, fold it up, and then in the daytime we unfolded it and ate on this little table. And that's how we lived.

When you arrived in Moscow, what did you want to do? Did you want to get married? To study? To work?

First of all I really wanted to study. When I finished the factory apprenticeship school, I really wanted to continue my studies, but I had absolutely no place to live. Furthermore, after finishing the FZU, we were required to work.

At the FZU, were you given training in a particular vocational skill?

Certainly.

Dubova in 1937

Which one?

Well the factory apprenticeship schools all provided seven years of education. Your specialization, however, depended on where you went to school, which factory the FZU you attended was attached to. The FZU I graduated from was attached to the Bolshevik cake factory, and I became a pastry cook there. What's more, I became a cake decorator, which was highly skilled work. I was good at making fancy designs on cakes with frosting.

Did you do a special design on each cake?

Yes, I did. But we also had five or six standard patterns, and so we did standard designs as well. These we could do quickly and that helped us to earn more money. As a cake decorator I was paid quite well, but I had no place to live, and so I felt obliged to keep giving people gifts in exchange for a place to stay. I would stay the night with girlfriends, and they were always glad to have me. At the time, I couldn't imagine why that was so, but later I realized it was because I spent a lot of my earnings bringing them things. Also, my family was having a hard time in Rzhev, so I would send my younger brothers things—sometimes slippers, sometimes something else. And all this time . . . all this time, until just recently, I was afraid whenever I saw a policeman, because it seemed to me that they could tell that something about me wasn't right. And I got married just so I could cover up my background. My first marriage was a kind of camouflage. I had no place to live. And my husband was from the bednota.[13] He was a member of the Komsomol and the secretary of a village soviet not far from Moscow. As a

---

13. This was a word used in Soviet times to denote the poorest peasants. They became a privileged group, from which the Party recruited people for positions of power and decision-making in the countryside.

member of the Komsomol, it was his job to identify and dispossess kulaks. You understand how . . . Marrying him served as a cover for me. And also we had our own little room. And when I went to bed, I would think to myself, Dear Lord, I'm in my very own bed. I experienced such happiness; it was like being in seventh heaven—I was that happy. But my husband drank a lot. He was a good fellow and kind, but he had become a heavy drinker. Because he was young and from the bednota, people tried to buy him off and were constantly treating him to drinks. They did this because they knew full well that they, too, were liable to be punished, and they wanted to protect themselves. And he drank, he drank a lot, and I kept dreaming and thinking, "Lord, if only I could marry a decent sort of fellow." I lived with him, but I dreamed about a decent husband, even though I had a daughter by him. And then, when he went off to serve in the army, such a fellow turned up.

When did he go off to the army?

When the war started. And then I got involved with another man, who, of course, left me in turn. Because I was so poor. And at the time, I had his seven-month-old baby, and he abandoned us. What's more, he pulled me away from the place where I had lived with my first husband. Then he left me.

And your first husband—did he come back from the war?

Yes, he did, and so I left him the living space we had, all of it, because I didn't want to hurt him.

Do you remember the birth of your first child?

I had my first child in 1939. My husband, as usual, wasn't home at the time. I would often sit around and cry. You know, I think it was because when I was growing up my father and mother always got on well, always did things together, whereas . . . And then, my father didn't drink, he didn't smoke, he never used foul language, nothing like that. I had expected to have that sort of marriage too. But everything had turned out just the opposite. When I was almost due, and still he was never home, I remember that I got ready and cleaned the room so that I could go off and have my baby and leave everything spick-and-span. I climbed onto the wardrobe—you know, they used to be very high—so I climbed up on top and dusted it, and at this point a friend of his dropped by and said: "Good heavens, did you climb up there to have your baby? Is that it?" Well, I went to my sister's and spent the night there. And then she took me to the hospital. We went on foot. And I had my baby. He didn't come to take me home from the hospital, either, because he was drunk. A neighbor came in a truck and brought me and the baby home. That's the sort of "homecoming" it was. You can just imagine what kind of shape I was in, how hard I cried. Then he came home, and things continued the way they had been before. All the time, of course, I dreamed of divorcing him, but I didn't know how or where to go.

And did you want his child?

I didn't think about it, really. It just happened, you understand.

You didn't take precautions?

No, we took precautions, but somehow . . .

And what about an abortion? Didn't it occur to you to get an abortion, since your husband was so hard to live with?

You know what, for some reason I kept hoping that . . . He was always promising to stop drinking. Moreover, he was kind. He was a good person, and in his own way, considerate. I kept waiting for him to stop drinking. He would say, I'll stop! I'll stop! And I believed him. Then I got pregnant very quickly. It just happened, and I didn't even think about getting an abortion. I did have two abortions—only that was later, when I was with my other husbands. Moreover, in one case I got blood poisoning because it was a back-alley abortion.

Did this happen when abortions were illegal?

Yes, that's right. It was terrible, absolutely terrible. So many women died, leaving small children, and so many were sent to prison. Women who had the abortions and suffered were sent to prison, and those who performed the abortions were also sent to prison. We were interrogated. I remember how after I had had the abortion I was lying there, weak from the loss of blood, and they kept questioning me, Who performed it, who performed it? And I was so weak, yet how could I send a person whom I had personally asked to perform the abortion to prison.

Were abortions performed for money or simply as a favor?

These were clandestine abortions, so, of course, they were done for money.

Was it easy to find someone to perform an abortion or did it depend on word of mouth?

It depended on word of mouth. For example, someone would say, That redheaded Polish woman performs abortions. And the way they were done. My God! I remember my second abortion. I had the abortion, and I felt so awful that on my way home I crept under the railroad platform and thought, I'll just lie here and die. And to think that two children were waiting for me at home!

You mean, you went home right after the abortion?

Of course, immediately. In this case it had been done under more or less sanitary conditions. It wasn't so bad. But one abortion I had—I went there and the abortion was performed by a nurse who worked at a day-care center. She pulled out a pile of dirty linen from under the bed and told me to lie down on it. And then there was a filthy sink where people washed their hands, and on it crude household soap. And she grated the soap and sprayed it up my uterus. Can you imagine? And I got blood poisoning and had to go to the hospital. I was deathly ill.

Good God, and they demanded to know who had performed the abortion?

Of course, of course.

That's terrible. And the doctors didn't recommend anything, any form of birth control?

No, of course not; nobody . . .

So the emphasis was on the need to produce children? Did you feel like you had to have children?

Yes, definitely. After all, it was wartime, and the birthrate had dropped significantly, so it was necessary to produce children. And in such circumstances, no one cared how we brought them up.

And at that time there was no maternity leave?

Look, my son by my second husband was born out of wedlock. And I never told anyone that I was an unwed mother and needed help. You know, sometimes I get irritated by all this talk now about the need to help single mothers. They're not the same sort of single mothers, understand? I'm not denying that there were unwed mothers among us, but nobody expected help from the government, because this was considered shameful.[14] In short, we tried to protect ourselves from being stigmatized and didn't reveal anything about our situation to anybody. By the way, I still have my tax book, which shows that they even deducted a tax from my wages for having too few children![15] Four taxes were deducted: First there was the "loan," which you had to make to the state; then there was the income tax; then the cultural tax; and finally, the union tax.

And what was the cultural tax?

How should I know what the cultural tax was. There were four taxes, and you had to pay—it didn't matter if you had enough to eat and drink. And then they deducted an additional tax if you had too few children.

---

14. A family law instituted in 1944 granted a small stipend to unmarried women who bore children, in order to encourage them to give birth and restore the birthrate, which had been severely depressed by World War II. This comment suggests that women were not eager to take the money. From the context, it is not clear why this assistance would be considered shameful.

15. The Family Law of 1944 put a high tax—150 rubles—on people without children. It was much lower—25 rubles—for people with only two children.

That is, if you were married?

I had two children. Once you had three, you were exempted from the tax. They had this law for two or three years. And that's the sort of life we had. And now, when old people with pots demonstrate,[16] I am always surprised: "Why are you doing that? You've lived a long time, you must remember the way things used to be." But then I think, Of course, there were a lot of people who were "given the green light," even those poor peasants, the bednota, who robbed us blind. They began to live better, understand. They never had anything, and now they just go through the motions of working and have everything.

When Stalin died in 1953 . . . I had a sister who was married to a military man. They're both dead now, God rest their souls. Her husband, of course, came from a poor family, and he was an ardent communist, a real one. He was a pilot. And she was "educated," with his help. And so when Stalin died, she wrote us a letter, "My dear sisters, how have you lived through the death of our father?" Our father! Can it be that she started writing this in 1940?—I thought to myself. But later, when she came to visit us, we constantly laughed at her.

She had Stalin's death in mind? Right?

That's right. When Stalin died, I was working in a military organization. And I remember that they immediately called a meeting of our section and announced his death. When I heard the news, I got very frightened, thinking that they would be able to tell from the expression on my face that I was very happy. [She laughs.] And I forced myself to look sad, so they wouldn't notice that it didn't upset me. Understand? And how many people they put in prison. I spent the entire period of "repression"[17] here in Moscow. You'd come home, and they'd say, Yesterday they took away Uncle Lesha. You'd go to work, and they'd say, Yesterday they took away Voronov. You'd go to see a girlfriend, and they'd say, We have an empty room now; they've exiled Andreitsev. And I in my naïveté thought that all of these people deserved to be in prison. I was brought up by my father to believe that the most important thing of all was to preserve my chastity. I wasn't afraid of anything, I was only afraid that I would be raped in prison. [She laughs.] I wasn't afraid of anything else.

---

16. Dubova was referring to anti-Yeltsin, procommunist demonstrations, which received a great deal of press coverage around the time of our interview with her.

17. This is the word that all of our narrators used in referring to the terror of the 1930s. It is a bureaucratic formulation, originally designed to present the terror as an aberration and not a crime, as in "illegal repression." The "illegal" has been dropped in popular usage, but the relatively mild term "repression" has evidently remained in circulation.

You mean, if you were arrested?

Yes, I was afraid that I would be raped, if I were put in prison.

And were you afraid of this because you thought that this might in fact happen to you?

Yes, of course. I had heard about this before, because I had an uncle, my mother's brother, who had served time in prison. As I already told you, her brother had also been branded a kulak and dispossessed. On some kolkhoz a potato crop rotted, and who was to blame? Only saboteurs could have done that. Aha, it must be Kudriavtsev. He's the one. So they gave him a five-year prison sentence. When he completed it, he came to our family in Rzhev, although they themselves were having a hard time. He arrived, lived in Rzhev for a while, and then one night they came for him, for no reason at all, took him away, and that was that. A troika [board of three] tried him, and that was the end for him. There was no trace of him for a long time. It was only after the war that he turned up again. And when he did, he was already an old man. They had given him twenty-five years, and where hadn't he been in those twenty-five years. You understand? And so he came to visit my mama, his sister, after Stalin's death, and he said, "If I had come to visit you when Stalin was alive, of course you wouldn't have received me." That's what he said. Then he went on, "But Stalin wasn't to blame." In spite of everything, he excused Stalin. And he said: "I went through so many camps, and in every one of them I would ask that at least they read out the sentence, tell me what I was in for and for how many years. And every time they answered, That isn't any of our business; we don't know. They've driven you here; let's get to work." He seemed to us . . . He was so young when they took him away, and when he came back, he was old and wrinkled, like a little potato. He looked so awful. To have to serve a twenty-five-year prison sentence . . . Perhaps he didn't serve out the entire term.[18] And he said: "Even if you were to stand me against a wall and ask me why I was put in prison, I couldn't tell you. They never published the sentence, they never told me anything. And I spent my entire life in prison."

You didn't become a communist?

No, no. I wasn't even a member of the Komsomol, although this was considered very important, and if I had been, maybe I would have lived better and would have gotten . . . Because most people treated me pretty well.

Let's go back a little. Where did you work in the beginning?

I began to work straight out of the FZU, at the "Bolshevik" factory as a cake decorator, and I worked there eight years. Then along came Griazo-

---

18. The amnesty of prisoners, declared three years after Josef Stalin's death in 1953, might have reduced his sentence by a year or two.

dubova,[19] and the three famous women pilots. Then we began producing the M–1 automobile, the "emka" [little em]. And the "call" went out: Girls, take the wheel! Girls, go into aviation![20]

What year was that?

I think this was in 1937 or 1938. And so I seized the opportunity and left the cake factory and went to train to be a chauffeur. But once I tried that life, I immediately gave it up. I was already pregnant with my first child in 1939, which gave me the chance to leave. And I suffered a lot for that. If I had kept working there during the war, I would have been well fed and my children would have been well fed.

Anna Akimovna, was your daughter born first?

Yes, she was. I've already told you all about that. Nobody met me when I came home from the hospital. And no nurse ever made home visits.

Did anyone prepare you for childbirth or tell you how to take care of a small baby?

How can you think that? Of course not.

And the birth itself. Do you remember what the actual birth was like?

Oh, how can you ask? Of course I remember it! It was so painful, I wanted to hang myself—only I couldn't find a towel. My contractions were very short. They seemed normal, but they were very intense and kept coming. I had no time to rest between contractions. I would lie there and watch the other women. They would cry out and then they would fall asleep, but I couldn't do that. I didn't even have time to take a breath between contractions; I was in such pain. I yelled and cried out, and nobody paid any attention to me! They would look and say, Everything's going okay. You understand how it was. That was that; there were no conversations. And I thought to myself, Where can I find a towel, I'm ready to hang myself. I just didn't have any more strength.

During childbirth what was the role of the doctors?

Well, they attempted to calm us, saying, Don't worry, everything's going okay, calm down, it'll be all right. And then when I was already in the de-

---

19. In September 1938, Valentina Griazodubova, Marina Raskova, and Polina Osipenko set a world's record for nonstop flight by women. During their flight, the radio broadcast hourly bulletins about their progress, and the entire nation listened. The three inspired thousands of women to follow in their footsteps.

20. The flight of the three women was part of a broader campaign that the government launched in the 1930s, intended to encourage women to assume work roles that had previously been occupied by men.

livery room, they prompted me, telling me to push; and they explained everything that was going on.

At that point you were working as a driver, a chauffeur, right?

That's right, only I had been transferred to light work. It was my job to give out tools to the other chauffeurs.[21]

Were there many girls who were drivers?

Yes, at that time there were. We trained in a school, and almost all of the trainees were girls. Everyone was young. And for that matter, I wasn't very old either. We were all so excited about going to the training classes. They would take us there in a bus, and we would sing songs all the way there and all the way back. Up to a certain point it was all very interesting. But when I actually started to work and had to bend over a motor and do repairs, it all became very uninteresting. Instead of frosting cakes and doing all sorts of wonderful things, I had to grease and oil engines; you can well imagine what that was like! And I immediately became terribly disillusioned. I was so happy that I was going on maternity leave, and when my leave was over, I didn't go back.

How long did you work as a chauffeur?

It must have been about a year.

What didn't you like about it?

You know, I didn't like anything about it. Even the garage where the vehicles were kept. At the factory where I had worked as a cake decorator, everything was clean, sparkling white, tidy—everything. And here, everything was soiled, greasy. Somehow the garage depressed me right from the start. And I couldn't keep my clothes clean the way I had when I worked at the factory, because at that time a chauffeur had to be able to do everything. Understand? If the carburetor went on the blink, you had to figure out what was wrong with it and fix it. I didn't like that at all.

And what was your living situation at the time?

At the time, I was living . . . I was already married. My husband was away on a business trip when I left the cake factory. What's more, he objected to the fact that I worked the evening and night shifts there because that meant we didn't get to spend the night together, like a real husband and wife, if you know what I mean. And so I decided to quit my job. For the good of the family, so to speak.

But he didn't object to your working as a driver?

No, he didn't.

---

21. She was given lighter work because of her pregnancy.

And this was largely day work?

Yes, that's right.

Then, after the birth of your daughter, who did you leave your baby with when you went back to work?

My daughter was born in late 1939, and I went back to work in early 1940. [At that time, women were given two months' maternity leave—a month before and a month after the baby was born.] There was no childcare available, and so I hired a young girl to look after her.

You mean to say that there was absolutely no childcare available?

Well, there was, but very little. And what's more, at that time it was considered shameful to put your child in childcare—as bad as it is today to put your newborn in an orphanage.

And why was that? Was it because children were not well looked after in day-care facilities?

Most likely it was because day-care centers were associated with orphanages, looked upon as shelters for abandoned children. That's the way it had been after the civil war, and that image of them was still fresh in people's memories. And there were so few day-care centers that they really were like shelters. And it was very rare for anyone to put their child in day care. Everyone tried to avoid that. And at the time, it was very easy to hire someone because so many people were needy. People were glad to get work as nannies or domestic servants. And so I had an old woman to look after my child.

Anna Akimovna, am I right in assuming that you found this old woman when your maternity leave was over?

That's right.

And you paid her something?

Yes, I did. She took care of the baby, and then for some reason she suddenly up and left us. And then the war began, and a young girl turned up who had come to Moscow and was completely without family and couldn't leave because it was wartime. So I took her in and gave her a home for the duration of the war, and she looked after the baby.

How old was she?

She came to me when she was ten years old.[22]

---

22. Before the revolution, too, peasant and working-class mothers commonly hired very young girls to look after their children.

[Anna Akimovna went on to discuss her living conditions, and then the conversation turned to her religious beliefs and the strict morality of her Old Believer parents.]

Anna Akimovna, on the level of everyday life, do the practices of the Old Believers differ from those of other Orthodox?

Well, to be frank, their hygienic practices differ. Among the Old Believers, men and women never bathe together. This is strictly forbidden. In general, their sexual life is totally hidden. My parents brought so many children into the world, and yet I never saw my father and mother sleeping in the same bed. Never!

Well, what did they do? Did they sleep in separate beds?

Yes, they slept in separate beds. But not because it was considered sinful to sleep together. That wasn't the reason. It was because there were many children in our family. As soon as a child turned two, Father took him, while Mother had the babies.

Did they sleep in the same room?

Of course. We all slept in the same room.

So you never witnessed tenderness between your parents?

No, I never did. I only saw my father kiss my mother when he was going off somewhere on a trip, and then he treated her just like he treated us children. He kissed us all.

Anna Akimovna, can you picture to yourself where their intimate life unfolded, where they made love?

You know, we had a lot of enclosed places—various sheds . . . And they toiled. They would get up very early, at the break of day, and they would work hard, and then—let's say—they went to rest in a shed, and . . . They had all the opportunities they needed. And then, when we children went off to school, there was also . . . We were raised to be very modest. When I lived in the hotel,[23] one of my roommates would walk around naked, and this, of course, really shocked me. At least I would want to have something on me.

Anna Akimovna, when they closed the churches, how did the people in your village react?

Oh, they took it very hard. You know, they were intent on killing those people, the ones who were closing the churches. I remember that the daughter of a former priest was the very first to join the Komsomol, and she would gather the young Pioneers and take them to the lake. And you know they lay in wait

---

23. This was not so much a hotel as a hostel, housing workers at the enterprise.

for her—this I remember—and wanted to kill her because she had joined the Komsomol and what's more had taken these young Pioneers. That's the way they reacted to it. People in my village reacted to it very violently.

So what did the authorities do after closing the churches?

Then they took everyone away, did away with everyone, including the priest. They also took away his son, my godfather. Nobody knows where he perished. And the rest lay low, just to stay alive. And the churches were looted. The poor peasants, the local *bednota*, looted everything, claiming it had to be done. They threw out the icons, burned them, and jeered at people who had them: Silly old women, what have you got hanging up there?

And you didn't save any icons?

No, I didn't.

But then how did you pray in the 1930s, '40s, and '50s?

I didn't, because the consequences for doing so were extremely harsh. I could have been fired from my job or even worse, I could have been shamed, subjected to public condemnation. I could have been attacked in posters, if, let's say, people had caught me praying or going to church.[24]

Did you wear a cross?

I wore one on the fastener for my bra, but not around my neck. That way it couldn't be seen; it was completely hidden. And I didn't have any icons. Nothing.

But you never ceased to be a believer?

No, I never stopped. But I concealed it. Deep down . . . I believed.

And your first husband—most likely he wasn't a believer, was he?

No, of course not. And I didn't give him the slightest reason to think that I was a believer. I never once prayed in his presence. My last husband belonged to the party, and he wasn't a believer either. And sometimes he would even curse. By this time, I had become more open about my faith. Let's say I was going to church to pray. He would say: "So you're going there. Don't you have anything better to do than to engage in such bullshit?" Just like that.

When you got married for the first time, who in the family decided how the money would be spent? Did you make the decisions together?

Oh, dear, we lived together for such a short time, only from 1938 to 1941. Then we had just gotten a place to live, and besides, we had so little money,

---

24. In the late 1920s, the government began to treat religion as a source of opposition and intensified attacks on believers, who might well have suffered in precisely the ways that Dubova envisioned.

there was nothing to decide. At that time there was a terrible influx of people from the villages, in the wake of collectivization. And many people lived in much worse circumstances than even I did. Understand? Why, *my* husband had the power to allocate living space. He had that little room. Then he allocated space to my sister who lived with us, so she had a little room. Then we got two small rooms, so it was as if we had a separate ... And at that time, people didn't aspire to live lavishly and buy things other than food and the bare necessities and something to wear. That was it.

Who did the shopping, for the most part?

He would shop. He would bring food back. It was easier for him to get the food. He was a master at wangling provisions. He had connections, they knew him in the store and everywhere else, everyone knew who he was, and he felt at ease everywhere[25]—all of which is to say that he was boss in the village.

Did you do the cooking?

Yes, I did. Oh, at that time, there were little kerosene stoves, and in our half of the house there was a brick stove. You could buy a lot of prepared foods then, understand. You could get cold boiled pork, ham, good fish, quality things. We're talking about 1939 or 1938; everything was pretty much available. So there was no real need to cook. To be sure, I prepared soups. But I didn't cook very much because he never ate. He would eat somewhere else, other people fed him, he got his fill. It wasn't that we didn't have food at home. He would bring home a whole bag of groceries—often he'd been drinking—and then—out the door. I would sit with the baby and cry, lamenting that I was all alone. Life was very hard.

And how did you meet your second husband? Was it during the war?

Yes, it was. Evacuees began returning to Moscow. Workers from his enterprise returned, and they were brought into our organization. And different organizations were giving out plots of land—you know the sort—for planting potatoes. They gave out plots to almost everybody, so people could feed themselves.

Was the war already over?

No, this was during the war, after the Germans had been driven back and were no longer a threat to Moscow. And these potato plots were all right next to each other. Well, here I was, all alone, and, naturally, a strong young man would help a lonely woman. And we began meeting there, exchanging hellos, and then I took him home. Evacuees lived in a dormitory, while I had my own place, so he began to drop by, and so on and so forth—

---

25. His party status gave him considerable power in the village.

that's the way we got together. I really liked his respectability. The fact that he didn't drink completely won my heart. I was very happy; he really was a worthy man. Of course, at home—understand—he was his mother's favorite. They were cobblers and lived well. And here he found himself with me and a baby—I had a little girl—in such poverty. His mother simply couldn't stand it: What had he gotten himself into and why? She was the one who took the initiative—in order to save him from this poverty, from this horrible mess. Well, and then he acted so stupidly when he left . . . not really stupidly, but despicably. It took me by surprise. And we hadn't saved up anything; we had nothing.

How long did you live with him?

I'll tell you in a minute. . . . About four years, let us say.

And you didn't attempt to register your marriage with him?

I couldn't. I hadn't gotten a divorce yet. At that time, you could only do it through the newspapers. First you had to file, then wait six months for them to publish the announcement in the newspaper, and then, if they thought there were sufficient grounds . . . then and only then would they grant the divorce.[26]

What do you mean by "through the newspapers?"

Well it was very simple: You went and filed for divorce. Then you waited until the announcement was published in the newspaper, that Dubova has filed for a divorce from so-and-so, for such and such a reason. The reason had to be given.

But it was as if we had gotten married. We trusted each other, and we lived together. And when our son was born—he really wanted a son—he was very good to him. But then when the baby was seven months old, he up and left, without a word. To tell the truth, there was nothing to talk about: We didn't have anything, not even a single ruble. To be sure, he had a lot of cobbling tools. He did know how to do things. At the time, it was the practice for people to have their shoes repaired. People were so poor that they couldn't buy things. So he had this suitcase full of cobbling tools. And I even brought it to him on the train platform. Well, what else could I do, once he had decided that he didn't want to live with me? I cried and cried, and that was the end of it.

And then I married this other man, whose photo you see here in the album. I didn't register that marriage either. We lived together like that for thirteen years, and then we registered our marriage. All told, I spent thirty years with him. He was very good to my son, but sorrow keeps gnawing

---

26. In 1944, as part of a campaign to strengthen the family, divorce became more difficult and more complicated to obtain.

away at me. I keep thinking, If only his own father knew what a decent fellow his son turned out to be, what a decent son he abandoned—without leaving so much as a trace. It's such a shame.

And what do you think? Just why did he leave you?

Because we were so poor. He couldn't stand it.

Did he earn anything?

Well, he worked at a factory, but at that time money was virtually worthless; it wouldn't buy anything. People didn't even earn enough to keep body and soul together. Everything was rationed. Yes, it was definitely because we were so poor. He must have lived well as a child. After all, he lived at home, they had some land, and he was well taken care of. And suddenly here he was, trapped by poverty. It was much easier for him on his own.

Anna Akimovna, what did you dream of becoming?

Well, when we were growing up in the village, no one even thought of going to the university. Father always said, I must give all my children vocational training so they can make a living for themselves. He sent my oldest sister to learn to sew, and he also wanted his son to train, to learn the cobbler's trade or the potter's. So my father did have a dream—to give all of his children vocational training in a trade—but the possibility of higher education for them never entered his mind.

But how did you see yourself? What did you want to be?

You know, I didn't manage to . . . I was very young and didn't have any goal.[27]

But what about later, when you had moved and were already living in Moscow?

In Moscow I had a burning desire to study. Where or what wasn't important; I wanted to study. But it didn't work out for me because I had no living space, nowhere to sleep, nowhere to work, nothing. But I really wanted to learn, and evidently, I was capable. But then I was thrown about: There was the war, I got married, I had a family, I suffered poverty. All my hopes were dashed.

Did you succeed in making a career for yourself or not?

Well, you know what, I can't complain, because I worked for many years in a construction design office, or KB, even though I had little education and no special training. And people there treated me very well.

---

27. It was evidently difficult for Dubova to review her life in terms of her personal aspirations. Girls of her age and social position were not raised to put themselves first.

Dubova in her garden in 1962

Did you work as a draftsman?

No, I worked in the technical division, with documents. You know, technical specifications, descriptions of blueprints, descriptions of any manufactured articles. Let's say they were making an airplane wing; there would be a description and technical specifications. It was my job to know them and to know whom to give what information and how to record it. Or let's take another example, standards. I had to know them. It was my job to change them when they changed, and they changed quite often. This work was—how shall I put it—I enjoyed the respect of others in my job.

Were you satisfied with your wages?

Wages, what wages! Why, we had a saying at work: "Without that piece of paper, you are an insect; with it, a human being." My lack of higher education prevented me from getting decent wages.

Did you feel that you never had enough money?

Of course, of course. It was very difficult. Thank God, I wasn't envious. People came to work well dressed. After all, it was the KB, a prestigious organization, so women there dressed well, while I . . . My clothes were nothing special, although I tried somehow to make "something out of nothing." I even took sewing classes later, to make my clothes look smarter.

Mama used to say: "Anna, you've had such a life. Good heavens, they could write a book about you." In my childhood ... I was merely a child, and this official, this secretary ... [28] I'll tell you what the real reason was, why they didn't deport us to Solovki: I promised to marry him, although I was only ... And he gave my mother a guarantee that he wouldn't touch me for five years. Then I barely got away! What a document I had to sign to get away! I had to write out an official statement that I renounced my parents, that I no longer had any ties with them. That's what really happened! I had to do that in order to get permission to leave!

Leave the village?

Yes.

So that you could go to Moscow?

Yes, and I kept that document for a long time, and then I misplaced it. What didn't I go through in my life. This secretary that I'm talking about, that I was supposed to marry ... Why I was still a child, and I remember he was such a drunk. You know, they would torment us. Oh, how they tormented us! If, for example, you were walking somewhere with your girlfriends, or with anybody for that matter, this secretary would say, Hey, you, kulak daughter, come over here! You'd go up to him, and he would give you a kick and say, Look, you know you can't walk with them; you know who you are. Just like that.

Did this happen in the village where your family was attacked and dispossessed?

Yes, yes. What do you think? It was so traumatic!

And did your past ever catch up with you?

No, no. We never suffered for it here in Moscow.

But you hid it?

Of course, of course. First of all, I never acknowledged it in any application for work. I thought, What will be, will be. I went by another last name, that of my husband. I used the last name of my first husband, and so did both my children. Therefore, I never acknowledged my past. I never did anything wrong, so why should I? We lived very honestly. You know, we didn't seek revenge or want to harm any of those people. We lived our lives very honestly.

If the revolution hadn't taken place, would you have stayed in the village?

I'd have stayed. As I told you, I feel as if I've lived someone else's life.

---

28. Here Dubova, without any encouragement from her interviewer, suddenly revealed these details of her family's escape during the campaign against the kulaks.

◼ Taking Advantage
of New Opportunities

SOFIA NIKANDROVNA PAVLOVA

At the time of this interview, Sofia Pavlova was ninety years old, the oldest of our informants and the highest on the social scale. For twenty-three years she had worked in the International Division of the Central Committee of the Communist Party of the Soviet Union (CPSU), and she also had been involved in such elite organizations as the Committee for Soviet Women and the Soviet-French Friendship Society. Precisely because of her successful career, we almost disqualified Sofia Pavlova for this book about "ordinary" Soviet women—she seemed too much like a Soviet-style heroine. The fact that Posadskaya knew her daughter, an activist in the Russian women's movement, also made us uneasy because we wanted to select narrators with whom we had no personal ties. However, other women kept telling Posadskaya that Sofia Pavlova was an extraordinarily interesting person and that she had lived a truly unusual life, especially during the first years after the revolution. And if Posadskaya did not interview her soon, she might never have the chance, they said, because Pavlova had been very ill. So Posadskaya went to see her.

Sofia Pavlova lived in an imposing building in a fancy neighborhood right in the center of Moscow, in the quarter known as the Arbat. During the Brezhnev era, many buildings like hers were constructed of solid red brick, nine to twelve stories high, towering above the prerevolutionary one-story private residences and apartment houses of Old Arbat. Until the liquidation of the Communist party in 1991, these red-brick buildings were unique, with a doorman standing at every door to prevent outsiders from entering; but during the years of perestroika, security became more lax. The doorman was somewhere else when Posadskaya arrived, so there was no one to ask which floor Pavlova's apartment was on. While she waited for the doorman to return, Posadskaya surveyed the entryway and recognized the signs of decline: The peeling walls and ceiling showed that nothing had been repaired for a long time; the doors of the elevator were covered with graffiti, just as in other apartment buildings. Yes, Posadskaya thought, observing that the Communist party was no longer in a position to guard or maintain the dwellings of its elite members, power had indeed changed hands. Pavlova was sharing an apartment with her younger son, a retired chemist, who was fifty-six years old. Contrary to Posadskaya's expectations, which were based on the widespread belief that all elite Communist party members managed to feather their own nests, Pavlova's apartment was small and her furnishings modest. Her main possessions were books, of which she had a great number in Russian and in French. Pavlova answered the door herself. She was a short, thin woman, with closely cropped hair, almost completely white. She was dressed in a jogging suit and hardly fit Posadskaya's mental image of an "old Bolshevik." Pavlova was not in good health and the conversation was continually interrupted by her shortness of breath and deep coughing. She occasionally took medicine for her heart. This evidence of Pavlova's ill health made Posadskaya feel so awkward about interviewing her that she tried to cut the interview short. But Pavlova would have none of it: She mustered her strength and went on speaking in a firm voice. Throughout the interview, Posadskaya was aware of Pavlova's tremendous will and could not help but admire it at the same time as she felt intimidated by it. Even in her enfeebled old age, Sofia Pavlova was still a formidable woman. How did Posadskaya find the courage to interview her, her Russian friends wondered.

"Are you really interested in these trivial details of my life—my childhood, my family, how I became involved in the revolutionary movement," Pavlova asked sternly at the start of the interview, when Posadskaya raised the usual introductory questions. "I could tell you about things that are much more interesting—about my thirty years of involvement in the Committee for Soviet Women and the Soviet-French Friendship Society, about my meetings with people like Maurice Thorez, Palmiro Togliatti, and Louis Aragon. They were my close friends!" [Thorez was a leader of the French Communist party and Togliatti of the Italian; Aragon was a well-known French Communist poet.] It was hard for Posadskaya to convince Sofia Pavlova that we were interested in other parts of her life, too, and that we very much wanted to understand how a working-class girl from Siberia finally ended up in the CPSU Central Committee's International Division, one of its most important sectors.

Pavlova's life is one of the "success stories" of the revolution. By the standards of the revolutionary period, during which the Bolsheviks took power in the name of the proletariat, she was doubly fortunate in her family background. She spent her childhood in the home of her mother's father, a railroad worker. From this grandfather she obtained her proletarian origins, while her uncles, who had formed an underground Bolshevik cell even before the revolution, drew her into revolutionary work when she was very young. Needless to say, everyone in her family supported the revolution.

Pavlova at home in 1996

Pavlova herself became one of the relatively rare working-class women who actively promoted its objectives. She fought on the Bolshevik side toward the end of the civil war, then took part in the campaign to wipe out illiteracy, making the rounds of peasant villages on foot. She agitated among Siberian girls on behalf of the revolution and organized meetings for women workers.

Despite the importance of her work among women and the stress that the party placed on women's emancipation, Pavlova denied any knowledge of this element of the Bolshevik agenda or any familiarity with the work of well-known Bolshevik feminists such as Aleksandra Kollontai. It is hard to know what to make of this denial: Does it mean that the drive toward women's emancipation was less widespread than historians have contended? Was Pavlova simply another of the many Communist party women whom we know to have been dismissive of anything that smacked of feminism? Or perhaps Pavlova's response was influenced by the eclipse of Bolshevik-style feminism after the 1930s, which might have effaced it from her memory as it did from official histories. Whatever the explanation, Pavlova benefited personally from official efforts in the postrevolutionary period to make the Communist party as well as the new political, economic, and intellectual leadership as "proletarian" as possible in its composition. This led to the rapid advancement of able (and sometimes, not so able) individuals of Pavlova's class. Gender contributed to Pavlova's advance as well: Working-class girls with her level of culture and commitment were rare. Note how few she counts among her fellow students.

Pavlova rapidly moved upward in the party hierarchy. In 1922, when she was eighteen, she became secretary of her local party organization and a member of its regional committee, the first step in her long and successful party career. "That could only happen in the provinces," she said of her rapid advance in the party, and added, referring to the criticism of Communist party rule currently widespread in Russia: "No one is interested in that now. No one needs it." Pavlova's ability and dedication won her other gains as well. They brought an invitation to Moscow to study at the Krupskaia Academy of Communist Education, and subsequently at the Institute of Red Professors. Under the direct purview of the CPSU, both of these institutions of higher education were established to train a new, communist intellectual elite to replace the prerevolutionary intelligentsia, which was tainted by its "bourgeois" origins. Pavlova benefited materially, too. She lived in comparatively spacious quarters at a time of dreadful housing scarcity, and she never had to worry about having enough money or getting enough to eat. She experienced the material hardships that were routine for most of the population only during World War II, when she was hastily evacuated from Moscow and found herself in unfamiliar territory and without party connections. But at the same time, Pavlova never lived luxuriously and evidently never aspired to affluence. A child of a revolutionary milieu that scorned material well-being and the comfortable "bourgeois" way of life, she never acquired the cozy domestic trappings that came to characterize the new Soviet "middle class," such as fancy lampshades and potted plants.

Pavlova's interview reflected her continuing loyalty to the system to which she had devoted her life. She seemed reluctant to criticize any Soviet actions, refusing to discuss the outlawing of abortion in 1936 and downplaying the fact that her beloved second husband perished during the terror of the 1930s. Only Posadskaya's persistent probing led Pavlova to acknowledge the harmful consequences to her son, who was born after his father's arrest and because of the new family code of 1936, was registered as having no father, that is, as illegitimate. Likewise, only as a result of Posadskaya's insistent questioning did Pavlova acknowledge that women's access to the higher reaches of the party might have been limited.

The anticommunist mood prevalent in Russia at the time of the interview made Pavlova defensive about her past. She often repeated the phrase, "Don't record that, no one is interested," especially when she discussed the important parts of her political work, those parts that could be considered real achievements. It was as if she was saying, That is in the past, and no one today is interested in the past. Each time she said this, Posadskaya had to coax her to continue speaking. Yet while Pavlova was convinced that no one was interested in her political achievements, she was also uneasy about revealing personal details. The first time Posadskaya interviewed her, Pavlova talked about her childhood, about her first and second marriages, her difficult move to Moscow, the births of her children, and her hardships during the war years. But then she had second thoughts. In her own opinion, her political work—her work for the party, in international organizations and the like—was what really mattered about her life, even though nobody was interested in it at present. After the first meeting, she telephoned Posadskaya and said, "My God, I said so many foolish things to you—about my childhood, about my husbands, about my children. Come back, and I'll tell you the truly important things, serious things about my activity in the Soviet Women's Committee and in the Soviet-French Friendship Society." In this chapter we have included both her personal history and that of her political work.

▨   ▨   ▨

Sofia Nikandrovna Pavlova: I was born into the family of a military man serving in the tsar's army, whose unit was quartered in Wilno [in Russian, Vilna]. Today this is Vilnius, Lithuania. I was born there, but I was born on December 27, 1903, according to the old style—that is, the Julian calendar, which is actually January 9. I always observe my birthday on January 9 and consider that I was born on January 9, 1904. That makes me one year younger. [Here she coughed.] My father came from peasant stock, from Kostroma *guberniia,* now Kostroma oblast. My mama was from the working class, from a long line of railroad men. Mama's parents lived between Belovezhskaia Pushcha and the town of Slonim [in Belarus]. And that's where my grandfather, my mama's father, worked, at a small way station. He had four sons and two daughters—my mama and an older sister. There were six children. Well, in terms of nationality, they were more Poles than Russians, because at home they spoke mainly Polish. And I spoke Polish and read books in Polish as a child—not as a teenager—when I was about ten or eleven.

My father soon died—when I was three years old. He died right there in Wilno, and Mama was left with three children, because my older sister Vera died at a very young age. And Mama took me and my two younger brothers and moved to her parents at this way station. And we lived there, at this way station, until the beginning of the First Imperialist War [World War I]— that is, until 1914. As I already said, my grandfather had six children, two daughters and four sons. All of them were railroad men, they all began by working for the railroad in the engine house, as assistants to the locomotive engineers, perhaps even as firemen. I, of course, don't remember exactly. But all of them later became railroad engineers with their own apprentices, and one of my uncles, Uncle Kostia, who was one of my grandfather's sons, even finished *realnoe uchilishche*.[1] One of my grandfather's sons, the oldest, moved to Siberia, and since family ties then obviously were stronger than they are now, he prevailed on all the others, and all his brothers, sons of my grandfather, also to move there. At the very beginning of 1914, very likely in 1913, perhaps it was even 1912, Grandfather left to join one of his sons in the Siberian town of Taiga. This was a major railroad junction, an important point on the Siberian main line, and from Taiga a branch went off to the city of Tomsk. Yes. And as soon as the Imperialist War began, we moved to Taiga to live with Grandfather and my younger uncle, Shura, to whom I was very attached and who then spoiled me and loved me very much. It was at the very beginning of the war, because I remember we went out on the railroad tracks at the way station where we lived and watched the refugees going by, and saw them throw away gnawed chicken bones, and such. Yes, and in the short time that we remained there after the departure of my grandfather for Siberia, my youngest brother died, and only two of us were left, I and one brother. Moreover, we all got sick with all sorts of childhood diseases—with measles and other things . . . with diphtheria and with pneumonia.[2] Evidently I had pneumonia, since father died from tubercular pneumonia. I suffered from pneumonia many times, even later as a young adult, when I was already studying here in Moscow.

It was a long way to school from this way station where we lived. They could have sent me to the town of Slonim, but that was impossible, and so a switchman who worked at the way station but was obviously sufficiently literate came to tutor me. He took me through the equivalent of the first and second grades. And when I arrived in Taiga at the end of 1914, I immediately entered the third grade at the elementary school.[3] And I was a pretty good student. But the instruction was also very good in this elementary school. I remember it so well, even now I have a vivid recollection of the French and German teacher. He taught both French and German. And so we lived in this little town of Taiga.

Grandfather and Grandmother had a little house consisting of three small rooms and a small kitchen. In one room lived Grandfather and Grandmother. Antoshcha, he always called her. That's Polish for Antonina. I remember there was an enormous samovar in the kitchen—it would hold a whole bucket of water—and Grandfather always sat near this samovar, and he always had a saucer, and turned upside down on this saucer—I'm not sure—I think it was a large mug, and on top would be a piece of sugar that

---

1. A six-year high school that provided a modern education, with an emphasis on mathematics and the natural sciences, before the revolution.

2. These were common childhood diseases in Russia at that time.

3. In the prerevolutionary period, it was quite common for children to obtain their elementary schooling at home and then to attend high school.

had been dunked in the tea but not completely eaten. Because Grandfather or Uncle Shura, with whom we lived, would buy loaves of sugar, lump sugar. They would buy these loaves, pyramids of sugar, and break off pieces from them. And so Grandfather could sit and drink and drink and drink, cup after cup of tea, without end. And the entire day, the samovar from which he took his tea sat boiling. And so these were the three small rooms in which we lived. Grandfather lived with Grandmother in one; in the second room lived my Uncle Shura—at that time he wasn't yet married—and in the third room the three of us lived: Mama, me, and my sole surviving brother.

Anastasia Posadskaya-Vanderbeck: Sofia Nikandrovna, do you remember what your daily life was like?

You see, Grandmother wasn't well. For the most part I remember her having to be in bed. Grandfather was always near her: "Antoshcha, stay where you are, stay where you are! Don't get up, don't get up, stay in bed!" And Grandfather did a great deal. And Mama. That's basically how the work got done. Uncle Shura, well, at that time he worked as an engineer's assistant, then he became a railroad engineer, and he . . . But more about that later. That's another story and has to do with my uncles' revolutionary influence on me—my uncles had an underground Bolshevik organization in the engine house in Taiga.

The streets in this town had no names. There was a bridge across the railroad tracks, and the train station was on that side. There was a first street, a second street, and a third street. We lived on the third street. And so they continued up to the seventh street. And the seventh street bordered on the real taiga, the forest. And even bears would come there. Yes. In this part of my life, what interests you, what do you want to hear more about? Have I left something out?

Well, it would be interesting to know more about your school: Were the classes large? What subjects did they teach, do you remember?

What subjects did they teach? They taught penmanship and they taught history. In actual fact, the elementary school was a preparatory school for the gymnasium.[4] Later, in 1917, I entered the first class at the gymnasium, but I wasn't destined to study there. And I think that was my good fortune. That's what I think.

Why do you think that?

They gave me a hard time. I had an enormous shock of hair, and it was curly. I would come home and comb it and even tie on a kerchief so it

---

4. An eight-year high school that provided a traditional education, generally including the study of classical languages (Greek or Latin), before the revolution.

would be smoother. Especially the French and German teacher and the religion teacher. Russian Orthodoxy was part of the curriculum in the school,
but I don't remember a thing; I didn't take it in. "Pavlova, go to the toilet
and comb your hair!" I would rise, go, wet my hair, comb it, and come
back. A little while later, the hair on my head would be standing up again.
Several times a day, during different lessons, I would have to go to the toilet, wet my head, and comb my hair. I went to school with cropped hair, cut
short, just like that.[5] Somewhere I have photographs where I'm wearing a
black apron. We had a brown uniform with a white collar and a black
apron, and we also had white aprons.[6] And even at that age I loved to read
poetry, and loved to read it aloud. I even read Nadson aloud from the
school stage. And many, many more. I read Apukhtin.[7] In general I think
the school was very, very good. When I think about it now and compare
the way my grandsons studied in school to the way I studied . . . With such
willingness! And it was because the instruction was interesting and they
didn't force children to learn; there was a real yearning, a desire to study, to
learn, and to prepare lessons. Yes.

*That's interesting. Sofia Nikandrovna, you said that 1917 was your first
year at the gymnasium. But apparently the revolution prevented you from
studying there?*

That's right.

Do you remember the beginning of the revolution?

How could I forget! I remember we all ran to the train station because political prisoners were traveling back from Siberian exile. It was a major railroad junction. Special trains always stopped there, meetings and mass
demonstrations in favor of the revolution were organized there, and we, all
us girls, always took part in these meetings and mass demonstrations. I remember Breshko-Breshkovskaia, who spoke here in Taiga.[8] First of all, her
speech was very emotional. That's the way I would characterize it now,

---

5. Peasant women and many working women in Russia kept their hair long, braided, and
covered with a kerchief. The fact that Pavlova cut her hair short and went about with her head
uncovered suggests that her family's views were quite untraditional.

6. Exactly the same uniform was reintroduced in the Soviet Union in the late 1930s. It was
abolished again during Mikhail Gorbachev's rule (1985–1991).

7. Semen I. Nadson (1862–1887) was a "decadent poet," popular in the early years of the
century. In the 1930s, his books were banned and removed from circulation. Aleksei Nikolae-
vich Apukhtin (1841–1893) was a prerevolutionary poet whose work Soviet critics con-
demned as having "stood apart from social struggle." In referring to these poets Pavlova is
demonstrating the independence of her aesthetic judgments.

8. Ekaterina Breshko-Breshkovskaia (1844–1934) was an activist in the radical movement
of the 1870s. Tried in 1877–1878, she was sentenced to five years of exile and hard labor. She
subsequently became a member of the peasant-oriented Socialist Revolutionary party.

very emotional. Of course I can no longer remember very well what it was about, but at any rate, it made a good impression on us, in the sense that the revolution, see, had liberated the political prisoners and they were going to Moscow, to the capital. And undoubtedly they would accomplish something good. And in general we too were full of enthusiasm. And already in 1920, after Kolchak had passed through Taiga and gone further east, I remember how the Reds crossed our courtyard. Our little house stood in a courtyard. Our little house, in which Grandfather and our family lived, was in a courtyard, and behind our house was a vegetable garden. I remember how the Reds crept through, and after that Kolchak's soldiers, and then back and forth again. Then there was a new wave of Reds, and they beat those Kolchak soldiers. But my brother and I weren't afraid of anything. We roared with laughter and watched and roared with laughter again. And there and then Grandfather took a spoon and beat us on the brow—I remember it—and said: "What are you so happy about? Why are you laughing? There's a war going on! A war! At any moment we may perish, and you are laughing. What are you so happy about?"

And how did your mama regard all of this, do you remember? What did she think of the whole situation? Was she afraid for you?

My mama was rather stern. Stern, and she was a very demanding woman.

Could she read and write?

Yes, but not very well. Not very well. But she was very interesting looking. Basically, of course, Mama did absolutely everything in the house. Because, as I said, I remember Grandmother being sick all the time, and then she died. So. Uncle Shura earned the money. He would bring it home and give it to Grandfather. Grandfather would go to the market. He would bring home rounds of frozen milk.[9] That's how they sold milk in winter. Yes. He would bring home frozen meat and so forth. I remember how on Sundays we would take turns, and all the relatives would gather, first at our house and then at someone else's, and we would prepare a meat filling and dough and make *pelmeni* [dumplings]. We would do this at the very beginning of winter. There was such cold weather there, God preserve us. Heavy frosts. And there was some big wooden thing, perhaps it wasn't wooden, I no longer remember exactly, a support . . . Not a support, and . . . not a tray for baking, but . . . a kind of board, a board. And so everyone would assemble the pelmeni. We had a kind of glassed-in cold porch, large, adjoining the house. And we would take the pelmeni out there, and they would freeze. Then, I remember, there were linen sacks, pure white, which were always got ready. When

---

9. This milk was not sold in containers, but as it was, frozen in some form that gave it a circular shape.

Grandmother was alive, she prepared them, but when she passed away, my mother prepared these sacks. And the pelmeni were put in them. Enough were made for the whole winter. There was also a larder. On one side was the porch, and on the other was this larder. And that's where these sacks of pelmeni were stored. And when there was a need, we went there, took some frozen pelmeni, cooked them, and ate them. The next Sunday it would be some other relative's turn, and everybody would gather there. And they would also assemble pelmeni and freeze them, and also prepare them for the whole winter. And that's the kind of stocking-up there was.

And did your mama also work outside the home?

She sewed. She sewed, and when we lived at that way station, she sewed well. And this was the way she earned money. She sewed all the time.

Did she sell the things or did she sew for acquaintances?

For acquaintances. Mainly for acquaintances who lived right there. I remember some kind of blouses with flounces. For some reason, it's mainly blouses that stick in my memory.

And did she have a machine? Or did she sew by hand?

No, she had a machine. And when we got to Taiga, she had a treadle sewing machine. It was no doubt Grandmother's. My mama was a coquette; you could call her that. She didn't have many outfits, but she had two pairs of fancy shoes. That I remember well. One pair was painted gold and the other silver. She had other ordinary shoes. But these were dress-up shoes; they were silver and gold. So. She loved to dress up. And because she sewed, she didn't dress badly.

And did your grandfather receive a pension? After all, he worked, he was also a railroad man. He must have gotten one, didn't he?

Yes, of course, he . . . But what kind of work he did I don't really . . . I think he was a simple railroad worker, because he read and wrote with difficulty. He could sign his name and everything, but he was semiliterate. And Grandmother was completely illiterate.

She didn't earn wages outside the home?

No, she didn't. But when we lived with them after coming from Wilno, they had a garden, they had bees, there must have been three or four—I don't remember—beehives, they had a cow, there was always a pig. But it was Grandfather who always prepared the food. They always celebrated Christmas in the Polish manner: They would set the table and cover it with straw, and Grandfather would bake *mazurki*. They're the tastiest Polish cookies. He had to soak the dough for a whole day in water, then he would take it out and roll out the cookies. Grandmother made jam from berries that we gathered, because there were woods all around; we were right next to Belovezhskaia Pushcha.

I remember there was a Russian stove. Grandmother cooked kasha [on it], and she shoveled the pies that Grandfather prepared into its large oven. The children slept together, as best I remember. But we didn't sleep on the stove.[10] Although it was a Russian stove and there was a place for sleeping on it. Yes.

And after the revolution did life change?

Yes, first of all, a Bolshevik organization immediately came to light at the Taiga engine house. And it turned out that my uncles, who worked and lived in Taiga, were all underground Bolsheviks. And it was my Uncle Shura who kept urging me, Join, join the party. And I would say, But I'm not ready, I can't. Just how old was I then? In 1917 I was almost fourteen years old. And he would say, Join, join. They were accepting young people. But we quickly organized a Komsomol organization with their help, and I worked, I immediately began working in this Komsomol organization. I was in charge of mobilizing the ranks of young people for a certain length of time. Then I was an instructor for work among girls, and I rode around the district on horseback. Then I was the editor of the district Komsomol newspaper, where I wrote my own poetry, or rather published my own poetry. Yes. So I immediately took an active part, and it was thanks to Uncle Shura's influence. At first, it was imperceptible; he didn't propagandize. As I said, I loved Uncle Shura very much, and he too loved us very much—especially me, he loved and spoiled me. Whenever he came back from a business trip, in the beginning, when he worked as a railroad engineer's assistant, he would say, Come here, look what I have in my pocket for you. I would run, knowing that I would find some kind of yummy candy.

Sofia Nikandrovna, what do you think it was that attracted you to this revolutionary work?

Well, I think that going to these meetings and taking part in these mass demonstrations on the square in front of the train station, of course, had an enormous influence on me. And then, undoubtedly, Uncle Shura also had some kind of influence. He was very well read, and, you see, at one time he had been secretary of this underground organization, before the revolution. Yes. Undoubtedly . . . I don't remember that he propagandized me. I only

---

10. The stove occupied a central place in Russian peasant houses. In cold weather, especially, peasants slept on it, in addition to using it for cooking and heating. The upper part of the stove did not reach the ceiling, leaving a broad platform on which people could lie. In warm weather, people slept either on the floor or on wooden benches that lined the walls. Pavlova's comment suggests that people slept on beds in her grandfather's house, evidence of their "semi-urban" way of life.

Sofia Pavlova in 1920

remember that later he would say to me, Join the party, join the party.
... No, I'm not ready, I'm not ready.

And why did you think that you were not ready?

For some reason I thought that I wasn't ready. But I worked very actively,
very actively. I was a member of ChON. I had a Mauser, and we would go
out to hunt down [rebel] bands—there were lots of them. Remnants of
Kolchak's soldiers.

ChON—what does that stand for?

Units on special assignment.[11] Yes. We fought these bands. Right after the
revolution. This was largely in 1920, the beginning of 1920. Yes. But then
all the same I joined the party. In 1921, I was accepted as a candidate for
party membership. And immediately—today this isn't of interest to anyone,
nobody needs this—immediately they made me secretary of the organization, the party organization, me, a candidate for party membership! Only
at that time and only in Taiga could that have happened.[12] The organization included all party members: those who belonged to the party's regional
committee, to the Komsomol's regional committee, to the police, and to the
court. Party members of all these bodies formed a single cell. That's what

---

11. ChON is the acronym for Extraordinary Units on Special Assignment. These were military formations composed of party members, Komsomol members, and sympathizers. Mobilized to fight in the civil war, they were supposed to be crack units. They operated outside of
regular Red Army channels and in close cooperation with the Cheka, the secret police.

12. She is explaining why it was that she was elevated to such an important position as secretary, when she had not yet been accepted as a full member of the Communist party.

they called it. I was secretary of this cell. Then, in 1921, actually at the beginning of 1922, we had a *chistka*,[13] or party cleansing. Here in Moscow it occurred earlier, in 1921, but ours took place at the beginning of 1922. And at the time of the purge, the party members met and decided that I should be promoted to full membership in the party. And they accepted me. So I've been a full member of the party since June 1922. Yes. Mainly I worked in the raikom of the Komsomol, and at the same time I was secretary of the party organization. How I combined the two, I don't know.

And was the party organization large?

Yes, it was quite large, because I would say there were approximately 100 people in the party raikom, something like that. It was large.

And were there many women?

Women? No, there weren't many women.

You were one of only a few women and yet they advanced you?

I don't even know. An instructor in the party raikom vouched for me. When I joined the party, he said that I was completely worthy of it. Yes. In addition to everything else, in addition to working in the Komsomol raikom and in the party raikom I would walk seven kilometers with my friend Roma Kvopinskaia. She was Polish. Her father had been exiled to Siberia, or rather her grandfather, in 1861, after the Polish uprising.[14] Yes. And his children had remained there. And so Roma Kvopinskaia and I became close friends. And we would walk seven kilometers out of Taiga, along the railroad tracks, surrounded by forest on both sides, in order to teach adults to read and write. And here's how they paid us. One person would bring a mug of milk, another a piece of bread. That's what we lived on. We would do this on our days off. Most likely, on Sundays—I don't remember any more—but every week, without fail, we would go to this way station. Then they would have "dried bread week." They would collect pieces of dried bread for famine victims on the Volga.[15] This was already at the beginning of 1922.

---

13. In March 1921, the Communist party tightened its recruitment policy and began to expel (or purge) members who for various reasons ("passivity," careerism, drunkenness) were considered unworthy of membership. About one-fifth of party members had been expelled by the start of 1922.

14. Late in the eighteenth century, Poland lost its independence and was incorporated into the Russian empire. Polish patriots greatly resented this subjection, and in 1860–1861, they staged patriotic demonstrations that led to clashes with the police and culminated in an unsuccessful rebellion against Russian rule, which was not suppressed until 1864.

15. In 1921–1922, a terrible famine broke out along the Volga river, threatening the lives of millions of peasants. It was caused by civil war depredations and the Bolshevik policy of forcibly requisitioning grain from the peasantry. It had already become the practice to mobilize people for a specific period and purpose. In the case of "dried bread week," people were mobilized to collect food for victims of famine.

Sofia Nikandrovna, you said you went out and carried on propaganda work among the girls, right?

Oh, it's terrifying to think about it, because several times ... There were many kulaks there. Siberians, you know, were really very prosperous. And there were the so-called *zaimki* [16] or settlements. And that's precisely where the prosperous ones lived. They kept livestock, bees, and so forth; they traveled around and traded, and so forth. Yes. It makes my skin crawl when I think about it. Sometimes we would be awakened in the middle of the night. I didn't travel alone; I would travel with one of the Komsomol raikom secretaries. He would be on one horse, and I would be on another. And they would wake us up at night: "Hurry, saddle your horses and get out of here. Get away, get away. They're coming to kill you." Yes. More than once we were warned like this. But even so, we would ride out again, again carry on our agitation work. We wanted to create a Komsomol organization, we wanted to involve the girls, because this was the hardest thing to do. The Siberian girls were rather resistant to such agitation. And already I considered myself an agitator and propagandist. Yes, I did.

How did you attract them? What did you say to them, do you remember?

No, I don't remember very well. I agitated for Soviet power, I said that it was good power, that it had given us freedom. "See, we can assemble, and could you assemble in tsarist times? Could you speak out, as I am speaking out right now?" I remember once I even said that. Although later one of the Komsomol secretaries said to me: "Why do you say things like that. You shouldn't. You shouldn't speak like that."

And what was it he didn't like?

I don't know what it was, but at any rate he didn't like it. And here the Siberian, or rather the Taiga period of my life draws to a close. At the end of 1922 the Komsomol raikom sent me and my friend Roma Kvopinskaia to Tomsk to study at the *rabochii fakultet,* the rabfak. We set off for Tomsk and enrolled. I don't remember whether we took any entrance exams or not. Most likely there weren't any exams; they simply accepted us. They made sure we could read and write, but of course we were literate because the elementary school provided a very good education, a very good education.

Sofia Nikandrovna, your mama didn't get upset when you left Taiga?

She cried a little and carried on. But I was very stubborn.

---

16. Separate farmsteads, at some distance from one another, were characteristic of Siberia, where the peasant commune was not so widespread as in the rest of Russia.

She wasn't afraid for you? After all, this revolutionary work was dangerous.

Of course she was afraid, because of the meetings. It's true we tried to conduct these meetings mainly in the daytime. At first, the streets weren't lit. Only later were there lights. The only parts of town that were lit up at night were the square in front of the train station and first street, where the stores and so forth were. And on the remaining streets, where the little shops were—there were shops—some kind of lanterns burned. But the lighting was very bad. So we tried to conduct all our work in the daytime.

Only the two of you were sent to the rabfak?

Only us two.

Just two girls? And who proposed you?

It was the raikom's decision to send us to study.[17] At the rabfak there were very few girls, in general. Mainly there were returnees from the civil war, young men who were already quite grown up, and for some reason there were Germans. The guys really courted us. They really went after me, for example. But you don't need to mention that. The student body was largely composed of returnees from the civil war. From the Red Army. Because everyone had either a Mauser or a revolver.

Did you have one too?

When I was in Taiga, when I was a member of ChON, then I did.

And did you arrive at the rabfak without your Mauser?

Without it. Without it. I turned it in. And it's such a pity that my documents from ChON were destroyed. During the bombing[18] of the history faculty on Gorky street, when a bomb fell right next to the windows of the history faculty, it caught fire, and the archive burned up, everything went up. And I didn't do anything to restore them. Although they were very important documents. It's true I wrote to the archive of the Soviet Army, when they were honoring former ChON members, but you had to have witnesses. Unfortunately, either the witnesses were no longer alive or I didn't know where they were. So I gave up. In general, I never attached much importance to the sort of documents that you were supposed to hold onto.[19] And so, at the rabfak, Roma and I were very good students. And very soon I was elected secretary of the Komsomol organization not only of the rab-

---

17. It is likely that Pavlova was awarded these opportunities because she was female and well educated, as well as a member of the working class. Working-class women were rarely as well educated or as politically involved as Pavlova, and the new government was eager to utilize their energies.

18. She was referring to the bombing that took place during World War II.

19. People needed documentary evidence of unusual service to obtain government awards and privileges including special treatment and access to scarce goods.

fak but of all the institutes of higher education in Tomsk: the Polytechnic Institute, the University, and the rabfak at the University. And I was secretary of this . . . You don't need to write that down, since, as I said, today nobody is interested in this. Absolutely no one. Don't, don't . . . And so I was secretary right up to January 1924. I was supposed to give a talk on the January events.[20] The University had an enormous auditorium. And suddenly, when I had already prepared myself to go out on stage and begin the talk, the secretary of the party organization took me aside and said to me, "You know, we just received the news, Lenin has died." Just imagine what came over me, how upset I got. And he said: "Now we don't need your talk. I'll go out and say that Lenin is no more, that Lenin has died." And that's what happened.

It is hard even now to convey the feelings that one experienced then. It's difficult to convey them. To convey the tremendous emotion, the feeling that Lenin was irreplaceable, that this loss was such a loss that—I don't know, I am thinking this, adding this now—it would affect our entire future. Most likely, of course, I am unconsciously adding that now. Probably at that time I didn't think like that, but I did think about the enormity of that loss, which we felt in conjunction with the death of Lenin.

Well, if you won't write it down, I can tell you some more about interesting moments in our personal life, that is mine and Roma's—how we went barefoot, barefoot to the theater, the wonderful Tomsk theater. And during the intermission we proudly walked around barefoot. Everybody turned to look at us, and we proudly walked around.

So you hadn't any shoes? Was that it?

Why do you say that? Of course we had shoes! This was our way of making a statement. We went to see a lot of things at that theater, and every time we went there barefoot. Moreover, if it was winter, we would go in short sheepskin coats, I had such a coat, but I didn't wear anything on my head, because I had an enormous shock of curly hair. I don't remember, but it seems to me that we took off our coats there. Yes, we took them off. But then again perhaps we didn't, since the building wasn't heated; in any case, our feet were red.[21]

---

20. This is a reference to the massacre that became known as Bloody Sunday. On January 9, 1905, a Sunday, tsarist troops fired on a crowd of workers and their families as they peacefully attempted to petition the tsar. Over one hundred people died, and many more were wounded. This event, which set off the revolution of 1905, was commemorated in Soviet times.

21. Pavlova and her friend might have been demonstrating their freedom from bourgeois propriety. Such manifestations were fairly common in the decade following the revolution, when enthusiasts rejected the old bourgeois order in action as well as word and symbol. For example, people sometimes dashed naked through streetcars.

Sofia Nikandrovna, did you live in a dormitory there?

Yes. I shared a room with Roma. Since there were so few girls. I don't remember the other girls. Or what they looked like. For some reason, I don't remember anything. I remember many, many young men—for the most part, in uniform. They were still wearing riding breeches and soldiers' blouses with a sword belt slung across the shoulder. They all carried a revolver or a Mauser.

Undoubtedly, you received some kind of stipend. Is that right?

There must have been a stipend. I don't remember what we lived on. Money we had. But in addition to being secretary of the Komsomol organization for institutions of higher education in Tomsk, I was also the organizer and leader of meetings for women delegates in the city.[22]

What does that mean?

Well here's how it was: We assembled women, we told them what Soviet power was, what it did. If some concrete task stood before us, such as collecting dried bread, we called upon them to do that. If it was necessary to collect donations, we called upon them to do that. So we also had concrete tasks and concrete goals that we summoned women to perform, in addition to our general propaganda work. That's how it was.

And how did women respond to this?

They listened with interest. For the most part, they listened with interest and responded with interest.

These were city dwellers, weren't they? Tomsk women?

These were women who worked at factories. We would go to the factories. There we set up meetings at the municipal level for women delegates. Yes. Or rather we convened meetings at the municipal level for women delegates and also for women delegates at the factory level. I was a member of the district Komsomol delegation and thus responsible for these delegate meetings. This continued until 1924.

In the summer of 1924 I got appendicitis. At that time, I was a third-year student at the rabfak. I had one more year to go before I would graduate. They told me that if I wanted, I could leave the rabfak and go to Moscow

---

22. Until the Zhenotdel was abolished in 1930, it selected women delegates from the factory floor who would temporarily be released from work to gain political experience. They attended literacy classes and meetings where they heard reports on political issues and learned how to organize facilities for working women, such as factory day-care centers. After three to six months, they would return to the workplace to share their experiences with their coworkers. Pavlova evidently organized and led meetings for such women, although her discussion of their activities makes the work sound considerably more "top-down" than do the accounts of most historians.

to study—supposedly I had sufficient knowledge to do that. But that summer I got appendicitis, and I had an operation. Everybody visited me and urged me not to go, to stay: "You're sick; how will you cope with everything?" But no, I was determined to go to Moscow. And so I went, planning to enter the Krupskaia Academy of Communist Education.[23] An academy had been created here in Moscow in honor of Nadezhda Konstantinovna. And so I was preparing to enter this academy. It was already August; that is, the time for exams was getting close. And so I traveled in the middle berth, not the upper one. And the ride was very bumpy, and I was so jolted by it that I barely made it to Moscow, and my stitches broke. Even now I have a terrible scar.

I arrived here in Moscow, I went to the academy, I found the admissions committee, and someone, I don't remember who, said to me: "And why did you come here? Do you write poetry?" "Yes, I do." "You should go to see Valerii Briusov."[24] And so I went to see Valerii Briusov. And I brought my poetry notebook, with excerpts of verses that had been published in our district newspaper. And Briusov leafed through them and read a line here and there. "My dear girl, you still need to learn a great deal, a great deal. You've come to Moscow?" "Yes." "Why have you come?" So I said that I had been sent to study at the Krupskaia Academy of Communist Education. "So do what you've planned and enter the Academy and study there. Write, and then we shall see." And that was Valerii Briusov's advice.

So I entered the academy, and for some reason I enrolled in the division that prepared teachers for factory apprenticeship schools. And that was the division I graduated from. There were very interesting people there, who later advanced into spheres of government. What did they teach there? They taught everything. They taught history, which I always really loved, they taught literature, and pedagogy. And we heard Krupskaia's lectures. It's true she didn't read them at our division but at the orgfakultet, that is the department for organizers, where people who already had some experience studied. People with experience, teachers from the provinces, and so forth. And that's where Krupskaia read her lectures. And we would go there to the orgfakultet to listen to her lectures. And so I graduated from the division that prepared teachers for factory apprenticeship schools.

---

23. The academy was an institution for preparing communist cadres. It was named after Nadezhda Krupskaia (1869–1939), Lenin's wife and a revolutionary in her own right. Krupskaia had had experience as a teacher and remained deeply interested in education. After the revolution, she played an important role in developing new school curricula.

24. Valerii Briusov (1873–1924) was a major poet and a leader of the Russian symbolist school. His prestige among poets meant that his approval would mean a great deal to an aspiring poet.

How many years did you study there?

Four years. And in the summer we did practical work, we would go to the Kuban and work there on horse-drawn harvesters and gather in the grain, as students.[25]

And did you have enough to eat during the years you were studying?

I don't remember being hungry, I don't remember that we went without food. But we did practical work in a printing office, for example. I worked in a printing office. This was where we did practical work in the winter time. At any rate, that's what happened in our division. And we also did practical work in factories.

Sofia Nikandrovna, how did you meet your future husband?

It was 1927, and he was a student in the same division. And at that time some couples didn't even register their marriages; at that time, you know, people paid no attention to that sort of thing.[26] In 1928, I had a son—this was my older son, who unfortunately is no longer alive. He's been gone eleven years.

When I got married, we moved out of the dormitory. My husband had a room on Bolshoi Komsomolskii Pereulok, in a large, communal, formerly bourgeois, apartment.[27] It was a very large room, a very good room. There were wonderful neighbors, bourgeois, but they were very fine people and treated me very well, especially when I moved in with my baby. My mama also came there to live, and she stayed with us while I finished up my last year at the academy.

Did she come to help you?

Yes, she came especially to help me. She even left her own son—to be sure, he was already an adult—he, too, worked in that same engine house in Taiga, I don't remember what his job was there. Yes. And then they as-

---

25. Students in the Soviet Union had to engage in "practical work," that is, do manual labor as well as study. This labor was supposed to keep them in touch with the "toiling masses" in whose name the revolution was carried out. It also often provided a convenient solution to labor shortages in key sectors of the economy.

26. Some people, young people especially, believed that the postrevolutionary challenge to "bourgeois" forms of existence made it unnecessary to register a marriage.

27. After the revolution, the state commandeered the spacious apartments in which well-to-do families lived and transformed them into communal apartments. The former inhabitants were sometimes allowed to keep a room for themselves. The rest of the rooms were settled by strangers, one person or family per room, or sometimes part of a room, separated from others by a flimsy partition. All of the inhabitants of an apartment shared the kitchen and bath. Such communal living arrangements predominated in cities until very recently. People continue to live in communal apartments to this day.

signed me and my husband to a factory in Iaroslavl. It was formerly the Ko-
rzinkinykh factory; after the revolution the Krasnyi Perekop. And there I
taught at the factory apprenticeship school. And my husband also taught
there. We taught social science. But I didn't teach there long.

*Sofia Nikandrovna, when you left Moscow for Iaroslavl, did you take your
son with you?*

Yes, mama came with us and the baby. And in Iaroslavl they also gave us a
tiny room. They gave us a room and some kind of entrance hall as well. So
it was like having two rooms . . . cold ones. And we also had neighbors.

*Sofia Nikandrovna, let's go back to the time when your baby was born. In
those days, there wasn't any kind of maternity leave. How did you manage?*

I gave birth in the Krupskaia maternity hospital. In fact, I spent several
days before the birth there. They taught me how to swaddle and take care
of the baby.[28] Even then there was some kind of preparation. And since
Mama came so quickly from Siberia, my studies weren't interrupted. And
since this was the last year, the year of assignments, we were assigned to
Iaroslavl.

I didn't work very long at the factory apprenticeship school. In addition
to being a teacher, I was also a member of the Krasnyi Perekop party
raikom. Krasnyi Perekop constituted a whole district, because it was a major textile factory. I was also involved in Iaroslavl with the Inter-Oblast
Party School, which was called a higher school. It served three oblasts—
Ivanovo, Iaroslavl, and Kostroma—and the students came from all three.
They took me on there as a teacher of world history, because, as I said, I
was always interested in history, I knew history pretty well, and I began to
teach history. World history. Moreover, in this Inter-Oblast Party School the
way things were set up for learning was remarkable. Very often professors
would come from Moscow to lecture. When I began to teach in this school,
they gave us two rooms. We had one room on the first floor and one above
it. But they were so cold, so cold! It was terrible! We froze to death, literally
froze to death.[29]

---

28. The Bolsheviks aimed to reduce the high prerevolutionary levels of infant mortality.
One way to do this, in their opinion, was to teach mothers how to care for their children properly. Because Pavlova had become a member of the elite, the Communist party, the quality of
this maternity home might have been particularly high. Compare this with Dubova's account
of childbirth around the same time.

29. Physical hardship, including suffering from cold due to lack of fuel, was not unusual in
those years. However, having two rooms for four people was a luxury and a measure of
Pavlova's privileged position.

Sofia Nikandrovna, did your husband continue to teach at the factory apprenticeship school?

No, no, they called him back to Moscow. They called him back to Moscow to *Komsomolskaia Pravda*.[30] Because he wrote articles. He was the correspondent for Iaroslavl.

And so you separated?

Yes, but not for long. We went to Iaroslavl in 1929, in 1930 I was already teaching in the party school, and in 1931 my husband called me to Moscow. And so I came back to Moscow in 1931, or rather my entire family—me, my son, and Mama—came back to Moscow. And once again we lived on Bolshoi Komsomolskii Pereulok. And in Moscow I also taught world history. There was KUTV—the Communist University for Workers from the East—and KUNZ—the Communist University for Workers from the West.[31] And I taught at both these institutions of higher education and also at the Moscow oblast Komsomol school.

Did you work simultaneously at all three?

Yes.

But your child was still small.

It was Mama! Mama saved me. I am eternally grateful to her.

So most likely you wouldn't have been able to do all this, if it hadn't been for Mama.

If it hadn't been for Mama, no doubt of it. And here I was completely free. I didn't breast-feed my baby long. Mama, in fact, bottle-fed him.

Sofia Nikandrovna, if possible, before we begin talking about how you taught at these institutes, universities . . . Your husband, where was he from originally?

I don't know, I don't remember.[32] He was virtually a Muscovite. His parents lived near Moscow, in Pushkino. At that time, this was a place where people spent the summer. His father worked as a bookkeeper. His mother didn't work.

---

30. *Komsomolskaia Pravda* was the newspaper of the Komsomol organization. It began publication in 1925, and by the end of that year, it had gained a circulation of over 100,000. It was one of the livelier newspapers in the Soviet Union.

31. Because of the relatively small number of communist intellectuals, especially in the early postrevolutionary years, professors at communist academies often taught at several institutions.

32. She was unwilling to talk about her first husband, from whom she later separated. His face had been excised from all the family photographs. It is likely that he got into political trouble during the terror of the 1930s. In any event, her account was an "edited text" of his history from which all but the most basic, harmless details were omitted.

And did he ever tell you what influenced him, why he became involved in revolutionary work? Were his family, his relatives also agitators?

No, no. Now I realize that this was a very ordinary, very ordinary, almost petty-bourgeois family.[33] There was nothing remarkable about it. As I said, his father worked as a bookkeeper. His mother was good, a fine person, but she never worked; she was a housewife her whole life.

Were there other children in the family besides your husband?

No, there was no one else. He was their only son.[34] And on the basis of my work at KUNZ and KUTV and at the Moscow oblast Komsomol school, I was sent to study at the Institute of Red Professors, to their institute of world history. The Institute of Red Professors had agrarian, economic, and party institutes, and it also had an institute of world history. Since I was a historian, I was sent to the Institute of World History.

Sofia Nikandrovna, going back to your work at KUNZ and KUTV, who were the students there?

I remember there were Turkmens, Uzbeks . . . [35]

And were there many women among them?

I don't remember women. I don't remember a single woman at KUTV.

And when you taught social science, was there anything about the role of women?

No.

No? And there was nothing about the role of women in the revolution?

Unfortunately for you, there wasn't. I don't remember. In my lectures there was nothing on that topic.

That's amazing. On the one hand there was so much work done among women, and in Taiga from the very beginning it seems as if you had . . .

Well, I simply talked about my own work, talked about Komsomol work, about my own trips to the oblasts around Taiga, to the settlements, to the villages. But I didn't talk specifically about the role of women, no. I don't remember doing that.

---

33. The Russian word she uses, *meshchanskii* (petty bourgeois), literally refers to the urban lower classes. His family may well have belonged to that social stratum, but she was also using the term petty bourgeois in a derogatory sense. For Russian socialists, the label "petty bourgeois" was a dismissive term, implying among other things vulgar material interests.

34. That is all she was prepared to say about him. She abruptly changed the subject back to herself.

35. Turkmens and Uzbeks are Muslim peoples who live in Central Asia.

Well, there were Kollontai's lectures.[36] In general did people know about Kollontai at that time?

Of course they did.

There were her famous lectures in which she . . .

Talked about free love and so forth. About a glass . . . [37]

Not only about free love. Yes, about that theory, but not only about it. There were also the lectures she read, as I recall, at Sverdlov University, about the place of women in history.[38]

Well, although Sverdlov University wasn't very far from us, I wasn't connected with it.

How did you view Kollontai at that time? How was she regarded? In general, what was said about her and also about other prominent women of the revolution, such as Inessa Armand[39] and Krupskaia?

Krupskaia, of course, we regarded with great respect, with love. I have photographs of her. There is a picture of the orgfakultet with her among the students. But I didn't have any personal contact with her; I only heard her lectures. I can't tell you how I viewed Kollontai or Armand at that time. I don't remember. I simply don't remember. Most likely, I didn't have any opinion on them at all; I don't know why.

Didn't they say anything to students about how the revolution was solving the "woman question," among other things?

Solving women's problems?

---

36. Aleksandra Kollontai (1872–1952) was the most well-known Bolshevik advocate of women's emancipation. She was a prolific writer and lecturer on women, socialism, and revolution, whose work pioneered in exploring the connection between personal life and political change. Her leadership of the Workers' Opposition, which was critical of Lenin's policies, marginalized her politically after 1921. In the second half of the 1920s, Kollontai came under increasing criticism for her treatment of sexuality and sexual relations as proper topics of political discussion.

37. Here Pavlova is repeating a false stereotype of Kollontai as someone who taught that having sex was no more important than drinking a glass of water to satisfy one's thirst. This kind of distortion of Kollontai's views helped the leadership to discredit her.

38. The lectures Kollontai gave were published in 1922 as a book entitled *The Position of Women in Connection with Economic Evolution* (Moscow: Gosizdat) and excerpted in *Changing Attitudes in Soviet Russia: The Family in the USSR*, by Rudolf Schlesinger (London: Routledge and Kegan Paul, 1949), pp. 45–71.

39. Inessa Armand (1847–1920) was another Bolshevik advocate of women's emancipation. She was a founding member of the newspaper *Working Woman (Rabotnitsa)*, intended for women of the lower class, and she became the leader of the Women's Bureau (Zhenotdel) of the Communist party in 1919. She died in a cholera epidemic at the end of September 1920.

Yes. In general, "solving the woman question."[40]

No, of course I don't want to say that, because if I do, then it will be the way we talk about these matters now. But how they were talked about then I don't remember. Perhaps they weren't discussed and perhaps they were.

Did they talk about the need for changing relationships within the family, about the need for a different division of labor?

These matters somehow didn't come up even within the family, because you felt you were on a pedestal, if I can put it that way. Seriously. In my family it was like that: I felt not only complete equality but sometimes even superiority.

How did you handle your expenditures? Did one of you make the decisions or did you make them together?

Mama made the decisions. Mama. We would turn our wages over to her. She took care of the household, and we would turn our money over to her.

And you would decide together what you would buy?

No. We didn't buy anything. And this was because we were so . . . Don't write this down. We had so absorbed, not so much a negative attitude but an indifference to comfort, to coziness, and the like, to going out and buying some particular thing, and that attitude has remained with me to this day. I often find I don't have this, I don't have that—things I should have thought of earlier, and they're not there. So those problems didn't trouble us at all. And we always had very simple furnishings. Always. That's how we were living when I entered the Institute of Red Professors, and I was assigned to the dormitory there. So we must have moved from Bolshoi Komsomolskii Pereulok to Bolshaia Pirogovskaia. At first we had only one room. We were all housed there in one room.

At that time you still had only one son, right?

One son. Then I left my first husband. This was when I was starting my second year at the Institute of Red Professors. I went to a sanatorium in Golitsyno.[41] And I was done for. I fell in love, and he fell in love with me. I came home and said that I would no longer live with my husband. But there was no particular need for us to get a divorce, since our marriage had never been registered anyway. And so I married for a second time.

---

40. Posadskaya was employing language used in the 1920s; Pavlova responded in language currently in use. Why did Pavlova say she knew nothing about efforts to emancipate women during the 1920s, when some historians claim such efforts were widespread? We cannot know whether she had forgotten about them, repressed the memory, or never experienced them in the same way that historians have described them.

41. Golitsyno is about forty kilometers from Moscow.

How did your former husband take it? He didn't want you to leave him?

H'm! No, he didn't! His mother ... It's true his father was already dead, but his mother tried so hard! She kept urging me not to leave Misha, not to leave him. But I was adamant. In such matters, that's the way it usually is; when faced with such situations, people are adamant. Love prevails.

You don't like remembering your first husband, do you? Were you in love with him? Was there something about him that didn't satisfy you?

Was I in love with my first husband?

Yes.

I don't think so. It doesn't seem to me it was real love. I must have simply been infatuated by him, although I had quite a few admirers.

When was that?

That was 1936 and 1937.

And what kind of work did your second husband do?

He was Assistant Public Prosecutor of the Iakut Republic. And by the time I graduated from the Institute of Red Professors in 1937, the year they liquidated[42] these institutes, I had been assigned to be head of a department at Iakutsk University.

And did you register this marriage?

Yes. I registered it.

But why? The first one you didn't.

But by the end of the 1930s the laws had changed,[43] so it seemed like we should register our marriage, and besides, my husband insisted that we register. Then I had children: First a daughter and then a son. And the children also had to be registered.

Did it seem to you that in this respect there was more freedom in the 1920s?

Yes, even now I believe that it was much better then. Unregistered relationships could be strong and lasting. Because those registered marriages ... Here's what happened: In 1937, when my second husband died, there in Iakutsk ...

---

42. The Institute of Red Professors was abolished in 1937 and replaced by a new system of higher party schools and a refurbished university system.

43. In the 1930s, the authorities began to emphasize the importance of registering a sexual union as a marriage. For example, married couples were more likely to obtain scarce housing than were couples who simply cohabited. A stable personal life also had become an index of a person's reliability.

In 1937! Good God!

In 1937. I married him in 1935,[44] and in 1937 he died. And he died from typhoid. Yes, the official reason given was typhoid and not something else. But later one of my friends, who was appointed chairman of the Sovmin [Council of Ministers][45] in Iakutsk, said that they simply did him in.

How awful!

They did him in because it was 1937, and that's what was going on then. In the beginning I was granted a pension.

At that point were you in Iakutsk?

No, I never went there.

So you were assigned there, but you didn't even go there?

That's right, I never made it there. I was about to give birth to Alik, and my husband was supposed to come for us and take us back with him.[46] But by the time my Oleg [Alik is the nickname for Oleg] was born, his father had already died; he was already gone. And there were difficulties with his [Oleg's] registration. Whereas when my daughter was born, my husband was still alive, and consequently they listed both father and mother on the birth certificate. But in Oleg's case they listed only the mother: Sofia Nikandrovna Pavlova, and the father's name they left blank.[47]

And you couldn't prove anything?

No.

And how did you feel about this?

How can you ask?! It was very painful, of course. But I didn't try to do anything, I did absolutely nothing, I did not pursue it.[48]

---

44. Pavlova's marriage took place a year before the promulgation of the Family Code of 1936, which rendered divorce more difficult and made it possible to identify illegitimate children. The timing suggests that even before they were inscribed in law, changing views of morality affected party members.

45. The chairmanship of the Council of Ministers was a very important position; thus, this man was likely to have had access to accurate information.

46. Personal needs clearly played little role in political assignments.

47. The fact that the birth certificate contained a blank space instead of the name of the legal father is another indication that Pavlova's husband was politically repressed.

48. It is likely that she did not investigate because she feared what she might find, as well as the consequences of being married to an "enemy of the people." She was unwilling to speak about the circumstances surrounding her husband's death and tried to put an end to that line of questioning.

Did it affect your younger son's fate, the fact that he had no father listed on his birth certificate?

No, I don't think so.

Did it sometimes put him in an awkward position?

Perhaps. Yes, in that sense it did. He sometimes felt uncomfortable because of it. And sometimes he still does.[49]

Am I right that the 1936 law that prohibited listing the name of an absent father on the birth certificate also banned abortion? Isn't that true?

Perhaps. I don't know, I can't really say.

You don't remember? Didn't people talk about it?

No, no. The people in my circle didn't discuss it. When I couldn't carry out the assignment and go to Iakutsk to be department head because I had two children, I was appointed to the history department at the [Moscow State] university, and there I taught world history.

Sofia Nikandrovna, when your daughter was born, did your mama help you?

At that time, we had a domestic servant who worked for us. At that time, you were still allowed to have a domestic servant. We had a young girl from somewhere near Riazan, I'm not sure where.

Did she help with the children?

Yes, she did.

And did you pay her something?

Certainly. She received wages. We registered her and drew up a contract with her.[50] That was required.

And how soon after your baby was born did you return to work?

It seems to me I went back within a few weeks, perhaps a couple of months.

---

49. A "proper" background, or in other words, being the child of a registered marriage, became significant when one sought to enter school, find work, locate housing, and the like, and had to present documents. A blank space where the father's name should have been inscribed suggested that there was something amiss in a person's background, and could prejudice officials against him or her.

50. Because Pavlova worked for the party, everything she did had to be open and aboveboard. In addition, having another person registered in her living space entitled her family to claim more room.

And if you hadn't had your mama with you or a domestic servant, would you have put your children in a day-care center, like others did?

They were actually put in day care. My older son was in day care. When we lived on Bolshaia Pirogovskaia, there was a day-care center attached to the Institute of Red Professors, and my older son went there. It was a very good center, very good.

Were there a lot of children in his group,[51] do you remember?

I had very little to do with these things. Mama did everything.

She took him to the center and picked him up?

The center was right near our building, so either she took him or the domestic servant did. It wasn't hard.

You said you didn't receive a pension for very long after your husband's death.

Well, I must have received it for almost three years. Two or three years.

And why did it stop coming? Nobody said anything?

They simply cut it off, and that was that.

And you didn't try to find out why?

No, I didn't make inquiries, because the money didn't interest me.[52] I worked, and I earned enough.

Was it enough simply because you lived so unpretentiously? Because your needs were so modest?

As I told you, we lived very simply. We never bought any special furniture or anything stylish to wear. We lived very modestly. We had a domestic servant—of course, we paid her—and still we had enough. Somehow, I don't remember that we ever went hungry, that we were ever too poor to buy basic necessities like bread, for example. I don't remember times like that.[53]

Were you still living in one room in a communal apartment?

It wasn't a communal apartment. By that time, we were living in the dormitory of the Institute of Red Professors. It had an enormous corridor, and on both sides of the hall were these little two-room apartments with tele-

---

51. In most day-care centers, the ratio of children to caregivers was very high. Posadskaya was trying to learn whether the ratio was lower in this center for children of privileged backgrounds. She did not receive an answer.

52. Pavlova's decision not to inquire about the pension was probably due to her fear of what she might find out, and perhaps of drawing unnecessary attention to herself, rather than to her freedom from financial worries.

53. That they lived relatively well suggests privilege. In these difficult times, virtually everyone went hungry and almost no one had enough money.

phones.[54] We had one large room and a second smaller one, where they had put a single woman. And when my daughter was born, they gave me the second room, and moved that woman into a room in someone else's apartment.[55] Each apartment was like that. Depending on the size of the family, it served either as a two-room apartment or as two single units, if the occupants were single. And each unit was also equipped with a phone. What's more, the dormitory had a very good outpatient clinic with a children's division. We lived in that apartment right up to the beginning of the war.

When the war began, they evacuated university personnel to the Tatar Republic. I got my whole family ready, put Mama in charge, and sent them off. I myself stayed in Moscow. Since childhood, in fact, I had had heart trouble. I don't know whether it resulted from diphtheria or from measles, but I had complications after one of those childhood illnesses, and so before the war I often had heart palpitations, very often. And the day I sent off Mama and the children—I'm not sure, it seems to me it was June 27, in any case it was the day when Moscow was bombed for the first time, and I was terribly upset, of course. There was a shelter in the basement of the dormitory, but I didn't take refuge there that time. I accompanied my family all the way to the train station. I kept thinking: Will they succeed in leaving Moscow, have they left yet or not, will their train be destroyed by the bombs. And right then, my heart began to act up, and I began to have palpitation after palpitation.

I had enrolled in nursing courses[56] that were being offered in the history department. Nursing courses had been set up there, and so I enrolled in them. But then my heart palpitations became so frequent that they told me to leave Moscow immediately and go join my family. At that time I was in the history department's party bureau. And the other members said to me: "Get out of Moscow immediately and go join your family. We won't permit you to take these courses; you aren't going to the front. It is categorically forbidden by order of the party." And they in fact sent me to the Tatar Republic. So I arrived in Kazan and went through a terrible time. I had no idea where my family was. The Tatar Republic is quite large, and they weren't in Kazan.

---

54. These were luxurious circumstances for the times, especially having access to a telephone. In addition, living in the dormitory meant that someone else cleaned Pavlova's rooms and did much of the everyday housework. On the other hand, it also meant that her private life was easily controlled and her public life was inescapable.

55. The government could move people around as it saw fit because it actually owned the housing, while people only had the right to use it. People were allocated free housing according to specific norms of living space per person. In Moscow, the norm was very low, at only five cubic meters per person. Members of the party, Pavlova among them, were allocated more space.

56. She was preparing to work as a nurse to support the war effort.

You mean you didn't even know where they had been sent?

I didn't even know where they were. When special trains would arrive in Kazan, they would jot down in a notebook—sometimes in pencil, sometimes in ink—where such and such a special train of such and such an organization was to be sent. So I was told to look, and if I was lucky, I would discover where they had sent the train. I didn't know the number of the train, but fortunately for me, organizations were listed. So I sat, I must have sat there for nearly two days, and I rummaged through those notebooks, and at last with great difficulty I found that so-and-so—I recognized the name—was in charge of the university's special train, and that it had been sent to the Kaibitsy district. I set out, but that district was quite a distance from the station—which station, I've forgotten. I reached the station, but could not tell whether people had already left for the Kaibitsy district or not. I went to ask the stationmaster; only with great difficulty did I persuade them to let me in to see him. He said to me: "It seems your train is still standing on the siding. We haven't sent it back yet. No horses have come from the kolkhoz to transport the people further." So I went along the siding, knocking at every car and asking, "Is my family here?" I was looking for my mama. And in one of the special trains standing on the siding—our university wasn't the only organization there, there were other organizations as well—I heard my mama's voice. At that point, my heart began to act up, and I felt awful. But Mama brightened up and said: "It's so good you've come! Little Alik has taken sick."

You mean to say they were right there in one of the train cars?

Yes. The evacuees were in freight cars with crude plank beds. In closed freight cars.

And had these plank beds been installed especially for the evacuation?

Most likely. I don't know. Perhaps these trains had been equipped to transport soldiers; they were already preparing to send soldiers to the front. Maybe they were transferring troops to the border. I don't know. Each car had a stove. Cold weather had already set in. It was already October,[57] already the beginning of October.

And you sent them off in June?

In June? Yes, June 27. And it took them all that time to get to Kazan; they were in transit for a long, long time. Often there were bombings along the way, and they were delayed, the train shunted onto a siding. Then the train stood for a long time in Kazan. Then they had to decide which district to send the people to. For the moment, they were sent to the Kaibitsy district.

---

57. The trip ordinarily took no more than a day, in peacetime; however, in the circumstances of war, it lasted months.

So this went on for several months—they spent several months in that freight car.

Yes, and Alik got sick; he got very sick with measles. And then there were complications—dropsy. His whole body was covered with blisters. When we arrived, they settled us with a Tatar family. The house was divided in two: The Tatars lived in one half, and we were put in the other. And in our half what do you think there was? Crude wooden benches that stretched from one wall to the next and a Russian stove. That's all. Nothing more. And so we all had to sleep on those plank beds, side by side. Since Alik was sick, he was last in the row. I slept next to him. Well, what could we do? I asked the chairman of the kolkhoz for a horse and wagon, because we were—I no longer remember exactly—about seven kilometers from the village of Kaibitsy, which served as a district center. I wanted to take my son there to the hospital so they could examine him; his entire body was covered with blisters. But the kolkhoz chairman wouldn't hear of it. And so our Tatar hosts gave me a baby buggy.

And why wouldn't he give you a horse and wagon?

He simply refused. In general, evacuees were treated very badly in the beginning, especially in the Tatar Republic. People were very suspicious of evacuees, afraid of them. And so our hosts said, "Take this baby buggy." And they gave it to me, a buggy they had made with their own hands. And so I put Alik in this buggy, and I trudged the seven kilometers to the hospital, pushing him all the way. When I arrived at the hospital, they examined him and said: It's complications caused by the measles; he's got dropsy. Give him sugar—four kilograms, no less. Four kilo, and the dropsy will pass. So I returned home and asked my mama if we had any sugar. She replied that there was a little.

Now my mama had not wanted to be evacuated. When she left Moscow, she didn't take along any winter clothing. She said, "We'll return in a month, at the very latest in two, so why bother." In Moscow we had been told to leave nothing in our rooms,[58] so we had thrown together all our things and put them in one corner of the communal kitchen at the end of the corridor. So we looked to see how much we had brought with us and found we had enough to exchange for four or five kilograms of sugar—no more. But we had no alternative; we had to save the baby. The rest of us would get by somehow. And so we fed Alik all that sugar, and that saved his life. We saved his life. Time passed, winter came, it got cold. The winter of '41 was severe, and it was bitterly cold in our half of that wretched hut. Mama hadn't brought any warm clothing. We had no blanket. I don't

---

58. They had to leave their apartment vacant in case someone else needed it. The apartment belonged to the party.

know what we covered ourselves with or how we covered ourselves. I don't remember. But somehow we managed to survive the winter. We virtually starved, because there was nothing to eat. Mama would go on foot to the district center, where there was a milk factory and some other kind of factory. She would get them to give her whey, the watery residue left over when they processed the milk, and bring it home. Then she would gather potato peelings at some other factory, bring those home, wash them thoroughly, and grind them up. Then she would go and beg someone to sell her a few eggs. She would beat in an egg, and out of this batter she would make flat cakes, and that's what we lived on. Somehow we managed to survive the winter. And in the summer our situation got a little better. I was given work. In the beginning they didn't want to give me work, but then they assigned me to keep tallies in the lumber industry. I would go on horseback into the forest to where the state was procuring lumber—logs—which then would be processed and shipped off somewhere. Now, the central office for this entire operation was in the district center. That meant I had to be transferred out of Kaibitsy. So they transferred me to the district center and gave us housing in a cold, unheated hut. We absolutely froze there.

No other people lived there? You were the only occupants?

No, one of my friends also lived there in the district center. She also had been evacuated, but her husband was at the front. So she received supplies, the so-called family allotment, whereas I received nothing.

What did family allotment mean?

They sent part of a military man's supplies to his family.[59] So she received this family allotment, and in addition, her husband would send her parcels. He even came to visit her now and then. Consequently, she lived very well, and from the very beginning she had been housed in the district center.

But didn't you at least begin to earn a little money, when you started working as a tally marker?

I was paid in bread. They would give me a loaf of bread.

You mean to say you didn't earn any money?

I don't remember anything about money. Perhaps they did pay me something, but for the most part, it's bread I remember.

---

59. Because the army was comparatively well supplied, these packages contained food, soap, and other scarce items. Pavlova, by contrast, was badly off. She evacuated Moscow in haste and lacked political connections for the first time in her adult life. Moving to the district center helped her to reconstitute them.

And did they provide anything for the children?

But tally markers . . . Now I'm going to tell you something very unpleasant. All the tally markers had lice. I got lice, and I was afraid to spend the night with my family, afraid the lice would spread to them. And that's the way I lived. It was terrible. Absolutely terrible. Yes. And so I worked as a tally marker for some time. What did I do? I would put numbers on the logs that the lumberjacks had piled together, then write those numbers in a book and bring the book to the district center, where the defense industry prepared lumber for shipment to the front lines.

Every day you had to travel to the district center?

Every day. And I couldn't spend the night in the district center because I had to ride out into the forest at dawn, actually before dawn. There would be a whole train of horse-drawn sledges, and we would go to the spot where the logs were to be loaded. After the logs had been tied together with ropes, I would mark them—indicate who had cut the timber, how many logs there were, and what kind.

Then somehow things changed. Obviously, some kind of directive came from Moscow, because the treatment of evacuees changed.

For the better?

People weren't as suspicious as they had been in the beginning, as negative. And so I was appointed a tenth-grade social science teacher in the district center. I began to work as a teacher, and gradually I cleaned myself up.[60] I felt like my old self again. The children began to go to a day-care center.

And was your mama still with you?

She took complete care of the children. As I told you, she was literally my savior. Then we arranged for the children to go to a day-care center, and my children actually began speaking Tatar.

What sticks in your mind about your work in this period when you were an evacuee? Does some particular episode stand out?

Well, I was immensely happy when I finally managed to get "clean" work and when, at last, I was earning some money. Moreover, my older son, who was already thirteen,[61] got work in a print shop, so he also earned something. I was very happy because now Mama had money to buy food—although, to be sure, that was not an easy task.

---

60. She had finally succeeded in having her party status recognized and had resumed her former role, escaping the unpleasant labor she had been forced by circumstances to perform.

61. He was the child of her first marriage.

Where did she find things to buy? At an open market?

Probably. I don't know. I don't remember. Most likely. Then I began to lecture to local party members. And in a short time they wanted me to come to Kazan. And so I moved to Kazan, and they gave us an apartment, an unheated one, on the second floor. It too was cold. But by this time I was working for the party obkom. Today nobody cares about this, so you don't need to . . . In the beginning, I was a lecturer. There was a lecture group attached to the division of propaganda. Then they made me head of this lecture group. I would fly on a U–2, a little airplane with an open cockpit. We would land in an open field. I wore *valenki,* or felt boots, of course, and I would wade through the snow to the village where I was supposed to lecture. But then I acquired a staff consisting of other evacuees and military personnel and began to organize lectures in the city of Kazan and not just out in the villages.

Sofia Nikandrovna, do you remember what the lectures were about?

Winning the war, naturally; what we had to do in order to win. That was the main thing. And we exhorted people to be more productive. So, when I would go out to district centers or to villages, I would exhort people to work harder, to do their share for defense. Then in March 1943 the Central Committee here in Moscow organized a seminar for heads of lecture groups, and I came to that seminar.

But that was at the very height of the war?!

Yes. And at that seminar I gave a speech and talked about the work of our lecture group, and then I went back to Kazan to my family, which had been living without me, going without food and suffering from the cold. But there was a certain Liuba Smirnova in the party organization, who helped me and helped my family a little in my absence.

Then it must have been at the beginning of 1944 or perhaps halfway through that year, I was summoned to the office of the first secretary of the party obkom. And I was told: "There's a call for you from the Central Committee." I got on the special line.[62] "Why haven't you fulfilled the Central Committee's directive? I am speaking on behalf of Dimitrov." At that time, Georgi Dimitrov was head of the International Division of the Central Committee of the Communist Party [of the Soviet Union] here [in Moscow]. "I am speaking on behalf of Dimitrov. You have been summoned by the Central Committee. Why haven't you appeared?" I said, "But I don't know anything about this." "How can you say that! Where is the first secretary? Put him on the line immediately!" So I handed him the phone. "Okay, okay, I will arrange her trip tomorrow." Yes. And the next day or

---

62. This was a special telephone that provided direct access to the center of party power.

Pavlova in 1943

the day after they bought me a ticket and sent me here to Moscow. And I didn't go back to Kazan. My family remained there without me. And I was appointed to the staff of the Central Committee's International Division.

And you began working for Dimitrov?

Yes, in 1944.

What were your duties?

The International Division put out a news bulletin, and I was made editor of that bulletin. Well, not the chief editor; the chief editor was Boris Niko-laevich Ponomarev, who later became a candidate for membership in the Politburo. I worked with him. And that's all. I worked until I was sixty-three.[63] I retired at sixty-three. That's all. Enough.

Did you have the same duties the whole time?

No, later I became head of a department, quite a large one, which took in several countries. In my work I dealt primarily with France, but I was also in charge of Italy, Portugal, Switzerland, and Belgium.

And did you have a chance to go there?

A chance to go abroad? I was in France—I don't know, I can't even count how many times I was there. I was in Italy three times, I was in Belgium

---

63. This was much older than the usual age of retirement for women, which is 55.

Pavlova in 1978

three times. Unfortunately, I never got to go to Switzerland, nor to Portugal. Most of the time I was in France.[64]

I remember so well my work in the Presidium of the Committee for Soviet Women. Also my trips in conjunction with this work. And after I retired, I became even more active in that Presidium and in the Society of Friends of the USSR and France, now Russia and France. These were my own private initiatives, but the work was akin to my interests, close to me and to my heart. So there you have it. I just wanted to add that.

Look, if you had been a man rather than a woman, would you have succeeded in achieving more? More, that is, measured perhaps by some kind of formal signs of recognition. Do you feel that being a woman somehow hampered you a little?

It's very difficult, of course, for a woman who has lived the life I have to imagine herself a man. It's very difficult to imagine how I in fact would have acted in that role. All the same, they didn't treat me simply as a woman. They demanded from me the same things that they demanded from a man, that they demanded from all the others. I was the only woman to head a department. And one of only three women at that level in the entire 5,000-member staff of the Party's Central Committee. And they treated me like a man. They made the same demands; they didn't make any allowances for me.

---

64. Travel abroad, especially to western Europe, was a rare and highly valued privilege.

They didn't make any allowances for you, but did they make it possible for you to advance? For example, were there any women who served as heads of divisions?

No. But there were women among the deputy heads. Not in our division, but in other divisions. Both the deputy head of the Division of Party Organizations and the deputy head of the Division of Culture of the Central Committee were women. Beyond that, I don't know of any other women who served as deputy heads of divisions. That's all I knew of and know of now.

Does it mean women weren't good enough?

No, it's not that they weren't good enough. I don't think that we weren't good enough. There were quite a few women who served as secretaries in the party apparatus. Immediately after the war, there were quite a few women secretaries in the party obkoms. True, they weren't first but second secretaries in charge of agriculture, even industry, culture, and science. But they also didn't get ... All the same, they didn't give women access to higher-level positions. There was a ceiling. It's the tenacity of tradition, and unfortunately, to this day, we haven't broken its hold. I don't know how long it will take to overcome it.

So what do you think: Compared to the present, were there more possibilities for women to participate in political life in the Soviet period?

It's very difficult for me to make the comparison. Very difficult. I can only say this: that the attempts being made now to blacken the record, to repudiate more than seventy years of progress in Soviet society, including progress for women, are nothing but lies. Out-and-out lies. While it can't be denied that millions of people perished in the Stalinist period, including women—I have to admit that many women in the vanguard perished—nonetheless, it was precisely in this period that women advanced. It was in the Soviet period that this happened.

Sofia Nikandrovna, what period of your life was the happiest for you?

For me the most interesting period was the initial one, when I was starting out. It was important and interesting for me, because I joined the movement, joined the revolution, as I understand it, and not as many "understand" it today. And of course, getting to know and working with such people as Maurice Thorez, Palmiro Togliatti, and others.

Sofia Nikandrovna, what does communism mean to you? How do you understand it?

For me communism means a great deal. It signifies the future, in the sense of justice—especially as regards the battle for a just society. It will come. It will come. Look, the ideas of communism are not dying; they are simply acquiring new forms. Communist parties may be changing their methods of work, but they continue to exist in almost all the countries of the world where they existed earlier. I tell you: They are changing leaders, changing their methods of work, changing the composition of their membership. They're changing everything. And this is as it should be. This has to be done. But they exist, and they continue to be called, if not communist, then socialist parties. Just look at the results of the recent elections in Hungary, where the Socialist party—that is, the former Communist party—won. And they're winning in a whole series of countries. Even if they are no longer called communist parties but socialist or social democratic parties, all the same they exist, and they are fighting for those new ideals, for those watch-words, for those principles, which have emerged in today's world. They are fighting to solve those pressing problems that have arisen in conjunction with the change in conditions, in society, and so forth. So I believe, I continue to believe in communism. I think that in the end—perhaps the victory will not come soon—but in the end, it will triumph.

▧ Daughter of
a Village Priest

VERA KONSTANTINOVNA FLEISHER

We found Vera Konstantinovna Fleisher living in the town of Zarechnyi, in the Ural mountains, near her son and his family. Constructed in the 1960s around the Beloiarsk Atomic Energy Station, Zarechnyi was a closed "atomic" city during Soviet times. "Closed" means that an outsider could visit only by special permission. At the same time, closed cities as a rule were especially well supplied and unusually clean, and people who lived there did not face the housing shortages that existed in other socialist cities. Generally speaking, closed cities were the choicest places to live in the "developed socialist system." Zarechnyi recently ceased to be closed. Its privileges have disappeared together with the socialist system, and the atomic station is operating at half its capacity because those who use the energy it produces lack the means to pay for it. But Zarechnyi is located in the midst of a forest, and the sparkling birch forest still stands. After the gray, soot-covered industrial city of Ekaterinburg, which Posadskaya visited first, Zarechnyi seemed almost like a fairy tale. Almost—because as she walked along the main street, she could see the dreary silhouette of the atomic power station, a plant of the same design as the one that exploded at Chernobyl.

Vera Fleisher lived in spartan surroundings. Her apartment was neat and uncluttered, which made it seem spacious although it consisted of only a single room and a tiny kitchen space. Fleisher herself seemed to Posadskaya very reserved and self-disciplined, as if she were perpetually taking herself in hand. A teacher's habit? Fleisher gave Posadskaya the impression that she was calm about the interview, but when she began to speak, her voice shook with agitation. "Can I bring you a glass of water?" Posadskaya asked. "No, it's nothing, I'm all right," Fleisher replied. But her frequent pauses while she attempted to gain control of her rapid breathing said otherwise.

Fleisher, the daughter of a clergyman, is among those of our narrators whose social origins stood as an almost insuperable obstacle to successful advancement in life. From the very first, the Bolsheviks regarded organized religion with animosity and set out to destroy churches and wean believers

Fleisher in 1994

from their faith. Church lands and properties were nationalized, and the facilities often were allowed to fall into disrepair. While a few church buildings in the Soviet era were still employed for religious services, they were more often used for other purposes, such as concerts or political meetings, or as warehouses or museums. Clerics were labeled class enemies, deprived of the vote, and taxed at a higher rate. More than a thousand were arrested, and many were killed. The children of clergymen were denied entry to institutions of specialized or higher education. "Our social origins weighed on me and my brothers and sisters like a stigma," Fleisher remembered. Only with great difficulty and only because one brother had joined the Reds during the civil war did she succeed in gaining entry to a teacher-training school. Much later, after thirteen years of work as a schoolteacher, she had a chance to continue her education and graduate from a teachers' institute. She spent the rest of her life teaching Russian language and literature in a small town in the north, in the Komi Republic, which she left only in 1988 in order to be near her son, one of her two children. Even so, her "bad past" limited her horizons: She never attained the level of education to which she aspired, and she was denied the honors and promotions that she believed she deserved. In addition to teaching, she coauthored the first Russian-language textbook written for the indigenous population of Komi peoples.

Fleisher also had difficulty remaining in touch with her parents. They were considered an "alien element," hostile to the revolution, and contact with such people put a person at political risk. The clergy and their families were particularly vulnerable to persecution in times of heightened political or ideological conflict—particularly during the years of civil war (1918–1920), the collectivization drive of 1929–1930, and state-perpetrated terror (1936–1939). Fleisher's father was arrested in each of these periods, and he perished in a camp at the end of the 1930s. Geographical distance and perhaps fear of association kept Fleisher from tending to her ailing mother in her final days. None of her mother's six other children made the trip either, and she died in the arms of strangers.

Fleisher married a physician, the son of a surgeon. She refers to him always as Iurii Glebovich, that is, by his name and patronymic, which is a rather formal and respectful mode of address and likely reflects her clerical origins. Through this marriage she entered the world of the professional middle class, a "cultured" milieu, in her words, where raggedy children such as her younger sister Lena had no place, and where it was a mark of degradation to play with the children of peasants. Men who belonged to this milieu earned enough money to keep their wives at home and might well insist that they stay there—quite rare in Soviet times, when most families required two wage earners. Fleisher, who took pride in her work, resisted the pressure. It was also unusual in the 1930s to have enough money simply to shop for what a person needed, as Fleisher did when her sister came to visit. The ties between Vera Fleisher and her husband appear to have been corroded by frequent, short separations and then the lengthier one that came with the outbreak of World War II; but it is hard to know for certain, because she was obviously reluctant to discuss the subject. What she did tell Posadskaya was that as a man of principle, Iurii Glebovich continued to send money to her and the two children even when he was no longer living with them. But she raised her children alone.

Despite the suffering that Fleisher and her parents endured at the hands of the Soviet government, she actively embraced the Soviet order, as did many—perhaps the majority—of her contemporaries. "I was a non-party communist," she asserted. Testimony such as hers is important because it indicates that even people who did not benefit from the regime's policies of advancing workers and poor peasants came to share its overall goals, and because her language shows that for her and surely for others, those goals became inextricably bound up with a kind of Soviet nationalism: "We worried about our motherland [the Soviet Union], strove to make her a great, flourishing power," Fleisher declared. Perhaps because of her embrace of the Soviet order, as a whole her recollections are very positive: "I have lived a full life," she told Posadskaya. She presented a positive view also of social relations. In her narrative there was nothing about fear or other people's suspicions. On the contrary, she spoke of support and mutual aid: "We had a golden rule, you know: Don't leave one another in need. And you know, those years were very hard, but there were such good relations between people! Warm, loving, sincere." Fleisher has maintained her integrity to this day: Unlike some who have hastened to revise their past to fit the needs of the current moment, she did not try to deny her former convictions: "I, like many of my colleagues, shared the ideology and was a proponent of the ideology," she acknowledged. "That's the way the times were, and our generation mustn't be judged from the perspective of today."

◇   ◇   ◇

Anastasia Posadskaya-Vanderbeck: Vera Konstantinovna, let's begin at the very beginning. When were you born? Where were you born?

Vera Konstantinovna Fleisher: All right. I was born in 1909, on the twenty-seventh of March, according to the new style—that is, the Gregorian calendar. Into the family of a priest. I was born in the village of Chistoe, in Perm oblast. My early years, the years of my childhood, were spent there. And then in 1916 our family moved to the town of Akhansk, also in Perm oblast, where I lived until the end of 1924. There were seven children in our family, I was the fifth. There were two boys and five girls. Mama was a teacher until she got married. But once she had a family and children, she didn't work but took care of the children.

I encountered the revolution when I was eight years old and was in the second grade. I don't remember very well what happened at that time, but the civil war years were fixed in my memory because our little town of Akhansk, the chief town in the district, was in the direct line of fire and passed back and forth from one side to the other several times. There were battles going on, and we had to hide in basements. The Reds would take up quarters in our house. Then the Reds would leave, and the Whites would come. For more than a month the town was under fire. All in all, quite— well—vivid memories of those years have remained with me.

Were you in school?

Yes, at that time I was in the third grade. In the spring, I remember, we were awaiting the arrival of Admiral Kolchak.[1] The town really went all out for this. We schoolchildren also got ready for the arrival of such—I guess he was that—an important person, but it didn't come to pass. Because a break-through occurred at the front, and the White Army began a hasty retreat.

---

1. Admiral Kolchak led counterrevolutionary (White) armies against the Bolsheviks (Reds) during the civil war.

Vera Konstantinovna, you said that your papa was a priest, in what church?[2]

Well, it was like this. In Akhansk there were two Russian Orthodox churches. At first, he was the priest at the Khlabishchenskii Church. This was a relatively small church at the edge of town, and we lived there in a house specifically set aside for the priest. But then later, perhaps it was in 1921, Papa became an archpriest and was appointed to the cathedral in town. It was a very large, very beautiful cathedral, similar to the cathedral in Perm, very much like it. All in all, it was a magnificent cathedral. Well, and I, like many others my age, got to be in the choir. I sang in the church choir. But I have to say that already at that time, even in the first years of Soviet power, priests and their families were really suspect. I already sensed that people didn't treat us the way they treated other children. And the older I got, the more strongly I sensed this. It should be pointed out that my older brother, Mikhail Konstantinovich, born in 1901, was a student in Perm at the time the civil war began, and he left school to volunteer for the Red Army. Because he was so young, he didn't take part, as they say, "with a weapon in his hands," but worked somewhere at headquarters as a clerk. That's the way it was. Papa was arrested several times. In fact, he was arrested many times.

When our town—this would be in the summer of 1919—had already become part of the "front," and the hasty retreat of the White Army had begun, an order was issued [by the Whites] to evacuate all the inhabitants of the town. We had no choice, nor did our family—several of the older children already were living in Perm at that time. We were still small and lived with our parents, and we also had to be evacuated quickly. A ship was sent specially so that the population could leave. An order had been given, it was compulsory, everyone had to immediately abandon everything and leave the town. But we weren't evacuated on that ship. Papa got hold of a horse and wagon, an ordinary wagon, somewhere, and we loaded it up with some of our things—my little sister was there too, you see—and we walked on foot almost 60 kilometers, we walked on foot all the way to Perm. We had relatives in Perm. That's the way it was. And Papa, soon Papa began to serve there as a priest in one of the churches. Somewhere on the outskirts of Perm, and we lived there. Not with our relatives. At first he served there. But you remember what those times were like. So, the front held for a long time in Perm. Then sometime in the month of July, the railroad bridge was blown up. The Red Army crossed to the other side of the

---

2. Posadskaya was asking about the religion of Fleisher's father. At this point in the interview, Anastasia was unaware that Fleisher was this narrator's name by marriage and not by birth. She assumed that because Fleisher was a German name, the narrator would belong to a faith other than Russian Orthodoxy. Fleisher understood the question quite differently.

Kama river and began pursuing the White Army. As soon as Akhansk was liberated [by the Reds], our father set out for it. He didn't want to go but did so of necessity. And here's what happened: As soon as he arrived home—he had worn his feet out by walking back the 60 kilometers—he was immediately arrested. "Why did you withdraw with the Whites?" But fortunately it turned out that my older brother was in the military unit that had occupied the town. Perhaps this had an effect or perhaps ... You know, the parishioners really loved and respected my father, and perhaps they came to his defense and that's why Father was freed. And soon we, too, came back. That's the way our life was, you see, after our town had been liberated, was again in the hands of the Reds.

Well, life returned to normal: There was school to attend. I went to school there until I was in the ninth grade. I remember, for example—this was in '24, I was then in eighth grade—when Lenin died in January. All those sirens, you know [factory sirens sounded, all at once, throughout the land to mark Lenin's death] and mass meetings to mourn Lenin—this I remember. This I also remember.

So. I was a rather good student, but there was no opportunity to further my education here. Our social origins weighed on me and my brothers and sisters like a stigma. And all of them, one by one, left Akhansk. We had relatives in Perm; whoever could, settled there. Worked somewhere, doing whatever they could. My older brother, since he had taken part in the civil war, had certain privileges. He had been on the side of the Reds, and, see, many doors were open to him. He was studying in the pedagogical institute. He was in charge of a *detskii dom* [children's home], and he wrote to me: "Come. You can finish high school here, and then you'll be able to continue your studies." And so in December 1924, I left Akhansk for Perm, and there I enrolled in school, and graduated in 1925. I did well, but it was the same thing: Because of my social origin—as the daughter of a priest—I was not given preference for admittance into an institute of higher education. I could only get into a teacher-training school.[3] I graduated from this teacher-training school in Perm in 1927. I was eighteen at the time. I graduated from the preschool division of the Perm Teachers' College, as it was then called. In addition to the program of study for the preschool division, I also passed all the exams that were required for the elementary school division and received a diploma with the right to work in preschool and in elementary school. Well, in the beginning I worked in a preschool, but the way things turned out, I didn't work there long. And then I started to work in a school, I worked in an elementary school.

---

3. Later in the interview, Fleisher acknowledged her debt to her brother, who helped her to gain access to this school.

What was your papa's situation at that time?

Well, now I'll tell you: My parents, you see, had moved back to Chistoe from Akhansk. There, one more daughter was born to them in their old age—we were completely taken by surprise—our little sister, Lenochka. She's now sixty-eight. Yes. Then my parents moved to another place that was near Perm, some small village. Except for my little sister, we were all adults already, with families. Each of us had a family of their own, their own worries. Well, and then, you know, things were such that we weren't even supposed to correspond with our parents [because the father was a priest]. It was like having a tie with an "alien element." But of course, we continued to correspond with them, and once in a while we visited them, but it was very difficult. And it all ended very sadly.

In 1933, I got married. At the time, I was twenty-three. And in 1936, my husband—he was a physician, a surgeon—was appointed head of the surgical division of the district hospital in the town of Kudymkar. At the time, we lived in Iugovskoi Zavod in Perm oblast. My husband's name was Iurii Glebovich Fleisher.

So Fleisher was his name?

Yes, my maiden name was Vorontsova. So he left for his new place of work. I stayed on in Iugovskoi with our son Volodia. At the time, he was two and a half—no, more, almost three—and I made up my mind to risk going to my parents, to visit them. A very sorry sight greeted me: Mama was seriously ill. She was paralyzed. Then she got a little bit better, and if someone supported her, she was even able to move a little around the room. Her speech made no sense at all.

And how old was she?

She was . . . You know, in 1936 she must have been sixty-one, sixty-one years old. But father took care of her, and then there was also a woman, very religious she was, and she helped her, she too, took care of Mama. Apparently she considered it a mission of mercy. At the time, my little sister was ten; no, she wasn't yet ten. Mama was fifty when she was born. And so my sister, of course, was neglected. You can well imagine what sort of girl she was—wild, you could say—she ran around with peasant kids.[4] Well, what could you expect? I remember my last meeting with Papa. I went with him into the vegetable garden, sat down on a bench under the birch trees, and talked with him for a long time. And he said to me: "One thing, Verusha, worries me. What will happen to Mama, if I die before she does? I beg you, don't aban-

---

4. She was clearly shocked that her sister had been permitted to play with the children of peasants. Her reaction indicated her sense of her family's social and cultural superiority to that class.

don Lenochka, help her to become a human being." And right then and there I swore to Father that I would never abandon my little sister. Well, I had to go back; I had a child at home, Volodia. At the time, he was still small. So I took Lenochka. "Let her stay with me for awhile," I said. And I took her home with me. I remember when we were on the train, the other passengers asked: "Is this girl from a *detskii dom*,[5] are you taking her from a *detskii dom?*" She was so badly dressed, you know. Since Mother had already lain sick for several years, well, you can just imagine what sort of child this was. Before I went to see my mother-in-law . . . my husband's sister was there too; she was also a physician. It was a very cultured family. My husband's father had been a professor, the dean of the medical school in Perm. By this time he had already died; I never met him. Well, it was a very cultured family, and I would have felt uncomfortable taking my little sister to their home in such a wretched state. When we arrived, the very first thing I did was to take the girl to a beauty parlor; they fixed her up. Then I went to the store and bought her a dress, a coat, shoes.[6] The girl was transformed. I could show her to my relatives. Iurii Glebovich wasn't there; he was already in Kudymkar. Well, we arrived, the girl spent the summer with us, and then she had to go to Perm to another sister because we faced the prospect of having to move.

Then it all began, in 1937. In '37, Papa was arrested, in the month of February, when the repressions began. He was sixty-three, I think he was in his sixty-third year. Right here—I'll show you—see, here are very interesting materials. The granddaughter of my sister who lived in Perm did research in the archives. They permitted her to do this, and she succeeded in obtaining all the documents connected with father's repression and his rehabilitation.[7] The documents are very interesting. Here's how it was: Father was arrested as an enemy of the people under Article 58, for counterrevolution. What counterrevolution? He was a sick old man. Well, as these documents make clear, he spent eleven months in prison in Sverdlovsk and then was sent . . . We only found out about this later. At the time we knew nothing and, what's more, we couldn't even make inquiries. Then he was sent somewhere, see, in the neighborhood of Novosibirsk, and there in one of the camps in April 1938 he died, apparently, performing heavy manual labor. Well, it stands to

---

5. In the 1920s, children's homes sheltered hundreds of thousands of children who had been lost or abandoned by their parents. Chronically overcrowded and underfunded, these homes lacked the resources to feed or clothe their charges properly, despite the government's commitment to children's welfare. Thus, these comments are evidence of Lena's truly wretched state.

6. All of the items she mentioned were extremely expensive at that time.

7. Taking advantage of the new openness that followed the collapse of the Soviet Union, many former Soviet citizens are exploring archives and contacting the authorities in order to learn more about their families' pasts, and in particular, about the fates of those who disappeared during periods of repression. We have translated the documents and letters concerning Fleisher's father's fate. They are to be found at the end of this interview.

reason, you know—a sick, old man. He was working somewhere where they were felling trees. Nobody even knows where he is buried.

Mama's life turned out to be even more tragic. We couldn't be with her. You see, I was expecting my second child. That's Volodia's brother. It was 1938, he was born on January 8. In December 1937, I received a telegram: "Mama has died." Here's what happened: She died in the arms of that woman who took care of her. She gave birth to and brought up, as best she could, seven children. Yet she died in the arms of someone else. We couldn't go to be with her, the situation was such . . . Of course, we helped her. I recall my dead husband. He would always say, "Verusha, did you send money to Mama?" He was a very decent person and, you know, was always saying, "Don't forget, you should send her money." We kept sending money. In a material sense, she was provided for, but we couldn't do anything ourselves. When I received the telegram, of course, I wanted to rush there—despite everything, I wanted to pay my last respects to my mother. But I was due any day, and my husband wouldn't let me go. He said, "I can't let you do that." That's how it was.

You know, at first I worked in a school for working youth.[8] And then I . . . in 1940 there was a teachers' institute in our town, and after working for thirteen years and having two children, I enrolled in this institute and studied. I worked and I studied. Well, and after graduating from the institute, I got a job working in a secondary school. I taught literature and Russian language in the upper grades. Well, I must tell you that during all those years—all of my life—my social origin was like a stigma. I was quite a good teacher, you know, and I had quite a few official documents attesting to that in my file, but whenever the question arose . . . More than once, my name was put forward for some kind of award, for an honorary title, but as soon as the matter of my "social origins" came up, that was it. They backed off. Sometimes it hurt, but what could be done? That's the way things were then, you know.

And in your file, did it say: "From the family of a priest?"

Yes, "the daughter of a servant of a cult" [the term used by Soviets for "priest"].

And you couldn't hide it?

How could I hide it?! How could I hide that?!

Well, let's say you were to leave and go somewhere else.

But why? How could I? I had a family, I couldn't go anywhere. Then, you know, that was somewhere in the upper echelons of the regime [that there

---

8. A middle school that workers attended in the evening, while they continued to work full time.

was such an attitude toward "alien elements"], but among my coworkers, no, among my coworkers, you see, I felt like an equal among equals. I worked there for more than twenty-one years, in the same school; all in all, from the moment I arrived, I worked in Kudymkar for twenty-six years, twenty-six years, until I retired.

And your husband, did he continue to work as a physician?

No,[9] my family life didn't turn out so well. The war changed everything. Even before our marriage my husband was a physician in the military,[10] and he only returned to civilian life for a short time, when we were having our family. Volodia came into the world. In 1938 a second son, Boria, came into the world. When Volodia was four years old and Boria four months, Iurii Glebovich was inducted into the army, in '38, as an officer [serving as a physician]. Well, it was '38, you yourself know what things were like, what the situation was then. At the time, the threat of war was already in the air. As a physician in the military, Iurii Glebovich was sent to Sverdlovsk. The family and I—there were the two children and then I had a nursemaid—were living, so to say, in a house in Kudymkar. Well, I remained there. Iurii Glebovich couldn't get an apartment in Sverdlovsk, he couldn't. He lived somewhere, you know, in some little room attached to a laboratory. Time passed. They decided to put another family in our house, since they thought we would be leaving. In fact, we had already packed our things. We were certain Iurii Glebovich would get an apartment any day and we'd leave. Now and then he would come to see us, time passed, nothing came of the apartment, and then in 1940 he was transferred to Ufa. And it was the same story there. Finally he got a three-room apartment in Ufa. But I still had to finish my studies at the institute. So we planned to move to Ufa in June.

Well, on June 19, 1941, my neighbor, also a teacher, and I were preparing for our last exam in the teachers' institute when they brought me a telegram. I unfolded the telegram, read it, and my heart sank. Here's what I read: "Plan on spending the winter in Kudymkar. I'm being sent on a long mission." You know, I almost burst into tears. I thought: I've got to spend the winter again in Kudymkar! What could have happened? I was very hurt. I thought, Just what sort of mission can it be? Well, what could I do? I passed the exams. I was an "A student," you know. I did very well on all my exams. Then on the morning of June 22, my little sister, Lenochka, arrived for the summer. Then later that day, for some reason, I went out into the courtyard. Suddenly I saw all the children running toward me: The boys were running toward me and also my little sister. "Vera! Mama, war! War!" What was going on? At that

---

9. She chose to answer in a much broader vein than the question required.

10. In the Soviet Union, physicians might serve permanently in the army. They held officer rank.

Fleisher in 1948

very moment, Molotov was announcing on the radio that the Great Patriotic
War had begun. It all became clear to me, what the long mission meant. And
when we met later, Iurii Glebovich said that as early as June 20 he had de-
parted from Ufa, moving west, together with the troops.

Well, did Iurii Glebovich write you later that he was at the front?

For a long time there was no news. The war began on June 22. I received
the first letter around August, in the month of August, perhaps even at the
end of the month. My certificate [of graduation] and his letter arrived at the
same time. All during the war we corresponded. Sometimes there wouldn't
be any letters for long periods. Iurii Glebovich went through the entire war.
Well, see, he was even shell-shocked, but he continued to work. He would
say, "Somehow, death spared me." He was at the front until the end of the
war, and then, without even coming home, he went to the Far East. Well,
see, the war with Japan was in progress. And then for a long time he . . .
Our troops, you know, were stationed there, in Korea. And then he was
transferred west again. So he only came home to see us from time to time.

When did he return home for good?

He never did.

He didn't return?

He never returned.

From Manchuria or from the west?

From the west. Yes, you know, he served after the war for a long time. He had more than twenty-five years of military service. Then he died.

You mean to say he didn't die at home?

He didn't die at home.

You were sent . . . ?

Yes . . . Then he died.[11] Well, the children were already . . . But, you know, he always sent us money. The main thing is that he helped out. But the boys were already grown up, of course. But I was happy, you know, in the midst of my family. We all got along very well. I was happy as a mother, you understand. I was happy.

Would you have wanted to spend your whole life at home, totally absorbed in family matters?

Spend my whole life at home? Incidentally, my husband had that view. He thought that a woman should devote herself entirely to her family. And he always held up his own mama to me as an example: See, Mama dedicated her whole life to us, to her children. And he was very insistent that I should quit work and devote myself entirely to my family. But I think just the opposite. That wouldn't have suited me. And it seems to me my children didn't lose out because I worked all my life. After all, they saw that I was not only a mama, that I bore not only the cares of the family. They saw that despite these obligations I had made something of myself, that people respected me, took me seriously, and for them, you know, that meant a great deal. And you don't have to sit and fuss over a child and say, Do this, do that. Serving as an example, being industrious, now that's . . . It doesn't do much good to talk to children, to try to convince them with words, but if they see that adults are serious about their own work—now there's a real example for them. And my children saw that their mama was a hard worker. Without a doubt, I was the last in the house to fall asleep, because I couldn't leave my work and go to bed until I had everything prepared for the next day. Anyway, I couldn't fall asleep until all the lessons for the next day were planned out and all the students' homework corrected, all of it.

Vera Konstantinovna, the fact that you strove so hard to get an education, where did that aspiration come from? From your family?

You know . . . I already told you that my educational opportunities were limited to the teacher-training school, and I got in solely thanks to the fact that my brother had taken part in the civil war. He was a Komsomol ac-

---

11. She was clearly unwilling to discuss this part of her life.

Fleisher with her two sons in 1951

tivist. And he worked at that school. Otherwise, I wouldn't even have had that opportunity.

Vera Konstantinovna, you never wanted to join the party?

You know, I'll be frank with you: I didn't join the party, but I was a communist at heart. I, like many of my colleagues, shared the ideology and was a proponent of the ideology. Well, look, we were children of our time, of our epoch, we couldn't have been other than we were, we couldn't have. You know, now they blame our generation for this and for that, but if others had been in our place, they wouldn't have acted any differently. That's the way the times were, and our generation mustn't be judged from the perspective of today. You know, when I look back on my life, I can say that I'm satisfied with the life I've lived, I'm satisfied. You know, if it hadn't been for my work, my life would have been meaningless. And I don't regret a thing, not a thing. I don't regret the hardships I endured, I don't regret anything. I'm satisfied with the life I've lived. If I hadn't lived as I did, how could I justify my present existence? How? I have lived, you know, a full life, a life filled with useful work.

Vera Konstantinovna, when you think of the recent changes, what do you applaud and what can't you accept?

What do I applaud? [There is a pause.] I applaud the fact that we have all become free and can freely express our own opinions about all the events that are taking place without being afraid of anyone or anything. No longer

Fleisher in 1979

need we fear that they will immediately take reprisal against us and send us away somewhere. That's positive. But on the whole, it's very hard for me as an old person, you know, to refashion myself [she uses here the verb *perestroitsia,* which has the same root as the noun perestroika], to adapt to the new situation, very hard. It's hard to give up your former convictions, your former way of thinking. But I understand that there's no going back to the past, nor will there be. But what especially troubles me . . . Of course, I'm very worried about the fate of our country. Our generation, for the most part, were great patriots—not in words, but in deeds. We worried about our motherland, strove to make her a great, flourishing power. We loved our country, loved her! And we were ready to sacrifice ourselves for the good of the motherland. And we resigned ourselves to all the hardships that befell us. So the fate of our motherland is very dear to us, at present the fate of our country worries us old people very much! It concerns us that we don't have peace. I would like the peoples in our country to live peaceably, as before; I would like this bloody internecine enmity to cease. It is tearing people in the Caucasus to pieces, and not only there. I would like to see the country revive, to see it become once again a power that the whole world would have to respect.

◆   ◆   ◆

[The following document was read into the tape recorder by V. K. Fleisher.]

"Office of the Public Prosecutor of the Soviet Union, Office of the Public Prosecutor of Perm oblast. Certificate of rehabilitation, citizen Konstantin Mikhailovich Vorontsov, year of birth 1876, city of Perm. Before arrest lived in Spasbarda, in the Tishenskii district of Perm oblast. Worked as a priest in the Spasbarda church. Date of arrest: February 7, 1930." Here it also says—apparently this pertains to the second arrest on September 3, 1937. [She reads aloud.] "Repressed on October 13, 1937, by decree of a troika [board of three] of the NKVD for Sverdlovsk oblast and on May 9, 1930, by decree of a troika of the OGPU for the Urals. Part 1 of Article 58–10 of the Criminal Code of the RSFSR: deprivation of freedom, ten years"—this was in '37. "Part 1 of Article 58–10 of the Criminal Code of the RSFSR: deprivation of freedom, three years for anti-Soviet agitation"—this was in '30. On the basis of Article 3, Section 1, Article 5, Section 1 of the law of the RSFSR, concerning the rehabilitation of victims of political repression, dated October 18, 1991, citizen Konstantin Mikhailovich Vorontsov is rehabilitated. Assistant Prosecutor of Perm oblast, Senior Counselor of Justice Semenov. In accordance with the law of the RSFSR, dated October 18, 1991, the rehabilitated have the right to the restoration of military ranks and special titles, to the return of orders and medals, and to payment of monetary compensation by the local agencies of social security at the rate of 180 rubles for each month they were illegally deprived of freedom, not to exceed 25,000 rubles, from the resources of the Republic's budget. Persons who were deprived of freedom, exiled, or deported, rehabilitated in accordance with the present law, if disabled or pensioners, have first priority for medical assistance and discounted medicines prescribed by doctors; also the guarantee of a free vehicle if there is medical evidence of need, the right to free travel on all forms of city transportation, excluding taxis, and also to public bus transportation available in the villages within the limits of the district of residence; the right to free round-trip travel once a year by railroad, and where there is no railroad, to water, air, or intercity bus transportation at a discount of 50 percent; the right to a discount on payment for living space, a discount of 50 percent for utilities, priority on waiting lists for telephone installation, the right to preferential access to grocery and manufactured products. A number of other privileges are guaranteed, which are also extended to persons rehabilitated before the present law was enacted. Members of the family of the rehabilitated will have priority on waiting lists for living quarters, if they were deprived of them in conjunction with the illegal repression and are in need of better living conditions."

▨   ▨   ▨

[An extract follows, from a letter written to Fleisher by the granddaughter of her brother or sister, also read aloud by Fleisher.]

"So I looked at all three files from 1919, 1930, and 1937, and of course, all these files illustrate the procedures and mores of that period; still, I was shaken when I saw the history I had read and heard about embodied in real persons, people close to me. The charges are absurd from today's perspective: General human concepts of goodness and honesty were turned upside down and represented as criminal schemes and acts. Facts were distorted and treated prejudicially; ordinary, everyday facts were used to demonstrate 'treason'. I don't know whether you are aware of what your father was prosecuted for, but I was simply stunned that such insignificant evidence led to such serious consequences. In 1919, he was prosecuted for saying a requiem for Whites killed in the civil war and promising them repose in the next world. In 1930, the priest was declared guilty by virtue of the fact that he called upon people to observe church fasts and did not condone organized forms of entertainment on those days and because he duplicated the services of ZAGS [the official state registry office] by recording births, marriages, and deaths in church registers. And in 1937, his official relations with his superiors were portrayed as the creation of an anti-Soviet group conspiring to subvert the government. Such nonsense. It's very distressing to read these documents, but also very interesting."

❖ Overcoming an "Incorrect" Birth

ANTONINA ALEKSANDROVNA BEREZHNAIA

Antonina Aleksandrovna Berezhnaia made her home in the Ural mountains, in the city of Ekaterinburg, formerly called Sverdlovsk.[1] The part of the city where she lived looked just like an enormous village: In order to cope with the housing and food crises after World War II, workers had been given allotments of land on the outskirts of town and encouraged to build their own small houses on them. Factories helped out in whatever ways they could. As a result, the streets were lined with one-story, single-family houses, each accompanied by its own small garden plot. Berezhnaia's home was in a different part of the city from where Posadskaya was staying, so in order to reach it, Posadskaya had to travel for a long time. It was early March, and the city was still heaped with filthy, gray snow. There was no one around when she finally got off the tram, and she had difficulty finding Berezhnaia's street. Good Lord, how does she get around in the dark out here? Posadskaya wondered.

No one would ever have guessed that Antonina Berezhnaia was 85 years old. She was tall and lean, with a bright flush on her sunken cheeks and a broad, open smile. She was clearly delighted to see her interviewer.

Berezhnaia was born in 1910 into a privileged class, the landowning nobility. Until 1861, when serfdom was abolished, members of this group had enjoyed wide-ranging authority over the peasants who worked their land, and even thereafter, nobles' advantageous political position enabled them to maintain economically exploitative relations with the peasants. The fall of the tsar signaled the end to noble privilege. During spring and summer 1917, peasants took advantage of the power vacuum to settle long-standing grievances. Rising up in enormous numbers, peasants drove the nobles from their homes and seized their land and property. When the Bolsheviks

---

1. After the revolution, as part of a larger effort to transform society from top to bottom, the new Soviet government renamed towns, streets, factories, and the like. After the fall of the Soviet Union, many of the prerevolutionary names were restored.

Berezhnaia in 1994

came to power that autumn, they upheld these peasant actions. All land should go to the tillers, they decreed in February 1918; no one should have more land than they and their families could work themselves. Faced with the kind of peasant hostility that Berezhnaia described at the end of her interview, many nobles fled the country. Others threw in their lot with the Whites and fought on the side of counterrevolution, and when the civil war ended and their side was defeated, they emigrated as well. At the end of the civil war, about 11 to 12 percent of the prerevolutionary nobility remained in the Soviet Union—approximately 10,000 noble families, or about 50,000 people in all. Revolutionaries regarded them as enemies.

Berezhnaia belonged to this group. As "a child with a bad past," she had to struggle from her earliest years, "first for my future, then for my work." The revolution deprived nobles not only of their property but also of many civil rights, such as the right to vote or to obtain a higher education. According to the decree of February 1918, nobles could only have an allotment of land if they tilled it on the same basis as the peasants—that is, without hiring labor. Some nobles tried to get around this ruling by setting up false collective farms of one sort or another on their former estates and appointing themselves as "specialists." According to Berezhnaia, her father became a specialist, an agronomist, for one of the new collective farms. It is impossible to know whether this was what really happened, or whether his collective, like many others, was a front. In any case, he soon died—in an accident, according to his daughter—leaving his family with no means of support. Berezhnaia and her sisters wound up in one of the thousands of children's homes established during the civil war to deal with orphans and abandoned children. These homes were miserable affairs, underfunded, undersupplied, and understaffed; nevertheless, they saved the lives of many children, Antonina Berezhnaia's and her sisters' among them. They also provided an avenue of socialization into the new revolutionary values: At the children's home, Berezhnaia became an activist and a member of the Komsomol, willingly shouldering a variety of chores. But her "bad past" remained an obstacle. In order to gain the right to further her education, she first had to spend time on the factory floor.

This was the part of her life that Berezhnaia really wanted to talk about. She embraced the values of her era, which emphasized production and work for the public good over personal life and private satisfactions. "Production was my life," she said. She joined the industrial labor force in 1930, at the very height of the campaign to transform the Soviet Union into a modern industrial society within just a few years by planning the economy from top to bottom. However, by 1930, all pretense of following the plan had been abandoned in favor of "storming the heights" of production. Workers were encouraged to increase their productivity by surpassing, or "overfulfilling," production goals. Those who succeeded were celebrated as "shock workers," or beginning in 1935, as Stakhanovites, after a coal miner by the name of Aleksei Stakhanov, who reportedly dug out 102 tons of coal in a single shift, rather than the 10 tons he had been assigned. Such achievements were trumpeted in newspapers under the slogan, "There are no fortresses that the Bolsheviks cannot storm." Shock workers and Stakhanovites were singled out for decorations, honors, and special privileges, among them the opportunity to improve their education and skills. Berezhnaia's exemplary enthusiasm for production brought her to the attention of her superiors. So did her activism: She joined the Communist party, was chosen as the chair of her factory's trade-union committee, and spent her free time in other activities that supported the goals of the revolution—for example, in organizing performances of the Blue Blouse workers' theater. This was a theater collective that performed in cafeterias and workplaces, acting out the day's news and commenting on current events, invariably with a political edge. Berezhnaia's commitment to the new order finally enabled her to overcome her "bad past." She entered the Urals Polytechnic Institute, graduated with a degree in engineering in 1940, and became the forewoman of a metallurgical plant.

During her interview, Berezhnaia described in great detail her work in the administration of the metallurgical industry of the Urals region, providing a valuable portrait of the inner workings of socialist industry. Berezhnaia initiated a number of technological innovations in the factories she administered, including rotary furnaces. In order to find the funds to modernize production in this way, she had to circumvent the rigidities of the centralized planning process, in which planners determined beforehand what factories would produce and then allocated them the necessary resources.

First, she had to convince the head of the planning administration to reallocate funds that had been earmarked for another purpose. Then she needed to get documentation guaranteeing the feasibility of her proposal. For this, she initially approached a local specialist, and when he proceeded too slowly, she went over his head and flew to Leningrad, where she convinced the chief engineer of the Institute of Refractory Materials to support her project and supply the necessary documentation. But before he would supply it, she had to sign an "economic agreement," in which both sides committed themselves to obtaining the resources necessary to produce an item that was not included in the plan and to accept responsibility for demonstrating to the authorities the necessity of paying workers overtime wages, that is, wages higher than those provided for in the plan. Only after overcoming these enormous bureaucratic obstacles was she able to introduce changes that brought significant economic benefits. We decided to retain for this chapter a large portion of Berezhnaia's discussion of her involvement in industrial production despite all the technical details, because it reveals her creativity, courage, and professionalism, as well as the seriousness with which she and others worked to implement the production-oriented goals of the Five-Year Plans. Although she was comparatively well paid and lived comfortably, money did not interest her, she said. Rather, "the chief satisfaction was that you had accomplished something and it worked." Berezhnaia's interview also shows how she and many other members of her generation tried to fashion their lives according to the regime's stated ideals. "I didn't take anything for myself," Berezhnaia told her interviewer, and her modest surroundings—a small, peasant-style house, lacking the conveniences of gas, hot and cold running water, and indoor plumbing— showed that she was telling the truth.

Berezhnaia's interview also reveals the difficulty of being a woman in a man's world and the obstacles that kept many other women from advancing in the labor force. She worked in heavy metals, an industry dominated by men. Sufficiently skilled at her work to be appointed regional director of the metallurgy industry in the Urals region, as a woman she had to overcome distrust and outright contempt when she assumed this position. Men ignored her and forced her to prove her worth, she told Posadskaya: "Sometimes I think it was so difficult because here I was a woman in the midst of men. Here you had to prove your ability to work, your knowledge, and only then did you earn their respect. Otherwise, they would have dismissed me completely."

In the process of adjusting to the new order, Berezhnaia turned her back on the painful aspects of her past. As one reads her interview, it is hard to avoid the sense that for the sake of harmony with the socialist order she was compelled to forget much of her past. That is probably why she so resisted talking about her childhood. "Do we really have to talk about that?"

she responded when Posadskaya first asked her about it. At the start of the interview, she briefly mentioned the fact that her father, although a former noble landowner, was allowed to work for a collective farm, but soon died as a result of an accident. Toward the end of the interview, when Posadskaya asked her to recall the early postrevolutionary years in greater detail, Berezhnaia said that she and her sister wound up in a children's home, but provided no information about why or how this happened. We can only guess that the family was persecuted on account of its privileged status under the old regime and that her mother gave the children to the home. But she did not tell what really happened to her mother or whether she was forced to renounce her family in order to work and study, as many others with comparable backgrounds had to do. Her childhood remained a realm of "silence" that she seemed determined to keep outside the bounds of the interview. Another realm of silence was her first, unsuccessful marriage, about which she said nothing at all. Two children from that marriage died in early childhood, but Berezhnaia likewise said little about those events.

In general, Berezhnaia provided very few personal details, and those that she gave all conformed to the ideal that emerged in the mid-1930s, of the socialist family as the source of stability for the nation. "Our family is strong," she said. In truth, she has enjoyed greater marital stability than many other women her age, the vast majority of whom lost their husbands long ago and in a variety of ways. She raised a daughter, has grandchildren, and has lived companionably for fifty years with her second husband, who also worked in the metal industry. At the end of the interview, Posadskaya met Berezhnaia's husband when he returned from shopping. He struck Posadskaya as being a very strong and stern old man, perhaps because his dark, military-style jacket reminded her of those worn by Soviet bureaucrats from the 1930s through the 1950s. He sat down on the sofa in the rather spacious room where she and his wife were conversing and looking at photographs. In a loud voice—evidently his hearing was poor—he began to comment on Posadskaya's questions and to correct his wife. It seemed to Posadskaya that he was surprised that she had come to interview his wife and not him.

◩   ◩   ◩

Anastasia Posadskaya-Vanderbeck: Please tell me about your childhood.

Antonina Aleksandrovna Berezhnaia: My father's name was Aleksandr Ivanovich Berezhnoi. He was a very intelligent, hardworking Ukrainian. He himself worked a great deal and kept his estate in model order. But after the revolution, see, he worked as an agronomist on a *sovkhoz* [state farm]. They invited him to work there because he was a big specialist, despite the fact that he had been a landowner. But he was killed there as the result of an accident. He worked there for five years and then was killed. We were left alone. Things had come to the point that, well, as a matter of fact, children with such a past[2] had nowhere to go.

How many of you were there?

There were three of us. Three sisters.

And your mama, was she still alive?

Mama was alive. But Mama managed to get us into a *detskii dom* [children's home][3] on the basis of a recommendation by the board of this sovkhoz where Papa had worked. We were in this detskii dom for five years. I studied in a model experimental school there and was a member of the Komsomol. Well, and then, see, it turned out that I couldn't get into a university because of my social origin. And so I went to work in a factory in 1930, the Tula arms plant. I worked there for two years, then started working two machines instead of one,[4] and was considered a "shock worker" at the plant. And when they had the first conference of shock workers[5]—they weren't called Stakhanovites then, but shock workers—fifteen people were sent from the arms plant, and I was one of those fifteen. See, I was at that first conference of shock workers. I have such memories of it; even today I remember it!

What year was that?

That was in '31. At that time, I was . . . I was born in 1910, so that means I was twenty-one. But I worked unstintingly, of course, and was the organizer of Blue Blouse performances. At that time there was a Blue Blouse theater movement in factories; it was very interesting! And I was a member of the town soviet, they elected me. That was the beginning of my work as an activist. Well, and then I got married and went to the Urals. And in the Urals things were also very complicated for me: I had a family, but all the same I entered an institute of higher education, and in '40 I graduated from UPI, the Urals Polytechnic Institute, with a specialization in refractory materials.

So by that time it was possible for you to get into such an institute, right?

Yes, yes.

---

2. Small children, of course, have no past. She is referring to her parents' social origins.

3. The recommendation of the sovkhoz leadership was required because children from privileged backgrounds were ordinarily not admitted to children's homes, however desperate their circumstances. See also Fleisher (p. 92, footnote 5).

4. Berezhnaia was referring here to the movement to encourage workers to increase the number of machines on which they worked, part of the campaign to raise productivity.

5. Conferences of shock workers were periodically convened for the purpose of disseminating the methods of the most advanced workers.

Berezhnaia in 1932. Handwritten on the back of the photo was a dedication: "A few words to my friend: Only by means of persistent struggle and lengthy work on the self can a person reach the heights of science. It is essential to value life and to know how to extract from it only what is good, uniting that with one's ideals. Then life will be interesting and full of happiness."

So your social origin was no longer an obstacle?

No, see, here's how I got in: When I was still in Tula at the arms plant, I was given recommendations by the party and union organizations, since I was a big social activist (she laughs). So that's how I got in. Well, and when I graduated from UPI here in the Urals, I went to work at the Verkhnesel-skii metallurgical works as a forewoman. I worked there for two years as a forewoman, and then, see, it was wartime. Conditions were very difficult at the works. We didn't even have dishes. Young people today haven't the faintest idea what things were like, then. We had to use metal cans for dishes. It was very hard, but the people really supported each other; they got along well. We worked twelve- or fourteen-hour shifts—not only at the factory, we even helped in the hospital, everywhere. That's how it was. But then I was promoted, and they made me head of this refractory shop. I worked in that capacity for three years. Well, how should I put it, production was my life, pure and simple. I really loved the factory, and I really loved my coworkers. We worked together very well. Things were hard, people would come and work fourteen hours, they would be hungry, but they had to go on working. I would go through the shop, and I used to sing them the song, "All Our Life Is a Struggle." They already knew that if our life was a struggle [she laughs], it meant we had to keep on working. They would run up to me and say: "Antonina Aleksandrovna, don't worry, we'll stay, we'll work another three hours."

Was this during the war?

That's right. It was during the war.

Were they women, for the most part?

Women and men. But there were fewer men, a lot of women. It's very hard to produce refractory materials.

You know, they make steel in open-hearth furnaces, they pour it into molds. Steel is used everywhere—rails, everything is made out of steel. And in order to make the steel pour—it's a very hot metal—you have to add a certain element so that it adheres, so that this steel flows like a stream along this, along these refractory materials and doesn't get contaminated. And in this way it solidifies into clean ingots. And it was these refractory materials that we made. But there at the factory, besides my work in production, I had . . . I was a member of the party. And I carried out agitational work, I worked with the people, I ran study groups—all that in addition to my work in production. And then they recommended to the administration of ferrous metallurgy that I be made chief refractory engineer. And when I transferred into the administration, it was the beginning of very important work. They introduced me to the managers of the factories of whom I was supposed to be in charge. You can just imagine: At the first meeting called by the head of the administration, all these guys gathered, big, important, seasoned. And suddenly, see, the head of the administration said: "I'd like to introduce your new chief refractory engineer. I ask you to love, favor, and help her. She will be in charge of you." Five factories, understand? And these were big and important factories. And I was from the shop floor, from the shop floor; on the other hand, I knew production well. But all the same, this was something completely different!

I was then forty-eight. Of course, I already had a great deal of experience. Well, so the meeting ended. The men said good-bye to me coldly and went their separate ways. I went to the head of the administration and said:

"You know what, send me back to the factory floor. I don't fit in here" [she laughs]. He laughed and said: "No, Antonina Aleksandrovna, I know you well, and you'll do fine in this work. We'll back you up. First, study each factory carefully, study everything; that way you'll figure out what you need to do." In addition, the Institute of Refractory Materials right here in Sverdlovsk was also affiliated with us, and this was an important organization, a research institute. Well, and so I began to work. I had a hard time, and my husband would say to me: "Just why do you need all this? Go back to the factory floor and take it easy." I said: "No. If I start something, I carry through with it to the end. That's the way I am." Period. Well, I began to go around to the factories. I went to one factory—I'll never forget it—the manager there, a big specialist, said: "Antonina Aleksandrovna, I'll give you the chief engineer, I'll give you the head of production, and they'll show you everything." I said: "You don't need to tear people away from their work. I know production. True, your factory is enormous, you supply the entire Urals with refractory materials, but I'll simply walk around and have a look at what is going on."[6] And so I stayed there two weeks. And I did the same thing at each factory.

What exactly was your task?

As the chief refractory engineer, I had to know what sort of technology and equipment each factory had, the quality of its output, and its prospects. These were precisely the things that lay in my domain.

And did you write reports?

Yes.

One for each factory?

I'll tell you about that later. First, I made a careful study of everything. Well, three months passed. Then I said to the head of the administration, "Well, it's time to get down to work." I drew up a plan of development for each factory. I'll tell you later what it consisted of. When I arrived at one of the factories, they assembled a lot of people for a meeting. Up to this point, when they had production meetings, I was very unobtrusive. Sometimes I asked questions, sometimes I listened—I always wrote down everything, studied everything—but I didn't express any opinions, didn't introduce any proposals of my own. But at this meeting, see, I heard them out, and then I talked about each shop, I showed them what was wrong with their technology, where their equipment was outdated, where the quality was poor and why, and drew up a plan of development. They were amazed, see. When I

---

6. Here, Berezhnaia clearly was resisting attempts to control what she saw, to hide anything that might be improper. She was acting according to the popular image of the leader who distrusts local authorities and gets to the bottom of things himself, or much more rarely, herself.

laid out everything to them at the meeting, they realized that I had exposed their hands, that they couldn't hide anything from me, because I had talked with the workers, with the foremen. Everything had become clear to me. And what they needed to do was to introduce a rotary furnace. Then the factory manager got up and said: "This is all very good, but we can't do it. Just who is going to give us the money?" I said: "You have to do it. Otherwise the metallurgical plants will keep expanding, and you won't be able to supply them with refractory materials." That's the way it was at that factory and at a second factory and at all these factories. And when I arrived at the administration, I found that the head had been replaced and there was a new one. He was a big specialist but a very rigid and tough man. After he had looked at my plans, he said: "You mustn't forget that we can't give refractory materials top priority; that goes to metallurgy."[7] I said that this was clear to me, because metallurgists always consider refractory materials secondary. But when the metal is of poor quality because of the refractory materials, then they always put all the blame on the refractory engineers. So, I said, the impasse had to be broken, the money had to be allocated. "But we can't allocate the money." Well, okay, I thought; my situation was very difficult. But I worked well with the others in administration. The head of the planning division, the head of the financial division, and the head of industrial and mechanical services[8] all supported me, understand. They understood that I really wanted to accomplish something. And so the head of the planning division said: "Don't worry. The only thing you have to do is get the documentation for the project through the Institute of Refractory Materials, and the rest, the money, I'll give you." "But how?" "At the expense of construction funds.[9] A great deal of money is allocated for open-hearth furnaces, but they don't use it all, they turn it around very slowly, money is left over, and I will give that to you." Well, then it was my turn: I went to the Institute of Refractory Materials, to the director there. He and I discussed the matter, but he was very indecisive: "Well, you know, this will take half a year; all of this will take a long time." I said, "No, we need to get this done quickly." I flew off to Leningrad. In Leningrad there was also an Institute of Refractory Materials, and in that institute was a remarkable specialist, the chief engineer of the institute, and

---

7. Branches and sub-branches of Soviet industry were organized hierarchically, according to their importance in the eyes of the government. The amount of capital invested in them was directly related to their position in the hierarchy. The metallurgical industry was of the highest priority, and therefore, was in a very favorable position; refractory materials, the branch of metallurgy in which Berezhnaia worked, was regarded as subsidiary.

8. Subdivisions within the metallurgy administration.

9. Because the central plan had allocated no funds to finance Berezhnaia's innovation, the head of the planning division proposed to take them from funds set aside for investment in equipment.

he helped me. He said: "Okay, we'll draw up an agreement.[10] Will you pay overtime?" "We will," I answered. And within three months they had prepared all the documentation. When they had completed all the documentation, the money was immediately transferred to the factory, and within two months they began construction. And after all this had begun, then the factory managers began to treat me quite differently, totally differently! And they would send a car for me and make polite requests: "Come, do come, even if it's just for a few hours. Look things over, check to see how things are going." That's how it was, and then the work went very well. But the work was very difficult, important, but also interesting, and I was very satisfied with it. Sometimes I think it was so difficult because here I was a woman in the midst of men, understand. Here you had to prove your ability to work, your knowledge, and only then did you earn their respect. Otherwise, they would have dismissed me completely.

Were there other women who were also specialists like you?

Well, there were women in the institute, but they did research. But, see, here's another reason why I had a connection with the institute: I invented many things. For example, one of my inventions was displayed at an agricultural exhibit: I proposed a device that didn't exist in the Soviet Union at that time for the pouring of metal. It was new technology. I really liked all this. I didn't do it for money; at that time, money didn't interest me. We had money, they paid us well, we lived well. But the chief satisfaction was that you had accomplished something and it worked. That's what was really interesting! Well, they did propose that I get an advanced degree at the institute. But I thought, I'm no longer young; do I really need to do this? I'll end my days in production. So I didn't go for the advanced degree. That's how it was.

Antonina Aleksandrovna, did they offer you yet another promotion, perhaps to a higher position in administration?

Look, I had . . . my position was a very important one, because I was the chief refractory engineer in the entire Ural region, understand!? In my field, see, you couldn't go any higher. Well, what could they offer me at the institute? Since I didn't have an advanced scientific degree, they couldn't put me in charge of a laboratory. Then, too, that sort of work, which was more sedentary, didn't interest me very much. If I had gone to the institute in the first place, of course I would have written a dissertation. But I preferred production.

---

10. When it became necessary to produce something that was not part of the plan, the customer and the producer concluded an "economic agreement" that allowed for some flexibility and required both sides to seek out additional resources or economize on those already in the plan and reallocate them.

You said that in industry during the war the majority of workers were women. What about after the war?

After the war, men began to fill the ranks, they came back from the front. So there were more men. And in the refractory works we already had a lot of men because there was a great deal of technical equipment in these factories. What's more, there were these new furnaces, mechanized furnaces, which women couldn't operate. Rotary furnaces for the firing of brick.

But during the war didn't women do heavy work like that?

Yes, they did heavy work. Very heavy work, especially in the refractory shop. But all the work was manual. It wasn't mechanized because they didn't have the equipment. There was nowhere to get it. And then there were factories that had been evacuated to the Urals from the south. They were set up in the open air, and they worked in the open, too. I'll tell you, people really worked!

And did women who had been evacuated do factory work?

Yes, they also did factory work. We had a lot of women from Ukraine. They worked in the foundry, in the open-hearth furnace. But just the same, they always did heavy work, because they weren't skilled. They couldn't be given lighter work.

Most likely there were also educated women?

Yes, yes. Educated women as well. A lot of them.

Antonina Aleksandrovna, look, in your life you had to work a lot with men, right?

Right. I'll tell you what was interesting about working with men in administration. It used to be like this: We'd have a meeting, a briefing session, and there would be eighteen of us, and I'd be the only woman! And in addition, I was the chair of the local union committee. And the head of the administration was very businesslike and knowledgeable, but he was really a tough guy and crude, crude.

Did he swear?

He didn't swear at the briefing sessions, but he loved to put people down. And we had one blast-furnace operator, he wasn't bad at the job, he was okay, but he was such a modest person. And the head of administration never called him by his name or by his patronymic. Just what did he call him . . . ? Aha, "Hey you, stand up, tell us, what's up in your shop?" But I, as chair of the local trade union committee, later, after everybody had left, I went up to him and said: "Why do you treat people like that, why? Don't you know how to treat people decently? Look, he's highly trained, he knows his work well. What gives you the right to humiliate a person like that?" I said: "You know what, cut it out. If you keep doing this, your be-havior will be discussed in the local [union] committee." And he said: "Are you trying to teach me something?" I said: "I was elected by the people, and I have the right to criticize you, because this doesn't become you, it's simply a bad example for the whole group." He and I had run-ins, big ones. Well, all the same, work is work. And at meetings he would always look for a reason to discredit me, to see if somewhere in my sphere something had gone wrong, either project documentation was lacking or somewhere a fac-tory hadn't met its deadline. But I didn't get flustered; I always gave him a good rebuff. And then, too, I had a lot of support from others in adminis-tration.

And, you know, what's also important, what's surprising is this: People weren't greedy for money, and that's surprising because in a material sense they didn't live very well, but nobody strove to earn money by dishonest means. Somehow things went along smoothly, people respected each other and were honorable when it came to their work. Everything was okay.

And now it's not like that?

Now it's not like that. What's most frightening . . . the young people. Our young people aren't bad, our young people are good, but you understand that all these hucksters have an enormous influence on them! Just why have they started being so carried away by this money? Because it comes easily. Strictly speaking, nothing is being produced now. The factory where I worked and my husband worked—we worked there all our lives—and now it's standing idle. Can you imagine that? How can that be? With that kind of equipment? And what about the people? How many people are without work? The main thing is there's no faith, that's what it is. It's very hard to have faith.

Do you still believe in those same ideals?

You know—by the way, I've been a member of the party for fifty years. I have to admit that there was a great deal in the party that was wrong and there were careerists, but the majority of people in the party were honest! My conscience is clean. In the course of my life, I did a great deal to ensure that factories ran well, to ensure that people lived better. I didn't take any-thing for myself. You see what kind of house I live in. I had more than one opportunity to get an apartment, but I didn't get one. Why? Because I had many women workers who had children and no apartments. I couldn't take one for myself. So I'm in this house, my husband and I built a house, and we live in it.

Antonina Aleksandrovna, would you recall your childhood for me, if you can?

Childhood was the most horrible time of my life.

Still, recall it for me, please. Tell me about your childhood.

I just don't know whether I should tell you about my childhood. Childhood was the most horrible time of my life.

Please do.

I was still small when the revolution began. And you know, even now I can still remember how we went out on the porch (at that time we had a two-story house on our estate)—our whole family went out, including Papa—just as a crowd of people was approaching, like a mass protest, and some of them were drunk. And some were armed with pitchforks and some with rakes and all sorts of things like that. It was awful! All of us, of course, were terrified. Prior to this, one of our stewards had been murdered some-where. But our father and mother were on very friendly terms with the peasants in the village. Once Father even saved the village from fire. He was tough but very just. And I will never forget—Mama used to recount this—how Papa went out on the porch and said: "Comrades! There was a time when all of this was ours. And now it is yours. I hand over to you the keys, I hand over everything to you, but I implore you to leave for my family what I can cultivate with my own hands." And they left him everything he asked for. No matter what, they respected Father. And so, you see, we were allowed to continue to live there.

And where was this, in what place?

In Tula guberniia, in the village of Rykhatko. Subsequently, we left for the village of Kurkino. No, wait, we left and spent a year in the village of Oga-rev, and then we went to relatives in Ukraine. Papa had four brothers in Ukraine. But in Ukraine at that time things were also terrible. Makhno was advancing and then there was Denikin;[11] it was all like that there. It was the revolution, and everything was very complicated. Still, it seems to me that we lived there for a couple of years and then came back. And when we came back, Papa joined the sovkhoz and worked there as an agronomist. And when Papa died, we moved again, you see, and Mama placed us in a *detskii dom* [children's home] where there was a model experimental school.[12] That's right. And here life was a little easier because it was a chil-

---

11. Nestor Makhno was an anarchist leader who enjoyed a considerable following among Ukrainian peasants. It is likely that Berezhnaia's family had fled to the province of Ekateri-noslav, because that is where Makhno's peasant forces briefly triumphed in late autumn 1919. Then they were driven out by an army led by General A. I. Denikin, a White general whose forces fought the Bolsheviks in the south of Russia.

12. These were schools that most assiduously followed the revolutionized curriculum of the first postrevolutionary decade. The new approach to education stressed the practical aspects of knowledge and its connection to the natural world, and students at such schools spent time doing physical labor as well as studying.

dren's home. And in this children's home I learned how to operate a milling machine. The children there not only received regular schooling but were trained, you see, to work in factories. Moreover, knowing that I was a person—how shall I put it—with such an objectionable past, in the children's home I tried to do everything. Not that I did it deliberately, I simply loved to work. I helped in the kitchen and I milked the cows when we went to the country in the summer. And then it happened, a terrible thing happened to me. I must have been about seventeen at the time, you know, when suddenly . . . Everyone has people who are good to them and people who are out to do them in. Someone denounced me, actually denounced us to the WPI [Workers' and Peasants' Inspectorate][13]—at that time it still existed— saying that children who were not from the working class were being housed in the children's home, and why were they there? And we got very upset, thinking that we would be expelled from the children's home.

There were three of you, right? Three sisters?

Yes, three sisters. This was a very difficult period!

What year was this?

I'll tell you what year. It was '29. And at that time, we were in the country. The children's home went to the country, to dachas in the summer. And a representative of the WPI came.

WPI, what's that?

WPI stands for Workers' and Peasants' Inspectorate. So they came in order to expel us. But the director of the children's home was there. He was the director of both the home and the school, Rimsha was his name, he was Latvian. A communist, but such a hardworking man, such a decent person. And so he spoke out, he said: "We will not expel Berezhnaia. Berezhnaia sets an excellent work example"—that's just what he said, an excellent work example. "She sets an excellent example in the way she gets along with others, everyone loves her, she can take the place of anyone, she can assist anyone, we will not expel her." And they didn't expel me. So this was really fortunate for me, for all of us. It was like a new lease on life. And so after that, I continued to study in the school. At the time, I was in the ninth grade, and then I finished the tenth grade. But when I applied to an institute of higher education—I wanted to enter a forestry institute, but you know, I wasn't used to concealing anything and I wrote down everything—I was re-

---

13. This organization was created in 1920 as a result of Lenin's belief that administration would become merely a matter of accounting under socialism and that workers would take over the process. Its role was to deal with citizens' complaints and improve the efficiency of production, with the active participation of workers and peasants. Under Josef Stalin it became a bureaucratic institution, but it remained active through the early 1930s, investigating, among other things, economic waste and mismanagement.

fused, on the grounds that there were no openings. Period. But later, I decided, no, come what may, I would graduate from an institute. I had such an unswerving desire, I could not endure injustice. Well, okay, Father was . . . [a member of the landowning nobility]. But why should I have to suffer because of it? And then I graduated, after all.

And your mama, what was her fate?

What happened to Mama? Mama was a simple person, she only completed four grades of schooling. When Father died, she worked on the sovkhoz, in the milk-receiving department. That's the sort of work she did. She worked there for three years, and then went to Ukraine to her relatives. She lived there awhile, and then in 1930, after I had begun to work at the arms plant, she returned to Tula, and we were all together—Mama and the three of us. One sister studied at a factory apprenticeship school, a second sister at a vocational college, and I worked at the arms plant. And they gave us an apartment, so we all lived together. And then I got married and went to the Urals.

[In the remainder of this interview, Berezhnaia discusses the fate of her family and gives her opinions, mainly negative, about the contemporary situation.]

❖   ❖   ❖

[AP reads:]

"Dear Antonina Aleksandrovna, the members of the administration of ferrous metallurgy extend heartfelt congratulations to you on the occasion of your fifty-fifth birthday and your twenty-fifth anniversary as a socially active engineer in the area of ferrous metallurgy. Your many years of experience working as an engineer have led to the improvement of technical and economic indices and to the technical perfecting of refractory enterprises in the Central Urals. Your colleagues in the administrative apparatus know you to be a social activist and a responsive and warm comrade. We sincerely wish you, dear Antonina Aleksandrovna, good health, long life, and success in your work and in your personal life. The head of administration of ferrous metallurgy, Selkevich, the secretary of the party bureau, Kamnev, and the chairman of the local trade union committee, Nepomniashchii."[14] This must have been in 1965.

---

14. The names indicate that all three of these officials were men.

A Life in a Peasant Village

IRINA IVANOVNA KNIAZEVA

Irina Kniazeva was the only woman we interviewed who had lived most of her life in a peasant village and who spoke about it at length. All our other attempts at in-depth conversations with peasant women—near Moscow, in the Sverdlovsk region, near the town of Novozybkov—were unsuccessful. Other peasant women either responded with monosyllables to Posadskaya's questions or took the conversation in a direction that was not useful to us. To our regret, this happened time after time. But we really wanted our book to have the narrative of a woman who remained in the village, so we did not abandon the effort to locate one. And then, when Posadskaya was in Tomsk, someone recommended Irina Kniazeva, a woman who had left her village for Tomsk relatively late in life, in order to live with her daughter and her family. Especially in winter, it is exceedingly difficult for an old woman to live alone in a rural village. Most village houses are heated with wood and lack all urban comforts, such as an indoor toilet, running water, a telephone, sometimes even electricity. Posadskaya immediately telephoned Kniazeva's apartment. Her daughter, a fifty-two-year-old woman with a tired, mournful voice, answered the telephone. Posadskaya's contact had told her that the daughter had lost her job at a factory, like many other women in Tomsk, and had practically no hope of finding another position. Her only option was to wait until she turned fifty-three and then to take early retirement. "Come over," she said. "But can you really be interested in my mama's life? She's illiterate, you know."

Kniazeva answered the door herself. The family was living in a standard two-room apartment in a typical building. The front room was immaculate, and along one wall stood the ubiquitous set of lacquered furniture: a bookcase, a simple china cabinet, and a wardrobe. A big television set, half-covered with a reddish, woven wool carpet occupied the central place near the window. These were the typical furnishings of a middle-income urban family during the twilight years of the socialist system. Since the system's collapse in 1991, the family had bought nothing new in the way of furniture or housewares—they hardly had enough money to pay for food, rent, and utilities. They had other financial worries, too. Irina Kniazeva confided: "My daughter says, 'Mama, you've got to save your money! We'll need half a million for your funeral,[1] and I have no money.' I've saved about 300,000 rubles."

Kniazeva seemed out of place in this urban setting. The years she had spent in Tomsk had not effaced her country ways. She was short, and her head was carefully covered with a white headscarf, worn in the village style. Although she could not read, she understood everything we said, and spoke clearly about her own life. But at first, she did have difficulty conceptualizing what we expected of her. It took Posadskaya's repeated questioning and encouragement to get the interview started. "I'm afraid everything I say will be jumbled up," Kniazeva asserted at the start. She wanted to know how she should begin. When Posadskaya told her to begin with her childhood, Kniazeva asked again: "How I was born, is that what you want?" Only after Posadskaya reassured her and asked the specific questions, "where, when, and in what year," did Kniazeva's narrative really commence. As the interview proceeded, she frequently stopped to inquire "What else shall I tell you?" or to say "I don't know what else to say." The open-ended structure of the interview was not easy for her, perhaps because her inability to read and lifetime spent in the village had given her little or no experience of the kind of consecutive account we wanted, or perhaps because she remained virtually untouched by Soviet ideology and its value system, which provided other narrators (Pavlova, Berezhnaia, and Ponomarenko, especially) with a framework for their stories. Kniazeva was born and remained a peasant. The events she remembered and recounted were the events of a peasant's life, and her ideal of the good life was a peasant ideal: a barnyard full of animals and a granary full of grain.

Kniazeva witnessed the events of her era with the eyes of a peasant, too. In her mind, Lenin and the Bolshevik revolution were inseparable: When Posadskaya asked her to talk about the revolution, Kniazeva in turn asked, "You mean, how people welcomed Lenin [who never visited her village]?" and she remembered that the people welcomed Lenin and the new freedom by parading about their village carrying icons and the Gospels. Their apparent enthusiasm for the revolution did not save the family from forcible grain requisitioning by the Reds as well as the Whites during the civil war, as both sides tried to deal with desperate food shortages. Her family's suffering at the hands of both sides may explain her indifference to the civil war's outcome: "Here's how I understood it," she explained. "Whoever wins, wins." Kniazeva had her own manner of speech, her own periodization of history, and her own idea of what the revolution was about.

---

1. In 1994, this sum amounted to about half of Kniazeva's yearly pension, or about $250.

Kniazeva's account of the patriarchal peasant family was much darker than Dubova's. Unable to support his large family on his allotment of land, her father went off to earn wages elsewhere and left the farmwork to his wife, as did tens of thousands of other peasant men in similar circumstances. Kniazeva's relationship with him suggests alienation, which could be the consequence of long years of separation: "I didn't seem like his kid and I didn't call him father," she recalled. Kniazeva's mother and father had ten children together, and her father brought two more from his first marriage. As her mother's first child, it became Kniazeva's responsibility to care for her younger siblings. For that reason, she never had the chance to go to school. Her father was not only terribly strict, as was Dubova's, he was also violent and abusive, beating her mother terribly, even while she was pregnant. Later, when Kniazeva's husband abandoned her, leaving her with two small children, her father began to beat and insult her, too, and eventually drove her from his house. He allowed her to live with him only on the eve of collectivization, when the government began to increase taxes and her father needed her labor to meet his quotas.

Despite the family's relative poverty and willingness to meet procurement quotas, they suffered during the campaign to dispossess kulaks that commenced in 1929. When the quotas were raised so high that her father could no longer fulfill them, the authorities put him in prison, where he remained for a number of years. The family lost their house, the implements they had managed to acquire in the 1920s, and all of their animals. To support herself and her children, Kniazeva found work at a grain elevator. Because she never earned enough to feed her family, every day she would put a handful of flour up her sleeve and then pass it along to her mother and the children. Pilfering grain in this way was a dangerous business. According to a law enacted on August 7, 1932, collective farm property was "sacred and untouchable." Those who stole it were regarded as "enemies of the people" and could be sentenced to death by shooting. To Kniazeva's religious way of thinking, it was also a sin. Until the end of her life she bore this "sin" of theft on her soul, unable to lighten the burden through confession because the revolution had shut down her parish church. As soon as she moved to Tomsk, a city where there was a church, she went to the priest to confess and beg forgiveness.

Hers was a life of destitution. Her father joined a collective farm when he got out of prison, and eventually, Kniazeva joined, too. She did whatever work was needed, but the payment for her "labor days" was miserable. Instead of helping, a second marriage increased her hardship. Despite misgivings, she decided to marry again after six years. But once more the marriage was a failure. Her husband left her, this time with five children. Her small daughter died of starvation. At the end of her life, for all the years of unrelenting labor she performed for the collective farm, she was granted the tiny

Kniazeva in 1994 with a photograph of her son

pension of twelve rubles, the minimum pension established for collective
farmers in the early 1960s, a time when the average pension for urban
dwellers was around 50 rubles. But before that, collective farm workers received no pension at all.

As she always did, at the end of the interview Posadskaya asked permission to photograph her subject. Kniazeva was embarrassed: "Oi, you
shouldn't!" Then she straightened out her headscarf and took from the
shelf a large photograph in a black frame—her youngest son, who died
while serving in the army. "Remember, I told you about him? I get a pension for him. Can you take a picture of me with my little boy?" So Posadskaya photographed them together: Irina Kniazeva, sitting on a little stool,
holding a photograph of her son.

◼   ◼   ◼

Irina Ivanovna Kniazeva: I'm afraid everything I say will be jumbled up.

*Anastasia Posadskaya-Vanderbeck: You won't jumble things up. Just tell it
as it was.*

Well, how should I begin?

With your childhood.

How I was born, is that what you want?

Of course. Where, when, in what year.

Kemerovo oblast, the village of Ostrovka [in Siberia]. I was born in 1910. Mama was due any time now, when Father went off to the mines, and the very next day, on May 1, I was born. When Father came back, I was already three. Father didn't take to me. I didn't seem to him like his kid, and I didn't call him "Father."

Had he gone to work in the gold mines?[2]

Yes, and Mother had to do the plowing herself and the sowing, see.

And did you have a large farm?

What farm? All we had were two horses and a cow. What else ... I was born first, just after my father married my mother. His first wife died. They had six children. Four died and two lived—a son and a daughter. And I was born, and my mama gave birth to ten children.

So that means you were the oldest?

I was the oldest. Well, we began to get on. I didn't call him "Father." But when I got bigger, they made me call him that. Father was awfully strict. Well, and so I grew up. There were no boys in the family, so by fifteen I was already plowing. First, they set me to harrowing. When I was ten or eleven, I harrowed the fields, and then, when I got a little bigger, I took up plowing, and I plowed and I plowed. And then Father hired a farmhand, such a good young fellow he was, he came from somewhere in Russia. He was awfully hard working, Fedor was. And we got to know each other, and he fell in love with me, it seemed. "I'll take you as a wife; I'll take you as a wife." Well, I turned eighteen, I was already into my nineteenth year, and he began to ask for me. Father did not want to give me to him in marriage, because Fedor was poor, had no roof of his own. He lived with the people he worked for. Well, all the same, it came to pass: The marriage was agreed on, we got married, had a wedding. So we lived in my father's house.

Didn't you want to marry him?

What makes you ask that? I loved him, and he loved me. But then look what happened: He took up with my girlfriend, Larka her name was. Well, my first child was a boy. Then I got pregnant again, and I didn't have an abortion. I was already seven months pregnant when he up and left.

Went to live with your girlfriend?

No, they ran off, left the village. And I stayed in my father's house. My second child was born, a daughter. Now, like I said, Father was mean and

---

2. In order to get to the Urals region or to northeast Siberia, Kniazeva's father would have had to travel hundreds of miles.

strict, and he said: "You got yourself a bastard." He drove me out of the house. He took down the cradle. Into the snowstorm, in the midst of winter he opened the door and threw me out, threw me out with the swaddling clothes, the cradle, the whole bit. "Get out of here." Life was hard. Grandma, now she's gone, would go to a neighbor and say: "Give Arina shelter for a little while. Our master has flown off the handle again. He's so mean; he's taken it into his head to drive out Arina." [Arina is a vernacular form of Irina.] I would move in, live at someone's for a week or two, no more, I had two kids with me, you know. Then it was back to Father. Every time he drove me out, I would come crawling back. And then we sowed a lot of grain [to have a harvest sufficient to pay the taxes in kind]. We weren't treated as "kulaks"[3] but as sure bets for fulfilling the procurement quotas. They would demand 500 poods [a pood is equal to about 36 pounds], and we would deliver it. I began to help out, and then he quit driving me out of the house. They would send men with a string of carts. I would deliver the grain. We gave up the 500 poods, got nothing back, and then they slapped on another 300.

This was a tax?

Yes, a tax in kind. And then there was no more grain left. And there were already eleven in the family. Mama had a lot of kids. There were seven of us: Three died, and seven were left. Then there were my two kids, there was Grandma, Mother, and Father. Then they put Father in prison, because we had no way of paying, no grain. Am I making sense?

You're doing very well.

He did his time. I don't know how long. Maybe three years, maybe five. Anyhow, a long time. And then they drove us out of the house. Just like that. All of us. Grandma went blind from grief. She cried all the time. We lived in a shed all summer, and then in the fall we started living in a small hut. A woman went away somewhere to her children. She let us live there, see. And so I went off to work. We didn't join the kolkhoz. We were scared, you know. And so they ruined us, they took everything. They took the animals, they took the horses, they took the cow—we had one cow—they took everything.[4] Now I went off to work at the grain elevator. The kids were already . . . well, they'd gotten a little bigger, and I left them with Mother and worked at the grain elevator. For six years after my Fedor left me, for six years I didn't get married again. Grandma said: "Be careful, don't get mar-

---

3. In 1927, following a severe shortfall in state grain procurements, peasants who allegedly hoarded their grain were labeled "kulaks," and force was once again employed to requisition grain.

4. Although she did not say that her family suffered dispossession as kulaks, this is precisely how kulaks were treated.

ried." I didn't even think about it; I didn't get married. And then a second husband turned up after six years. He seemed to be okay. He kept asking and asking. But I was afraid to get married. I said: "I have two children. How can I marry? Their own father threw us out. Is this one going to feed us?" And so it turned out. Well, all the same, I ended up marrying him. He wouldn't leave me alone. So I got married, but he was not a good man. Oh, he was not a good man! God forbid there should be such people. He beat me and cursed me out and swore all the time, and he drank and drank and drank. That's how it turned out. So, I got married for a second time. He was the father of my fourth child. One died; three were left. And Iurka had just been born—he was only twelve days old—when he [his father], too, took off, left me. Again I was abandoned. And all I had was an awful little hut.

What year was this?

What year? It was 1945. He wasn't sent to the front. So they sent him to work in one munitions factory after another. That's what happened, and I took it very hard. I thought: I've got three kids, the baby's with me, there's no day care. Good God, what am I going to do? He didn't pay any alimony, he didn't help, nothing. Well, somehow I managed to raise Iurka, somehow. When he reached the age of two, I left him and the other kids at home and went to work on the kolkhoz. And I worked for fifteen years on that kolkhoz. Yes. Before that I worked at the grain elevator, like I told you. And then I left. It was very hard, very hard. Well, the kids grew up. Only when Iurka, the youngest, turned fourteen did the authorities find him [Iurka's father]. He'd been hiding out somewhere near Moscow.

They searched for him in order to make him pay you alimony?

Well, Iurka was fourteen.[5] He was working, and so were the other kids. The girl, Zina, was working, and the oldest, Sashka, already had a job as a tractor driver. They didn't go to school very long, only completed five grades. Well, he came back [Iurka's father]. He came back, and we took him in. And Ivan said: "I didn't come back to live with you, but I'll put up a house for you." Well, our little house was really bad, so we said yes. "Let him, Mama, let him build us a house." He built the house, and then he went off again. That's how he was.

And you kept living in Kemerovo oblast?

Yes, there in the village of Ostrovka.

---

5. When a husband disappeared and failed to pay child support, his abandoned wife was entitled to go to court, initiate a search for him, and attempt to force him to pay. It is unclear why Kniazeva seemed reluctant to respond directly to Posadskaya's question.

Irina Ivanovna, you said that you still remember what life was like before the revolution and that you remember the revolution itself.

Yes, yes.

Talk about it, please.

You mean, how people welcomed Lenin?

Yes.

Well, when freedom was declared, everyone went to the church, the people gathered in the church, and we dragged out all the icons. Our village was good. The streets were straight and even; the houses were good. So we marched around the village with these icons and the Gospels. My grandfather welcomed the revolution with the Gospels, too, but he was the first to be branded a kulak and dispossessed. So we welcomed Lenin by walking around the village with these icons, with prayers. Free at last, free at last. We went round the entire village, and then we put the icons back in the church.

When was this? So they rejoiced that the revolution had taken place?

Yes. This was when the revolution was over, when Lenin was already there.[6]

And how did your family respond to the revolution? Did they react to it positively? After all, there was the civil war. And then some sided with the Whites, some with the Reds.

Well, the Whites came, then the Reds. Day and night they came. We had a house. Of course, it only had one room, but it was big. So they would come for the night. The yard was large. It could hold lots of carts. The Whites would pass through, and then the Reds would come: "Have the Whites been here?" "They've come and gone." The Reds would pass through, and then the Whites would come: "Have the Reds been here?" "They've come and gone." Many times they spent the night at our place. An iron stove was kept lit, and one soldier boy—I remember it as if it were today, I wasn't asleep—one soldier boy sat near the stove and said: "Lice, lice, lice." Grandma said to him: "Sonny." He was young, he was handsome, and he was Russian. "Granny," he said, "the lice are eating me up." And so they came, oh, they came day and night. I don't know how many.

---

6. It is unclear what period she was referring to here. Perhaps it was the February revolution, which overthrew the tsar; or perhaps it was indeed the October revolution, when the Bolsheviks came to power. She also might have been referring to the end of the civil war and the onset of the New Economic Policy in spring 1921. Regardless, it is clear that Kniazeva conceived of the revolution in a very different way than did her interviewer, who conceptualizes the revolutionary process in terms of the chronology of history books.

And your family—were they closer to the Reds or to the Whites, or to neither?

Neither to one nor the other. Whatever happens, happens. Here's how I understood it: Whoever wins, wins. The Whites would come, they would go into the granary to see what was there—oats—and they would take it. Then the Reds would come, and the same thing would happen: "Do you have any oats? We need to feed our horses." "Shucks, no, the Whites have already been here and cleaned us out." "Well, we'll get our hands on what's there. Come on, open the granary." And that's what happened. Life was very hard. So, what else can I tell you?

Could your mama read and write?

No, no. All the other kids could read and write. I was the oldest and the only one who couldn't.

They didn't send you to school?

Well, Mama took me there. She took me there when she thought it was time. It used to be you had to be nine years old, and I was maybe eight. The teacher patted me on the head—I already had a long braid, like this, all plaited—patted me, and said: "Well, next year bring her for sure." And then the next year Mama had a baby, she needed a nursemaid, and, well, what could I do? I was the oldest. And so I wasn't sent to school. That's how it happened I stayed home.

So you had to look after the younger kids?

And so they didn't send me to school. I stayed home, took care of the babies. They would take me with them to the fields. When I was five, six, I already looked after the babies in the field. Mama would hang the cradle on a birch tree, and I would sit and rock it, while Mama would reap, work. That's how we worked.

Irina Ivanovna, and was the house big? How many rooms were there?

There were two rooms. That's the way it was in the village. There was a kitchen and then there was another room, a common room, but that room wasn't heated. There was no real place to sleep. There was one cot; only the little ones slept on it. But there was a large Russian stove, and some of us slept on it. Mother and father always slept on the floor. Always. Those children who were grown up also slept on the floor. Only the little ones were put down to sleep on the cot. On the cot or in the cradle. That's how we lived. Well, I don't know what else to tell you.

Irina Ivanovna, did your father beat your mama?

Oh, did he.

He did?

He beat her.

Hard?

He beat her.

Did she cry?

Oh . . .

Well, how did the others react to that? Did anyone come to her defense? Did she run away from home?

She would run away. Grandma would defend her more than anybody else. He beat her. He was jealous. Oh, terribly jealous. My father was thirteen years older. He had been married before, and mother, well she was younger than he was. And our mother was really pretty, although, see, she was short, like I am. Really pretty. If he saw her with anyone, if a man said anything to her, he would pick a fight, he would.

What about other women? Was wife beating widespread? Did it often happen in other families?

Did it happen to other women? Wait a minute, I'll tell you: Our neighbor really beat his wife good. About the rest, I don't know. The rest didn't beat their wives. They got along okay. Our neighbor, Uncle Rodion, he also beat his wife, he beat her good.

Well, why do you think your mama put up with it? Did she talk back or do something about it?

She went . . . She came from another village, twenty kilometers away, my mama did. Once he beat her so bad, it was awful. They carried her out on this, on a rag. Father hitched up the horse, put in pillows, also sheepskin coats, and took her to the hospital, thirty kilometers away.

He beat her to a pulp, and then he took her to the hospital?

He beat her to a pulp. He beat her so bad, heaven help her. But she recovered and went to her father's house and said . . . I was three or four at the time—I don't remember it. Well, she went to her father and said, "Pop, take me in." She was pregnant at the time. He beat her like that, even when she was pregnant. And the boy was born unharmed. He died, passed away when he reached the age of four, he did. "Pop, take me in," she said. But her father replied: "The priest married you. When you were married, we lit a candle for you,[7] we prayed. Bear with it. Whatever fate God sent, you must live with it."

---

7. Her mother's father was referring to particular elements of the marriage ritual. He was repeating these details in order to emphasize to his daughter that she and her husband were bound together in holy matrimony and that he, her father, could not interfere by giving her shelter.

So she returned to her husband?

And she went back to her husband. But they lived together for ages. He died first. He was older; God took him first.

So your family was very religious?

Yes, that's right. We all went to church, we always went. The church was five doors away, really close. The church bell would ring and Grandma would say: "Get up, get up! Let's go to morning service." Early in the morning.

Do you believe in God?

Yes, yes, yes. We believe.

So what happened later, when God was outlawed and they closed the churches?

Yes, they closed the church. They destroyed the church, they burned the icons. They destroyed everything. Just the walls were left. When was it? I saw it three years ago—the walls of the church are still standing.

But when everything was outlawed, what did you do? Did you pray at home? There was no priest?

No priest. At home we had icons, Mama blessed me with one when I was married. I still cherish that icon. So we prayed at home.

Irina Ivanovna, what did you think of Lenin after he died? Had anything changed? Do you remember?

Everyone praised him for one thing or another, said that Lenin had given us freedom. Let's say they began to produce those things—the things you plow with—plows, and father bought one. Up to that point they made them in the local smithy, and they didn't work very well. Then Father bought . . . Ah, I plowed with an iron plow. The horses moved easily. Father bought a winnower. There hadn't been any. There hadn't been anything, anywhere. Even if you had the money, you couldn't buy a thing. Nothing at all. And then winnowers appeared. In our large village we had to make do with only two or three winnowers, and that's how we winnowed the grain. It wasn't easy. And then we got our own winnower. But we only had it for about two years, and then they took it from us. Collectivization began, and that was it. That was the end. They took the plow, too, and the winnower. Everything.[8] And we were ruined. We were left with nothing.

---

8. This section suggests the extent to which peasants like Kniazeva remained outside the revolutionary process. In this period, many changes took place: Agitators came to villages to generate support for the revolution, and campaigns were launched to abolish illiteracy. Nevertheless, this narrator continued to experience the revolution strictly in terms of her own peasant interests.

You didn't want to join the kolkhoz?

Well, in the beginning Mama said something like: "How can we go to the kolkhoz?" But then when Father finished doing time and came home, he went to the kolkhoz. He was a carpenter, a real craftsman. He made rakes, he made pitchforks. Whatever was ordered, he was the one to make it. Why not, he was a carpenter. And he made everything. And he began to get on. He bought a little house, he bought a cow. And they began to get back on their feet. They lived that way till they died. I don't know what else to say.

And how were things for you on the kolkhoz? What sort of work did you do there? Hard work?

Oh, it was wartime, and then after the war . . . hard work, day and night. In the daytime, we would reap—there were only us women to do it—and at night, when we had already cut the rye, we would drive home the threshing machine. We had to do the threshing at night on the threshing floor 'cause we had to get them the grain fast. To the 'levator. All the time we were taking grain to the 'levator. In the daytime, the whole day long, we would reap, and at night, as soon as evening came, we would go to the threshing floor to thresh the grain. How many rows . . . I was short, so I used to thresh three or four rows. No, more—five, almost six—more. The kids, all three of them, would be asleep, and I couldn't get into the house. "Now don't hook it shut," I'd tell them. I would knock and knock, but they just wouldn't open up. I would take a thin pole and unfasten the hook. The hut was small, it stood all by itself, on the edge of the village. I would shake and shake the children, and they would wake up. That's how it was. Nights were like that all during the harvest. I would say: "Don't make me work at night. Look, I have kids." "The kids aren't going anywhere. Get on with it, work." It was hard, hard. We worked day and night. There were no men, after all!

Didn't you want to get some training, so you wouldn't have to do such hard work?

And how could I do that? I didn't even know the alphabet, didn't know a thing.

Well, wasn't there a likbez, that is, special courses for people who couldn't read and write?

There were, but I didn't have the time, I worked. They wanted me to come. I went there, two or three times. I learned the letters—A, B, C, D. That was enough. Well, I can scratch out my name.

Can you read?

No.

How much did you get paid for your work?

We got 400 grams of grain a day, if we made our work quota.[9]

That's very little.

Very little. And we worked day and night. And when you were paid, you got one small sack of grain. You'd take it to the mill, and they'd take half for grinding it. You'd bring home just that. I pulled wood myself on a sled, I hauled hay myself. One day I would go for hay, the next day for wood, then again for hay. And I would leave my kids. Oh Lord, dear God, they were such good kids. They didn't start a fire and burn the house down—[although] I had to let them light the stove by themselves. But then things got better. They sent Fedor Ivanych from the district center to be chairman of our kolkhoz.[10] Ah, he was such a fine man! And he saw me hauling the hay myself, loading it on the sled like a cart. "Hey you, who do you belong to?" "My name is Kochetkova. I'm the daughter of Ivan Ivanych Kochetkov." Well, they lived side by side, my father and the kolkhoz chairman. They had given the chairman a kulak's house. "I know him. Don't let me ever see you again hauling wood or hay yourself." So I said, "Fedor Ivanych, they won't give me either oxen or horses." "They will." And they started to. I would go, take a horse, and bring back hay. Everything by myself. One day I would bring hay, the next day I would have the horse to bring wood. And that's how I got on.

How was the work organized on the kolkhoz? Were there brigades?[11]

Yes, there were brigades. There was a kolkhoz named Five-Year Plan and a kolkhoz called Victory. In our village, there were two kolkhozes. It was at Victory that I worked.

And who was the brigade leader?

You know, it was wartime, then it was after the war; there were no men. One man named Zhuravlev came; he was a cripple. Then a second, Ivan Brusimenko. There was also something wrong with him, something with his eyes. These were the brigade leaders we had. Only cripples were left behind. Then there was Efim Balmaev; he couldn't see very well. They weren't

---

9. The "work day" provided the basis for calculating the payment in kind received by collective farmers. Because collective farmers had the "privilege" of a small individual allotment of land on which they could grow food for themselves and for the market, they were paid much less than their contribution to the collective's output. Sometimes they received no compensation for meeting production targets. A natural economy prevailed in the village, and money was rare.

10. The kolkhoz chairperson, the most powerful individual in the village, was in charge of the management of the collective farm. His (sometimes her) primary responsibility was to fulfill procurement quotas set by the central government.

11. Work was organized according to groups called brigades, each of them under the command of a brigade leader.

sent to the front, although Efim was healthy. So, these three men. These were the men we worked with all the time.

And what sort of pension were you given?

Oh, twelve rubles. And then when my son was killed,[12] they took away the twelve rubles. "You can't have two pensions." And they gave me twenty-one rubles. It's on account of him that I'm getting it.[13] As if my labor didn't count, as if I had never worked. All those years of work, and no trace.[14]

Irina Ivanovna, what was the hardest period in your life?

All of it, all of it was hard. Well, from the time I was young, I harrowed the fields and plowed. That's how our family was, everybody worked. Then my husbands left me with kids to raise on my own. I was desperate, starving. I would gather rotten potatoes, mash them up, feed the children. Then the war, famine . . . Ah.

When was the famine, do you remember?

In '30 and '31, when they wiped out everything, took away our animals, our house, everything. We lost everything. That's when there was famine. Well, and when I went to work at the 'levator, I'll tell you how I sinned: I would pour grains of wheat into my pocket or into my mitten. I was living at my aunt's. I would come to her and pour them out, pour them out. It wasn't much at all. I stole it. Today a little, the next day a little, and I would send it all to Mother. My kids were with her, and that's where I sent it all. There were millstones, they would grind the grain, so I would gather the leavings. I worked at the 'levator, so I would take stuff from there. And I wasn't the only one; everybody did. I would pour grains of wheat right here into my pocket or into my mitten, and then I would come home and pour them out into a little bowl. I was living then at Auntie Iulia's. Don't get caught, she would say. And I would answer, No, I won't. That's how I fed my family one winter, one whole winter. That's my sin, that's how I sinned.

Quite the contrary: It's a sin the state acted that way.

Governments don't care. The priest already . . . I went to confession, said to him: "Father, I stole. It was like this: I stole wheat out of hunger." "Do you repent? Well, then the Lord God will forgive you."

---

12. Her son died in the army during peacetime, just a few days before he was scheduled to be sent home. She was told that he had been in an accident, that he fell under a train. However, it has recently become well known that many conscripts died in peacetime because of the way they were treated in the military.

13. Because her son died while fulfilling his military obligation, Kniazeva was entitled to a benefit.

14. She was referring to the fact that she was receiving no pension in return for all her years of arduous labor.

And just when did you go to the priest? Was it recently?

No, it was a long time ago, when I moved here to Tomsk. In the village there was no priest. And as soon as I moved here—I was already up in years—I said to myself, You've got to confess your sin.[15] Yes.

Irina Ivanovna, what was the best period in your life?

Well, when my old man built us a house and left, and the kids were already big. Iurka was already fourteen . . . fifteen . . . already sixteen years old. My old man left and the house was a big one, had two rooms. My son was working then as a tractor driver. That was the time I would say was good.

What do you think: If the revolution hadn't taken place in '17, how would you have lived?

I can't say how. I don't know whether things were good or bad under Nicky [Tsar Nicholas II]. It seems to me that things were good. We had animals, our barnyard was full, the granary was full of grain.

---

15. Kniazeva moved to Tomsk sometime in the 1970s. This meant that she was burdened by her sin of theft for approximately forty years.

From Peasant to Journalist

ELENA GRIGORIEVNA PONOMARENKO

Elena Ponomarenko is the only woman we interviewed who was still working. At the age of eighty-two, she was still heading the museum of labor
achievements at the Sibelectromotor plant, a top manufacturer of large engines. She was the factory's oldest worker.

She and Posadskaya met for the first time in the city of Tomsk, at the entrance to the plant. As a result of the movement away from a state-controlled economy, the plant was practically idle—almost no one wanted its
products, and those who did, had no money. Nevertheless, the old order remained in place. Posadskaya had to present her internal passport for verifi-
cation and to sign a register. "She's a writer who's come all the way from
Moscow to see me," Ponomarenko announced proudly to the guards, two
elderly women. The museum was located on the third floor of the plant's
administration building. This would not be so bad if the elevators were
functioning; but as part of the effort to economize, the elevators had been
shut down. So Elena Ponomarenko had to climb the steep staircase. She
leaned hard on her cane and stopped frequently to catch her breath.

Ponomarenko's life seemed intertwined with that of the museum. In
1956, she had come to the plant to set it up. By the time of our interview,
however, when half of the workers at the plant had been fired and those left
had not been paid for months, no one was interested in the museum. Ponomarenko, too, was almost never paid. The factory administration had proposed that she take an unpaid leave—"until times get better." So her work
was now practically voluntary. They had "cut back" on her assistants, and
she herself was in constant risk of being laid off, too. "Of course, the first
ones to be fired are us, the old people," she said with a sigh. For the time
being, the director was protecting her position, but no one could tell what
would happen next.

All large industrial enterprises once had museums such as the one that
Ponomarenko established. These were usually created at the initiative of
the Communist party. The rituals of socialist production took place in these

Ponomarenko in 1994

museums—the "consecration of workers," which was a solemn ceremony celebrating a worker's first wages; the honoring of worker dynasties; the meetings with worker delegations from other plants; and the award ceremonies for shock workers of socialist labor and victors of socialist competitions. Thus, a museum of this sort functioned not simply as an educational or cultural center; it also had an important ideological role to play. For that very reason, just a short while earlier Posadskaya would not have taken an interest in the displays of such a museum—the ideological element would have put her off. But by the time of her interview with Ponomarenko, the museum, like everything else that was "socialist," served as a reminder of a very different social and economic order, one opposed to virtually all the changes taking place in what was once the Soviet Union. It is almost impossible to imagine how a museum like this could manage to survive. No one was interested in it any longer, everyone was busy getting by, earning their daily bread; and yet, despite all that, the museum continued to exist. "I won't let them close it while I'm alive," Elena Ponomarenko said firmly, offering "resistance" even at the age of eighty-two.

Elena Ponomarenko's attentive blue eyes peered from behind eyeglasses. Her straight, gray hair was cut very short. There was something soldierly about her—a kind of restraint and self-control. That impression was intensified by her clothing: She wore a long, straight, dark blue jacket, stiff at the shoulders, in the style of the 1940s and 1950s, and a straight skirt made of the same fabric. She appeared firmly planted on her feet, but this was an illusion: For many years she had walked with the help of a cane, and she recently had undergone an operation on her knees.

Ponomarenko was born in Ukraine in 1912, to the family of a peasant, a landscape gardener. Her father did not have enough land with which to support his seventeen children, and twice he moved the family to Siberia, where, it was said, there was land sufficient for everyone; but they never succeeded in escaping their poverty. So as was typical of the peasantry, Elena went to work at a very early age, helping her father and brothers plant trees, herding animals, and taking care of others' children. Her father's death and the need to work forced her to leave school after only five years, which she regretted for the rest of her life. Her first real job was selling books and newspapers at a kiosk; subsequently, she was assigned to a bookstore. In conformity with the values of her era, which celebrated manual labor and production and looked askance at any kind of commercial relations, she claimed to have hated engaging in commerce. She embraced the new era in other ways, as well: She was the only one in her family to join the Pioneers, a Communist youth organization for children of between ten and fourteen years, and then the Komsomol, the League of Young Communists, where she found the kind of social controls that characterized traditional peasant life and that she evidently preferred—"iron discipline," she called it. Then, when she was around twenty years old, her elder sister died of typhus, leaving three small daughters. Despite her embrace of the new order, Ponomarenko evidently never considered giving the children to the state to raise: Claims of family still came first. She herself took on responsibility for raising the children, thereby ending all her chances for further study. She also had to give up her job in the city and move to the country, where she took over her sister's work. In her interview, she talked about some of the hardships that she, an inexperienced nineteen-year-old, had to face: procuring food in an unfamiliar setting, preparing it when she had never cooked before, becoming a grownup and a single mother overnight. Not long after, she got married, but she lived only three years with her husband. Those years were far from happy: He cheated on her and lied to her, and she finally left him, taking their two-year-old son with her. After that, alone with four children—"a whole kindergarten"—and an aged mother, she faced the problem of keeping her family alive.

Ponomarenko's subsequent career is a "success story": It shows that the revolution did provide an avenue of upward mobility for at least some of the formerly dispossessed, prompting the beneficiary to embrace the system uncritically, even when members of her own family suffered terribly at its hands, as happened in Ponomarenko's case. Having finished five years in a village school, Ponomarenko managed to complete two more years of school in evening classes for working youth. Overlooking her lack of formal education, an exiled revolutionary gave her a start in a journalistic career in the small Siberian town of Maslianino, where she became a correspondent for a local radio broadcasting station. After she learned to type, she wrote articles about local events, which appeared in a wide range of publications. At the same time, she joined the Communist party, which solidified her position as a journalist. Throughout her career, Ponomarenko staunchly and uncritically upheld the correctness of the state's policies. When Posadskaya queried her about whether she was ever troubled by the tight ideological controls imposed on all media, Ponomarenko claimed never to have noticed them. She herself actually took part in the campaign to dispossess the kulaks, as became evident in the interview: She described the process by which an alleged kulak, one Makhov, was exiled on the basis of her radio broadcast. Her account of his alleged sabotage conformed so closely to accounts of sabotage that filled the newspapers during the early 1930s that it is hard to know whether to believe it. Only reluctantly and only in passing did Ponomarenko acknowledge that one of her brothers was exiled to Central Asia as a kulak; and only late in the interview did she "remember" that another brother, Grisha, spent ten years in the camps for cursing Stalin. And she served up Grisha's story in order to challenge the veracity of Alexander Solzhenitsyn's publications on this subject. Solzhenitsyn was one of the Soviet Union's most biting critics. His writings, particularly *The Gulag Archipelago,* chronicled the lives and sufferings of prisoners in the Soviet penal camps. Ponomarenko was employed as a journalist for various publications or for the radio until 1956, when she began her work at the factory museum.

The interview with Ponomarenko is one of our longest. The fifty years she worked as a journalist evidently affected the way she remembered things. When she spoke of her life, her narrative sounded less like a life story than a series of well-crafted sketches with no clear threads connecting them and no underlying themes providing continuity. We nevertheless chose to retain a fraction of her narrative (roughly 20 percent). In addition to material treating Ponomarenko's early years and her career as a journalist, we have included her lengthy description of her unhappy marriage. The marriage provides an extreme but vivid illustration of the inability of the government to strengthen the "socialist family," having itself destroyed the traditional values and community supports that had earlier reinforced personal stability.

◈ ◈ ◈

Elena Grigorievna Ponomarenko: I was born in 1912 in the village of Bogorodichnoe, in the district of Slaviansk, Kharkov oblast [in Ukraine], into a large family. I was the youngest of seventeen children. It happened like this: Mama was a pretty girl of seventeen. A handsome man came up to her—he had seen her, see—he really took a liking to her, and he began to beg her to become his wife: "Take pity on my orphans. I've got three daughters and a son, my wife died, and my boy is only six months old. There's no one to look after them." Well, for a long time, you see, she couldn't make up her mind. Her parents didn't like it much. After all, there were four children; it was no laughing matter. But he was so practical, so serious; in the end, she consented. He lived in the neighboring village. They were married, and he took her there. And in the very first year she had a son, Nikolai Grigorievich. My father was a gardener. At one time, he worked for a count as a gardener, as an ordinary gardener, and he learned to do the work there. And so, see, we had a large family, and things were very strict. My parents were very religious people, very religious. And we were all brought up in the fear of the Lord, as they say.

Well, Father, you see, they lived there, he loved Ukraine, Mama loved her native land, too. But they had ten sons and seven daughters, and while each son had the right to an allotment of land, daughters weren't allotted land in those days.[1] And so when the "Stolypin reaction" set in, people immediately said to him: Grigorii Pavlovich, we all respect you, you are an excellent gardener, an excellent fisherman. You know, Siberia has such wealth. Bread grows on trees there, it's the land of milk and honey. There's lots of land there—you can take as much as you want—you should make this northern country your own.[2] They really enticed him that way. Go, you won't regret it, go, in order to feed your family. Here you'll have a hard time putting bread on the table, go.

Anastasia Posadskaya-Vanderbeck: And did your papa and mama welcome the revolution?

Papa welcomed the revolution. My mama, Mama prayed for Lenin. She even, you know, requested that Lenin's name be put in the *pominalnik:* "Be

---

1. Among Russian and Ukrainian peasants, land traditionally was held in common by the community and allocated to each household according to specific formulas, usually only to adult males. In some areas, however, a widow with sons might obtain an allotment until the boys grew up.

2. Following the revolution of 1905, Russian prime minister Petr Stolypin instituted legislation that encouraged peasant households to withdraw land from communal holdings, set up farmsteads of their own, and enclose their property. It also enabled peasants to sell their holdings and leave their villages permanently. At the time, peasants regarded Siberia as a kind of Utopia, and tens of thousands moved there; but many of them were disappointed and eventually returned to their native villages. The Stolypin legislation was aimed at creating a strong, independent, capitalist peasantry that would serve as a source of stability and support for the government.

sure to write down Vladimir, be sure to."[3] And she prayed for him. Because, see, we always, our whole life, were very poor, but when the revolution came, there was this new order, and somehow we started to find work and started to live much better. Death was no longer at our door. It used to be that we lived from hand to mouth, but now, you see, we were really living—well, it was also very hard, but it was completely different. Mama, for example, she welcomed the revolution, and the kids also welcomed it.

And were you in school at the time?

It was terribly far to school. [She had to walk to school, a distance of seven kilometers.] I didn't go to school very much. Either I didn't have any shoes, or I didn't have anything to wear, or I had to do something at home. Until late autumn I tended the cows. When I was seven, after father died, in the summer I started to earn my own bread. I tended other people's cows. All in all, it was awfully hard, but I loved school, I would have walked even further. I wanted so much to learn! Oh! You cannot imagine how much! Well, I finished the fourth grade here [in Siberia], and then we went back to Bogorodichnoe, the village in Ukraine where I was born. It was very pretty there. And I liked the place and everything, but I didn't like the way people treated me. "Siberian contingent," *katsapka* [a mocking Ukrainian epithet for a Russian]—that's what they began to call me at school. I had done very well in school, and here suddenly I was getting twos[4] in Ukrainian language. In Russian I had fives, but in Ukrainian, twos. This made me terribly indignant. Well, I wanted to get out of there at any price, and I did. One of my older brothers came; his family was in Siberia. I cried and cried, day and night I pleaded, and they finally let me go.

But your mama stayed behind?

Mama and my older sister stayed there in Ukraine, but I went to my brother's [back to Siberia]. And I went to work. I must have been fourteen when I started to work. Well, you couldn't get along unless you worked, and he got me a job at a Soiuzpechat kiosk. (At that time it was called Kontragenstvo pechati, but now it's called Soiuzpechat.) And so I sold books, newspapers, this and that. Then I worked in a bookstore as a salesperson. I graduated from the bookstore school. I worked. Then they sent me, they assigned me after graduation to Aleiskoe, to a bookstore. I absolutely couldn't stand commerce, but that's how things turned out. There was

---

3. This request indicates that Lenin held a special place in their hearts. The *pominalnik* was a book that was kept in the parish church, in which people wrote the names of those for whom they wished prayers to be said—ordinarily, their close relatives or children.

4. Russia and the Soviet Union used a five-point grading system, in which five was the highest grade. A grade of two was very poor, as the grade of one was almost never used.

nothing I could do: You went wherever they sent you. I was in the Komsomol and quite active. Well, and I had also been a Young Pioneer.

How did you join the Pioneers?

This was in school, of course—in school. They accepted only the top pupils. What did I like about the Pioneers, the Komsomol, and the party? It was the iron discipline. If you broke any rules, that was it, you were out, you were no longer trusted, it all was terribly strict. But I never broke any rules; somehow I always had people's confidence. That was important: People trusted me.

Did your other brothers and sisters join the Pioneers, too?

No, nobody else was in either the Pioneers or the Komsomol.

But still, why did you want to join? Okay, there was the discipline, but what else?

What I liked best, of course, was the discipline! I really liked the fact that everything was so strict, that everything was so wise. There'd be tasks to perform, you'd perform them, and they'd say to you, Well done! They'd praise you. I'm not overly fond of praise, but still it made you feel good, somehow, when . . . And then I saw that in that environment a person developed more quickly, more doors were open. They had their own circle. I moved right up from the Pioneers into the Komsomol; they advanced me. And from the Komsomol I moved into the party. So in my case, one followed the other, yes. And in the Komsomol things were also very strict. If a girl, for example . . . Even if a girl was good, if she stepped out of line, she was expelled, yes, they expelled her from the Komsomol.

But how can that be? Look, in the twenties there were all those theories about free love . . . [5]

God forbid! You know this . . . You shouldn't pay any attention to what people say now, no, not under any circumstances! There're so many lies circulating now. Look, I lived through all this, I lived through all this myself.[6] I'll tell you straight. I'm judging by what I experienced: In our circle, it was

---

5. In the 1920s, sexual mores were in fact more diverse than the question suggests. It is true that some intellectuals and young communists preached or practiced "free love"; but V. I. Lenin and most of the party leadership were far more conservative on sexual matters, advocating at the most a kind of serial monogamy. And lower-class women were often more conservative still, resisting any attempt to weaken the family, which provided for their economic welfare and that of their children.

6. The intensity of Ponomarenko's response may in part reflect the fact that she came of age in the late 1920s, when official attitudes toward sexual issues had already begun to move in a more conservative direction.

considered shameful if a girl hung out with a guy, went off with him some-where to have a good time. That was it.

What kind of tasks were you given to perform in the Komsomol?

There were all sorts of tasks. Let's say that somewhere there was an old woman living alone and she was in poor health. So you had to go and tend to her, clean up her place, scrub the floor, everything. All this had to be done. We ourselves did the scrubbing, we whitewashed the school, scrubbed the floors, scrubbed the windows. We painted the windows, painted the floors, we did everything. In a single summer, we made the school shine like a cucumber. All this the Pioneers and Komsomol members did, they were the only ones. So there were all sorts of tasks, lots of them. You'd go somewhere or clean the street, or ... in general, all sorts! Then we also had to help, you know, those students who had trouble with school.

How did you meet your future husband?

Oh, you know, that's a real story. Well, I lived alone all the time. Here I was a girl, and I was all alone.[7]

Did you rent an apartment?

No. I lived in Novosibirsk. I lived with my mama, I worked there.

The two of you lived together?

The two of us, my brother lived with us too. Mama had already come back from Ukraine. Now, my sister—one of my older sisters, Anastasiia Grig-orievna—lived in Iurga. Her first two children died; she almost went out of her mind. They got scarlet fever, and in the village there was no way to save them. And so she was left with two little girls. Then her husband died. Now, about this time, there was a typhus epidemic, and she caught it. And all of a sudden I got a telegram: "Come immediately, sister in a bad way." I was working in Novosibirsk, I had a good job there, but I left. I took a leave and went off. I arrived, and she remained alive for nine days. An old man, a feldsher, was attending her. He was such a drunk, he didn't under-stand a thing. I even flagged down a train and begged them to send a doc-tor. Well, one came, said something, gave her some medicine, and left. There was nobody else who could help, and, well, she never regained con-sciousness. The whole time, she was delirious, and then she died. I was left with those children. I was just a girl, I wasn't even twenty. Here I was, all by myself, with three children, and the cow didn't even give milk yet. There was no food, nothing. So on the third day—she died on March 1—on

---

7. As becomes clear from what follows, Ponomarenko was not alone at all. What she meant when she used the term was that she lacked a husband, a breadwinner.

March 3, I went to the village soviet and said, "We're dying of hunger, I don't have a thing to feed the children, what should I do?" The chairman [see Kniazeva] said to me, "Look, there's a kolkhoz nearby, go there." [The kolkhoz was eight kilometers away.] "Go there," he said, "and ask for something." My sister had given them . . . Well, I'm not sure whether it was a plow or a . . . something, one of their farm implements. After her husband died, she didn't sow any crops—they had such a small field, but after her husband died she couldn't do it, and she let the kolkhoz have everything. I set out. It was muddy! Rain mixed with snow was coming down, mud mixed with snow. Well, it was March third, it was still cold. I was wearing boots; I had put on boots and set out. Water poured into the tops of the boots, mud. I got to the kolkhoz, and the officials there opened their eyes wide in amazement. What was this! I said: "Look, the children are dying of hunger. I've come to you, you've got to help! The village soviet told me that the kolkhoz is duty bound . . . " "Yes, we are." They gave me a pood of flour. Look, I was just a girl. True, I was quite strong, I was sturdy, but I was a girl. They could have given me a horse and wagon, after all. I couldn't ask them, I was shy, and, what's more, I wouldn't lower myself. I just couldn't ask. So I lifted the flour up onto my shoulder and set out. I walked awhile, and there was nothing, not even a bush. Ahead there lay a bare field, all the way to Iurga, an empty vale, as they say. I kept walking through the mud, everything was soaked, I couldn't put this sack down on the ground. So I lowered it down on my back, I was able to wiggle my shoulders. I kept shifting it back and forth like that. I got as far as the first hut in the village . . . a bench. I collapsed on it with this flour, burst into tears, and then went on home. When I got to the porch, I heard singing inside. I opened the door, the kitchen was right there with its Russian stove. And on that stove with their legs dangling down were all three of my nieces, see, the little ones Nina, Lilia, and Falechka, and they were singing "Forgotten, Forsaken." I used to sing them to sleep with that song. They sang it beautifully. Oh, how I began to wail, I collapsed on the bench and wailed. They slid down: "Aunt, don't cry, don't cry." Here I was, just a girl, and they were addressing me formally, with *vy*—me, Auntie Lena, with *vy*. [Russian, like French and German, distinguishes the formal "you," or *vy*, from the informal *ty*.] Nastenka [her sister] had taught them to do this. "Don't cry, don't cry." And suddenly, they too began to wail. And I thought: What am I doing? Why am I tormenting the children? I wiped away their tears and said: "Come on, we'll get something ready to eat." But I didn't know how to cook, after all, I had a job, I always ate in cafeterias. I didn't cook anything myself. Okay, I could make soup, but I didn't really know how to cook. Well, I took a cup of flour, some salt—oh no, I forgot the salt, that's right. I stirred it all together, lit the stove, heated the frying pan. I found some old lard, it had almost turned green. Well, we made flat cakes, ate them—see—sang, had tea, everything. Life started again. After that, I never cried in front of them again, never!

[Ponomarenko remained with her sister's children, took her sister's place at a wayside station for the military command, and never returned to Novosibirsk.]

And at night, I had to receive officers arriving by train, lay out cots for them to sleep on, feed them, everything. And I would lock the kids in, it was scary. The train station wasn't far away, it wasn't far at all, and I was really scared. At night, I would run home at least twice to see how my girls were doing. I'd open the door very quietly, tiptoe in, they'd be sound asleep, I'd leave again. Well, that's why I decided to bring Mama from Novosibirsk, and then I felt much better! Mama was there, now. She was old, she wasn't in good health, but just the same she was there with them. Someone was with them.

Now, right next door, the head physician, Arkadii Ivanovich Koriaev, and the head agronomist, Vladimir Ivanovich Suasar, had their offices. Suasar was an Estonian, but he was born here [in Siberia]. Lord, how they fell in love with me, both of them. Well, okay, I wasn't bad looking. And then they saw how well I took care of things at home. I tended the cow, and, when spring came, I dug beds and planted onions and radishes and everything, and in the yard I planted potatoes—the yard was big. I did everything, everything myself, I got up at six in the morning, I even . . . And they would often come out on the porch and look into the yard. Then it turned out they made a bet. They argued about which one of them would marry me, and they both began to court me. But I didn't pay any heed to their attentions. I had absolutely no need of them, I had no time, I was busy day and night. I had to milk the cow, then I had to take care of the kids, and do the wash. I washed at night, I would get two hours of sleep, it was very hard. But they made this bet and began to court me.

How old were you?

Twenty, by that time, I was already twenty. Well, I'd come home and Mama would say: "You know, Lena, Vladimir Ivanovich came by and chatted with me; he's such a fine man. He talked with me, he played with the girls, he even got down on all fours and let them ride on his back." Yes. He was such a strong man. Arkadii Ivanovich also came, but he would come and ask for a hunk of bread and a cucumber. Incidentally, they all collected dry rations for us, whatever they received. After all, they weren't married—there were a lot of guys—and they would give everything to Mama. And I begged Mama: "Good heavens, Mama, don't take anything from them." "Lena, look, the children want to eat. Why are you making such a fuss?" And she hid the rations from me, but she kept taking them. Well, they kept coming, and this Arkadii Ivanovich made me a formal marriage proposal.

Now, when they began to court me, they came to Mama and began to try to win her over, so she in turn would win me over. And Mama would talk to me, and I would say: "I'm not going to marry anyone! I don't have the time right now to get married." But then Mama would sit there and say: "You know, Lena, you shouldn't marry Arkadii Ivanovich. Sometimes he has a drink, he'll come here with a little vodka and drink it down, but Vladimir Ivanovich never drinks. He's a fine man, really fine." I, on the other hand, preferred Arkadii Ivanovich.

Well, things went on like that for six months. They both kept courting me. Vladimir Ivanovich took to dropping by. Once, he came on his day off and said: "Look, Elena Grigorievna . . . "—by that time everybody was calling me Elena Grigorievna, well, three children, here I had a whole kindergarten, I was so serious—and he said: "I really like you, and I have serious intentions." I replied, "I don't have any serious intentions except to raise these children," and parted with him very coldly. Finally, he said that the summer was coming to an end, they had to leave, and he had to get married, bring his mama, his grandpa and grandma—his family, that is—a wife. I said, "I won't get married." "Yes, you will get married." I countered: "No, I'm being serious with you. I can't get married. How can I? You have no need of my children, or perhaps you'll actually want them, but your mama or somebody else there won't want them, and then where will I go with three children?" And just what do you think they thought up? One night I was washing clothes. I'd begun, see, in the evening, there was such a heap of clothing. Three little girls, oh, how dirty they got everything. I only had time to do it at night. I was washing, and suddenly a messenger from the village soviet came running and said, "You're wanted by the village soviet." Well, I had a cow, they must want me to pay some kind of tax, they must be collecting taxes there. So immediately, without even taking off my apron or anything, I dried off my hands a little and rushed off to the little wooden house of the village soviet. I got there and said: "Where? What's this all about?" There wasn't a soul around. On the table lay a book. The messenger said to me: "Sign here." I signed, and, see, just as soon as I signed, he said: "That's all! We've got it!" A door opened, and in came the director of the sovkhoz and various comrades. Arkadii Ivanovich wasn't there, he was absolutely opposed. Well, and everybody came into the room, and Vladimir Ivanovich immediately ran up to me, as if he was going to embrace me. I literally pushed him away, began to wail, and said, "Just what is this?" Well, and how did I figure out what was up? I figured it out as soon as he closed the book, this kid [the messenger] closed the book, and on it was written "Marriage Registry." I thought I was signing for the tax, and here it was the marriage registry. Vladimir Ivanovich immediately signed as well, and everything was done, and I was already married. Well, everyone began to talk, everyone. I ran away. I ran home wailing, fell down onto the bench wailing. Mama said: "What is this? What's the matter with you?" I couldn't say anything, there were already footsteps on the porch, the whole bunch of them had come. They'd gotten together all sorts of food, wine, each of them was carrying a big pile, and they'd come to celebrate. Here I went into the small room with the kids, shut the door, and refused to come out. They kept knocking until it was almost morning. I didn't go out, absolutely refused. By this time, Mama was crying and pleading with me. I said: "No, I'm not coming out! I'm not getting married!" Just before morning, everybody left, and he knocked, saying "Lenochka, open up, please." I said: "Get out, get out of here! Get out, so there's no trace of you here! Get out." Well, of course, he didn't leave, spent the whole night sitting on the *zavalinka* [a mound of earth around a Russian peasant hut, serving as protection from the weather]. It was already September seventh when the registration happened [the marriage]. It was cold. Now, see, the next day he came again. I immediately went to the kids and busied myself with my own things. He talked with Mama either here in the room or in the kitchen. Two nights passed that way. I was still a virgin. He left, crying. He'd gotten chilled to the bone and was crying. On the third night, he couldn't take it any longer, he'd gotten sick, had a fever. Mama came to me: "Well, don't you understand? It's a done deal. You're already married, you both signed the registry, everything was done on the up and up. Now you're a married woman, you can't torment your . . . . Just look at what's happened to him. He's not eating anything, he's sick as a dog. Well, only on the fourth night did I become a woman. Lord, how I wailed! And he! He seized me in his arms—he was such a strong fellow—and ran to Mama: "My little girl, my little girl!" And he flew out onto the street with me. I pushed him away, but he kept crying, "My little girl!" Everybody had already gathered, everybody. Evidently he had complained, and everyone was standing on the porch and watching [she laughed] this tragedy. Well, that's what happened.

So that's how I got married. We lived for six months in Iurga—no, less than six months. Well, anyway, then we went to his mama's, outside of Novosibirsk. They had their own house there, and that's where he took me. The house had three rooms, no, two rooms and a kitchen. In it lived his mama, his brother with his wife and child, another unmarried brother, his grandma and grandpa, and then us—the whole bunch had come. Here's how the two of us slept: Mama's bed—that is, my mother-in-law's bed— was on the floor, and we made up a bed and he lay on one side and I on the other, and in the middle were the kids. We didn't yet have a baby. But then a baby appeared. Lord! How hard it was!

You know, once his mama did something nasty. I didn't know how to cook. I baked pierogi and put them on the table, and his mama also baked pierogi and put them on the table. And when everybody sat down at the

Ponomarenko in 1946

table, she pushed my pierogi aside and gave him her own. And from that point on, I felt deeply offended by her. Up to then, I had put up with everything: Day and night I fetched water, I did everything, I worked in the vegetable garden in the summer, I never objected to a thing. All the neighbors were amazed: "Well, they've gotten themselves a domestic servant." That's just what they said. And then he went to . . . He again became the head agronomist for the state enterprise Soiuz Zoloto—he was an agronomist by profession—and he took business trips all the time, went to where they had their farms in the country. [Enterprises often had farms associated with them, which supplied their workers with produce.] One day, a guy came from there, he brought a whole box of tomatoes. Everybody was at work. Only Grandma and Grandpa were home—and me with the baby. Nobody else was there. Well, this guy arrived, and I ran out and bought half a liter of vodka. Well, once a man made an effort . . . , that was the thing to do— Grandpa whispered to me to do it [as a kind of tip, according to the rules of etiquette]. I ran and got the vodka, and they put out a spread, we sat down to the table, and this guy turned out to be quite a drinker. Now, Vladimir's grandma really loved the bottle. I would buy her a half-liter of vodka, and as long as it lasted, she and I were the best of friends, but as soon as it was gone, she began to get angry at me, swear, you name it. Well, this guy drank the half-liter and said: "Just what is this, it makes you wonder: Such a wife, the picture of health, pretty, and there, what a broad he's living with, sleeping with." How I restrained myself, I don't know. He'd already finished the vodka and gone off. And here I was with the buggy—the baby was asleep in it—and I bent over him, I was crying, I began to sob. And Grandpa came up to me—Grandpa was an amazing person—he patted me on the head—he always took my side—and said: "Lena, don't cry, don't cry. Why are you crying like that?" I said: "Grandpa, look, he's already a father, we already have a son!" He stood there and said: "Silly, silly girl, this isn't his first child. He had a daughter, and she died when she was four months old. He was married." Good God, he'd never said a word about that to me, everyone thought he was a bachelor, no one . . . . I didn't know. It was awful! I was crushed. "What's more," he said, "that's not all. He got divorced—no, while he was still living with his wife, he began to live with her sister, and a boy was born. He lived only two months and died." Well, I called my brother in Novosibirsk. "Grisha, come, come and get me. I simply won't live another minute with Vladimir." Now, all my brothers respected me and loved me, and they thought that whatever I said must be true. He came, came in a horse and wagon, got me, and took me back to Novosibirsk. Took me there, and I lived with him, he lived in a dormitory for pilots. Well, that's how it was. And then he [Vladimir] appeared! With suitcases in hand, and everything. He came straight to Grisha and said, "Grisha, you understand, I don't know how it turned out this way. Did I do something wrong, was I drunk?" All in all, somehow he made amends. Grisha said: "Well, this is Lena's business. If she wants to, she can live with me." Grisha respected my husband, by the way; all my relatives respected him. Well, my husband said: "Look, I'll go to the manager, ask for an apartment, and we'll move there, into an apartment." Now right there at Soiuz Zoloto there were apartments on the fourth and fifth floors.[8] And that was it. We went there and got an apartment, a separate room—true, the hallway was communal and the kitchen was communal. Well, I was used to hardship, I wasn't afraid of anything, of any difficulties. We moved there. Soon I forgot about all that.

You forgave him?

I forgave him. I'd already forgiven him for what had happened. It was difficult, but I thought "What if that guy lied?" I had never noticed that he had cheated on me before this. Yes. We lived in this apartment, I was also given work, at the library. So everything was okay, I worked in the evenings. In his department—he was the head agronomist—there was an accountant, Katka. She was really huge, you know. Well, she took to dropping by, well, that was all, they laughed, joked, and the like. But then he began to step out. He would come home in the wee hours of the morning. Once he came home drunk. In general, he didn't drink that much, but this time he came home drunk. He lay down in bed and said "Still, you're better than all the rest!" You know, it was like someone had hit me on the head. I had begun to no-

---

8. State enterprises often provided their workers living quarters.

tice that he and Katka had some kind of special relationship, he and this Ekaterina, and here suddenly there was this remark. Well, and I, see, immediately pricked up my ears, but I didn't say anything about it. Well, once in the evening I was sitting in the library, gazing out the window at the street. I looked and I looked, and suddenly I saw him coming, and with him was Katka. And he had said he was going out of town on a business trip. And there he was, with her arm on his shoulder, and they were leaving. And it was already about ten o'clock—most likely even later, I worked until about eleven. When they needed me, I even worked until midnight. I saw the two of them together, and I fainted. The cleaning lady was there, mopping up, and she immediately called the ambulance. [Ponomarenko explained that after this she moved into another room on the same floor, and then she became aware that Katka had begun to sleep in her husband's room.] I sent a telegram to my sister: "Vladimir and I have split up, can I come?" And she telegraphed back, "Come." But I still haven't told you the most important thing, why I sent this telegram. When I saw what was going on, I took the baby in the middle of the night—it was 2 AM—went out with him onto the fifth-floor balcony, and almost threw myself off. Mama cried and carried on, it was awful. She said: "Lena, what are you doing to us? What are you doing?" I didn't say anything. She said: "Well, have pity on us, have pity! Just what are you doing? You're throwing us to the whims of fate, I won't be able to bear it. The girls . . ." She kept on. The girls, too, kept sobbing. Well, that was when I sent the telegram and went to my sister's. I arrived, they were living in their own house. Well, they, too, had a large family, it was cramped. And then I had to decide what to do about my work. I went to the head of the district office of education. He said that somebody else was working in the library, that there was nowhere to send me. Well, he began to think, where could I work, what could I do. He thought a long time, yes. In that village there was an editorial office for radio broadcasting, and a revolutionary who at one time had been exiled to Siberia, Nikanor Petrovich Kirilenko, was working there. I'll never in my life forget that man. He gave me, you could say, my start in life. Yes. The head of the district office of education talked with him and said: "A woman's coming to see you. Talk things over with her, Nikanor Petrovich. Because she worked in a library, she must be an educated person." I had read a lot, books were my "university." I was well read, knowledgeable. Yes. I set out and went to see him—he was such a gray-headed, gray-headed old man. Well, I told him my whole story. He turned out to be a very fine person. He took me, began to teach me, I lived there in this radio studio. Literally lived there! He sent to Leningrad for a typewriter; the "Leningrad" was such a good typewriter. I learned to type, I worked at it nights, around the clock, literally. I wanted to learn as fast as I could, I wanted to show everyone . . . Yes. When my husband was courting me, Mama said to him: "You have a higher education, while Lena isn't educated, she only finished five grades. Doesn't it bother you?" "I'll teach her, once we get to Novosibirsk, I'll enroll her in classes, she'll go to school." Later, we had our first family disagreement about that. Well, we had lived there for a while, about six months, and I said, "Volodia, I'm going to enter the evening school for adults." He said: "For that you have to have an aptitude. You have to have an aptitude in order to study."

He came right out and said that?

Yes. And that was our first disagreement. Oh! How he hurt me, you know! Here I was in the city, and I wanted to study something awful. And at that point, I began to cry. Later, he tried to smooth things over, well, okay. But I couldn't forgive him.

Was he himself educated?

Yes, he graduated from two colleges, engineering and agriculture. Now, see, this Nikanor Petrovich right away sent me to evening school for adults, and I went. I worked in the daytime, and in the evening we studied until almost 1 AM. Well, I finished seven grades; I studied for two more years, in all. Well, we lived there and I kept on working. [She had become a journalist.] Oh, I had to travel a lot! And wolves attacked me, and bad people attacked me, all sorts of things happened. It was horrible. But all the same, I was really eager to do this work, I really loved it. I wrote for *Soviet Siberia,* I even wrote for *Pravda,* wrote for *Krasnaia Sibiriachka* [Red Siberian Woman]. Well, in general I wrote for every paper I could. You know how many paid assignments they gave me! Well, most of the journalists knew my fate [that she was raising four children on her own]. I became friends with all the journalists from All-Union Radio and from Novosibirsk, with all of them; we all corresponded. I always sent them the latest local news.

I arrived in Sukhumi [in Soviet Georgia] in 1939 and joined the radio committee immediately. They had given me very good references there in the old place, excellent ones. There, too [in Siberia], they had pushed me to join the party, it wasn't my idea, but ... What happened was that I had written an inflammatory article for *Soviet Siberia,* I had written that, well, everybody sat around in the raikom, everybody sat around in the raiispolkom, while I went to the fields, and everything was just lying there, the wheat was burning up, the flax was rotting, everything was rotting, and I wrote about all this for *Soviet Siberia.* I wrote an expose. On Sunday we received *Soviet Siberia,* and I read the article to Mama. She said, "Well, Lena, we'll have to pack our bags, we won't be able to live here any longer." I went for bread. I was walking across the square, and Evgeniia Vasilievna, first secretary of the party obkom, came walking toward me. Oh, how nervous I got! I approached her, she took my hand, shook it firmly, and said: "Well, good for you! How smart you are! We just sit around, wearing holes in our skirts and pants, while you, just a slip of a girl, went out, saw every-thing, and wrote about it all. What's more, you don't belong to the party." I said, "Well, yes, I'm still in the Komsomol." "We'll give you recommenda-tions. So, girl, get ready. We're going to take you into the party." Well, see, I didn't really aspire to this, but the fact of the matter was that earlier I had worked in the editorial office, and I found that there was more faith in communists and members of the Komsomol. I was already beyond Komso-mol age, I had almost been excluded from it on that account, yes. Well, what could I do: They brought me the recommendations, very quickly they persuaded me to join, see, arranged it all, and took me into the party. Then we went to Sukhumi. [She and her son moved to the south due to the lat-ter's ill health.] We arrived there, and I went into the editorial office as a party member, so of course . . . In the beginning, they made me an instruc-tor for mass work with activists, worker-correspondents, and rural corre-spondents.[9] Well, I worked for a little while, and then they sent me to Tbil-isi, to a school for editors I'd been assigned to. I went there, and I graduated from the school with honors. There were others there who al-ready had degrees, but I worked day and night, I sat up way into the night writing these, well, what are they called . . . [synopses]. I returned from Tbilisi [in 1940], they had already made me editor, confirmed me as editor of the Russian edition. I was doing good work, our life began to settle down.

You say that you really liked to study, Elena Grigorievna. How did it seem to you: Could you openly ask questions about society or did you feel that there were things you couldn't talk about?

No, I didn't notice that.

Didn't you see around you, well, that there were repressions, that people were disappearing, and that sort of thing? How did you react to that?

You know, here's the essence of it, how we reacted to that: I even, some-where I even have a piece I wrote about that. For example, I was working in Maslianino district [in Siberia], and there I had a friend, the amazing Akulina Potapovna, famous throughout the country. [She had performed great feats on the labor front.] This was a time when terrible acts of sabo-tage were occurring on kolkhozes. Once she came to me and said, "Elena Grigorievna, come, see what is happening on the kolkhoz." I got there, and we went to where they kept the flax seeds—these were the very best, the ones that were sent abroad for export, sold at very high prices. The kolkhoz had become very rich on account of the cultivation of these seeds.

---

9. These were unpaid volunteers who regularly wrote to Soviet newspapers, usually to ex-pose wrongdoing.

Ponomarenko in 1946

And so Akulina Potapovna took me to this granary, and there we saw something terrible: We opened the door, and there was a pile, an enormous pile of flax seeds of the highest quality, like gold—they literally sold them for gold. And from that pile, streams of smoke were going up, the seeds were on fire, and they were all destroyed, the kolkhoz lost millions. And this was the work of Makhov, who headed a work brigade. He was the son of a kulak who had been repressed and exiled to Narym.[10] And he had actually gotten into the Komsomol.

You didn't try to talk with him, with this . . . Makhov?[11]

No, I didn't talk with him. I wrote all about it, came back, and immediately broadcast it on the radio. And I passed it on to the oblast, to the oblast radio committee, and I reported the whole thing myself on the radio. [At some length, Elena Grigorievna described how as a result of her broadcasts, her life was endangered. In addition to her son's illness, she said, this forced her to move away.]

Just what happened to this Makhov?

He, too, was exiled to Narym.

You mean to say he was exiled together with his family, yes?

---

10. Ponomarenko provided no evidence that Makhov was really responsible for the fire, apart from the word of the woman she quoted. It is entirely possible that he was innocent and that the fire resulted from carelessness. On the kolkhoz, nothing belonged to anyone, so no one took care of collective property.

11. Posadskaya was really asking whether Ponomarenko tried to investigate the truth of the accusation. The publication of a story about his (alleged) sabotage would have had terrible consequences for Makhov, as Ponomarenko was well aware.

Most likely, together with his family, but perhaps not. I don't know how it turned out. But this wasn't only on account of my broadcast. He was involved in lots of other things, too. The MVD[12] was investigating him, they were investigating him, as it turned out, even before this. Anyway, it was sabotage. I witnessed sabotage with my own eyes, nobody can prove to me that it didn't happen, I saw it all with my very own eyes. What I saw is exactly what I've told you about. Yes.

Elena Grigorievna, among your acquaintances, no one was repressed, your family wasn't affected?

Well, why do you say that? I've already told you that Vania, my brother, they repressed him as a kulak, exiled him to Central Asia.

Well, did you write about this, did it ever occur to you that this was unjust, that somehow you could say something or write something about this?

Well, why not? We did write about this, we wrote, I even wrote about this, that . . .

At the time?

Yes, that some had unjustly been exiled, we wrote about it. Later they were returned, some of them were returned. Even there, they proved their worth. What's more, another of my brothers was repressed, I forgot—Grisha.[13] He too was repressed, he was exiled somewhere in the north. He was repressed because he cursed Stalin. His friends put him up to it. And he honestly, so to say, "served his time." There he also worked as a gardener, proved his worth, and he served ten years, this brother did, and then he returned and worked, and that was the end of it.

Elena Grigorievna, I'm simply asking you these questions because I myself am trying to understand . . .

You know, I'll tell you just what my brother said: Things there were very bad. But what has been written by that, what's his name, our famous . . .

Solzhenitsyn?

Yes, Solzhenitsyn, he wrote a lot that wasn't true, a great deal. He exaggerated everything so terribly that my brother was simply outraged and said: "No, it wasn't all like that, the way he says it was." It wasn't all like that. Everybody worked, received . . . Well, there were times when they went hungry. Once or twice, for example, I sent him lard, sent him dried crusts. It was

---

12. Most likely she meant the NKVD, the political police.

13. The fact that she remembered her other brother's exile rather late in the interview, and only after Posadskaya had questioned her persistently, was no doubt a measure of how deeply she repressed the memory. Having two brothers who suffered under Stalin's regime is likely to have been a significant obstacle to Ponomarenko's advancement, if not an actual danger to her.

hard, but the way things are portrayed in Solzhenitsyn—I was horrified, too, when I read it. My brother was there for ten years, he saw all this and he knew. In general, he disagreed with what Solzhenitsyn wrote. He said that not everything that Solzhenitsyn wrote was the truth. Yes. Well, of course, my brother was outraged at some things. Well, those who suffered there were largely the alcoholics, the real bandits, those were the ones who were dealt with very strictly, very strictly![14] Sometimes even other inmates really beat them up because they were such beasts. While those who worked honestly . . . My brother worked honestly. He was respected for that.

Elena Grigorievna, how did you figure out who was a kulak and who was not a kulak?

Well, we figured it out immediately, of course. They lived better than others, they lived very well. They had cows and sheep and pigs and horses and good, strong log houses. Well, and they ate better. For example, when we were teenagers, we would go to parties in the village. We lived in town all the time but went there to get a decent meal, we would go to the village to eat. And so we would go to a party, and they were all, they were all there in stylish silk dresses or wool skirts, kulak girls—you could pick them out immediately.[15]

What kind of shoes did they have?

They had leather shoes, leather, while we had *lapti* [crude sandals]. Our mama also sewed for us all, she sewed us a kind of cloth slippers. We really had a hard time, a very hard time. Mama was illiterate, my older brothers set up separate households, they already had large families with nine, eight, seven children apiece, and all of them were illiterate. I was the only one to receive any sort of higher [sic] education, out of all seventeen of us.

Elena Grigorievna, doesn't it seem to you that if you had been a man you would have been promoted more quickly?

I should have been born a man, because since childhood I've worn a cap. Never in my life did I wear a scarf on my head, I always did the work of a man, just look at these hands, see? They are so tough, so strong. I've been like this since childhood. Well, I was born a woman, so what can be done?

---

14. Virtually all accounts of camp life give a completely different picture, in which decent and hard-working people suffered most and criminals occupied privileged positions.

15. The sort of elegant dress that Ponomarenko described did not necessarily indicate that a young woman came from a well-to-do family. A marriageable young woman's clothing was an important factor in her ability to attract a good mate, and by the early twentieth century, manufactured goods superseded homemade ones in the hierarchy of village tastes. When they came of age, marriageable young women often sought work in order to earn the money they needed to buy the silk and wool dresses required for successful courtship. Ponomarenko's assertion reflects her "outsider" status in the village.

Ponomarenko in 1957

Of course, I envied men, envied them. I should have become . . . And some even compared me to a man: With your energies, your matter-of-factness, you're more like a man. Yes. I've never had a braid in my entire life, I've always worn my hair cut, like a boy's. But you know it was my work and the conditions of my life that made me like that. So I went about all the time in a cap, in pants, in a jacket.

Elena Grigorievna, what's your opinion, why didn't you advance further in the party?

They did try to advance me, but I refused. When I arrived here in Tomsk from Kolpashevo, they offered to make me head of . . . , I've forgotten what department, the main department in the gorispolkom. They offered it to me, but I said, "No, not on your life!" Later, they offered to transfer me to *Red Banner,* but I didn't feel capable of it. I thought that I wouldn't fit in, why should I go there, when I didn't have a higher education. I didn't have a higher education, while they were all college graduates.

Red Banner—you mean the newspaper in Tomsk?

Yes, the Tomsk oblast newspaper, *Red Banner.*

So, you yourself didn't agree to it?

That's right. Only now do I understand. I look around and see how some people work [that is, poorly], and I think that at the time I undervalued my-

Ponomarenko in 1956

self, simply didn't give myself credit. I did everybody's work, literally every-body's. The head of our radio committee ... I would come back from out in the district [she would be out in the field, doing very difficult work], where death looked me straight in the eye—all the time, not just once. I would turn in an essay or something, and he would take it and "mix" it with verses of Maiakovskii or Esenin or with something else, and then un-der his own ... [publish it under his own name] and give himself a double fee. But I overlooked it all because I was afraid I would lose my job. I had a family, I was responsible for a large family. I was responsible for their lives, for their schooling, for everything, and consequently I was afraid to lose my job. Simultaneously I had ... , some people took advantage of me, took ad-vantage. They gave me ten party assignments simultaneously, and I fulfilled them all.

What sort of assignments did you have?

[Elena Grigorievna described at some length the "voluntary" work that she, like most citizens and all party members, was expected to perform. Then Posadskaya asked her a personal question.]

Elena Grigorievna, you said you blamed yourself for your mother's death?

I was to blame. When I worked in the radio committee, they sent me to gather material at a kolkhoz, in the middle of winter. I told them that there was no firewood at home, no coal. My son had gone off somewhere on a school trip. I told them that Mama had gotten sick and that I couldn't go. And you know what the head of the radio committee said to me? He said: "Elena Grigorievna, you're a communist! And for a communist, the politi-

cal takes precedence over the personal." And so I went. And when I returned home, it was already too late. [Here she began to cry.]

How old was your mama?

Eighty-six, but she was still strong. [Very quietly:] She would still have lived
a long time.

Well, and that man who sent you wasn't concerned about her?

We had a horrible apartment. They had made me a room out of the hallway. They hacked a window in the wall and made a room, and it was cold.
They installed an iron stove in it, but there was no wood, nothing. So that's
what happened. They took care of burying her [while Elena Grigorievna
was still traveling], [very quietly] they did everything and nothing.

▧ Under a Sword of Damocles

ELENA TROFIMOVNA DOLGIKH

Before Posadskaya met Elena Dolgikh, she already knew that Dolgikh was a native Siberian, had worked most of her life as a teacher, had been a member of the Communist party, and had raised three children. In addition, despite her lack of higher education, Dolgikh had become an amateur ethnographer and published a unique book of riddles of the peoples of the Soviet Union, which she herself had collected.

When Posadskaya visited Dolgikh's home, she was met at the door by an attractive young woman, who said "Granny is waiting for you." This was Dolgikh's granddaughter, herself the mother of two young children. When Posadskaya saw Dolgikh, the first thought that came to her was, How fortunate that she doesn't live alone! "Granny" was tall but looked frail. She moved quietly about the room, and spoke just as quietly. Sometimes her voice on the tape was so weak that we could barely hear it. In her soft voice, the first thing she asked Posadskaya was "Are you hungry?" It was obvious that whatever Posadskaya's reply, they would feed her. She was served tasty boiled potatoes and homemade pickles, then strawberry jam and tea. Like most families in Tomsk, Dolgikh's survived on food they grew in the summer. Posadskaya's own mother spends her summers in the countryside growing and preserving food. Perhaps for that reason, she felt completely at home with these two women, as if she had known them a long time. She was quite moved at seeing how tenderly and attentively the granddaughter treated her granny.

The interview took place in Dolgikh's room—one of three in the small but comfortable, standard apartment located in a multistory building in one of the newer regions of Tomsk. As they sat on the sofa talking, Dolgikh sorted through Siberian "miracle berries," small berries believed to cure virtually every illness, separating the fruit from the stems with her blue, almost transparent fingers: "At least I can still do something useful," she said. She was clearly nervous. Posadskaya could barely hear her voice. "I must start somewhere. . . . I can't collect my thoughts." It occurred to

Dolgikh with her granddaughter in 1994

Posadskaya that Dolgikh was so weak that she would be unable to talk for very long. But Posadskaya was wrong.

Elena Dolgikh was another woman with a "bad background," which she never fully escaped; fear was an important theme of her story. Yet her parents were perfectly ordinary people. She was the child of two teachers, of peasant background on her father's side, of clerical background on her mother's. Elena's mother had obtained her secondary education at a church-run diocesan school, as had many women who taught in a rural elementary school in the early years of this century. After Elena's father died in 1917, her mother did not return to the schoolroom; instead, she took her five children and went to live with her husband's family, a common practice for peasant widows. Her father-in-law was a stern and hard-working peasant, and Elena and her family lived decently. Then, when she was ten, Elena was sent away. This, too, was not unusual: Her aunt, her mother's sister, had married and had a baby, and Elena went to care for it as a nursemaid. Later, the aunt and her husband, both teachers, adopted Elena and provided her with educational opportunities that her brothers and sisters, raised as peasants, were unable to share. With the help of her adoptive parents, Elena finished school and enrolled in a school for teachers. She was the only child in her family to obtain any education.

In her youth, Elena embraced the new society that the Soviet leadership was struggling to build. At the teachers' college she became an activist, editing the school's wall newspaper, an instrument of propaganda that set out the party line as it applied to the school. Despite this evidence of loyalty, the "sword of Damocles," her background, caught up with her: Someone denounced her by sending a letter to the school, declaring that she came from a family of kulaks. Only at that moment did Dolgikh learn that her grandfather had been labeled a kulak and deprived of his property and that her mother and younger brothers and sisters had suffered along with him. The campaign against the kulaks destroyed the family. Her grandfather died of a heart attack; a brother, Serezha, was sent to perform involuntary (slave) labor in the Kuzbas, one of those inhospitable sites with abundant resources—coal and iron, in this case—where involuntary laborers ensured the success of the industrialization drive.

Despite the fact that her adoptive parents were teachers, Elena Dolgikh suffered as well. She managed to finish her teacher's training only with enormous difficulty. Even though she signed a statement renouncing her family, she was driven from the school where she had begun her studies, completing them instead in another school, in the town where her adoptive parents lived. Assigned to teach in a peasant village, she lost that position, too, after someone informed on her once again, possibly because she had given shelter to her mother and two of her siblings, all of whom were clearly refugees from their village. An article appeared in a local newspaper, asking why a person of kulak background was permitted to instruct the village children. After she was fired, she was able to find another position only because the persecution of teachers from "incorrect" backgrounds was not an official policy and so was applied inconsistently. Dolgikh's background always left her feeling vulnerable at work.

Her background affected her life in other ways, too. Pavel, the man she loved and a party activist, was ordered by his superiors in the Communist party to sever his connection with her on account of her kulak origins. When he refused to obey, someone instructed the postman to withhold the letters he wrote to her. She married another man, who subsequently abandoned her with three children. "He fell in love with someone else," she acknowledged without rancor. Although he paid some alimony, the family lived in need because Dolgikh earned so little as a teacher: "We were really hungry. Lord, how hungry we were!"

Dolgikh was the only one of our narrators who referred to the inferior economic status of Soviet women. As in the West, the labor force in the Soviet Union was stratified by sex. Women were clustered in poorly paid sectors of the economy, even when they occupied professional positions. As a teacher, she earned "only a little more than a cleaning woman," Dolgikh said. She criticized the Soviet government for exploiting teachers and physicians, professions in which women predominated: "All my life I've felt the government was to blame for the pitiful existence teachers and doctors led." Industrial workers, who became a relatively privileged group in the Soviet era, earned

Dolgikh in 1994 with her book collection, featuring the series "Great People in History" (all men)

considerably more. That explains an apparent paradox: During World War II, a period when rationing was instituted and most people suffered terribly, Dolgikh's family, at last, had enough to eat, because she went to work at a factory producing goods for the front and began to receive workers' rations of 800 grams of bread (about one and three-quarters pounds) and grain for the children, twice the ration she had received as a teacher.

It was this terrible poverty that led Dolgikh to join the Communist party. Party membership offered the chance for professional advancement and somewhat higher salary, and thus, some relief from the family's destitution. She was frank about her party membership: "I was a party member simply because I had to be." In Soviet society, positions of responsibility and power had to be filled by party members, to ensure loyalty to the system and its values. If Dolgikh wanted to work as inspector of primary schools in her region, as she was invited to do, she had to become a party member. So she joined the party, despite her fears that her "kulak origins" might resurface, particularly during periods of cleansing, or "purges," when "class enemies" were identified and removed from their party positions, and sometimes suffered in more serious ways as well.

Only after she retired did Dolgikh become fully free from fear. She said old age was the best period of her life: "When I retired on pension, I became free, absolutely free," she declared. "It is really terrible to live under the weight of fear," as she had to do for much of her life. In her old age, she wrote her memoirs. Their tone is very different from the tone of her oral narrative, which is unaffected and devoid of bombast. By contrast, the written memoirs reflect "Soviet-speak," the language that saturated the media. The stylistic differences suggest that private, conversational language may have remained relatively untainted by "Soviet-speak." We have included a small section of the memoirs at the end of this chapter.

◈   ◈   ◈

Elena Trofimovna Dolgikh: I think that I've had a rich and interesting life. A creative life. I've read a lot. That's been my lifelong passion. I was born into a family of teachers. Both my papa and mama were teachers. There were five of us: two boys and three girls. Papa died very young. He was only thirty. He died in Tomsk. And we were left orphans. When he died, I was seven years old.

Anastasia Posadskaya-Vanderbeck: So he died in . . . ?

In 1917.

And you were born . . . ?

I was born in 1910, in the Altai region. I was the oldest, long-legged and skinny, playful, but very obedient. We loved Papa very much, Mama too. We lived in the sacristan's house, because Papa was the village sacristan. He was held in high esteem in the village; the village was Solonezhnoe in the Altai. Papa died in '17, and about a year later we moved. We went to Grandfather's, to the village of Mikhailovka, 150 kilometers from Solonezhnoe. The revolution had not yet reached Siberia. The civil war took place before our very eyes.

You remember the civil war?

I can tell you about individual episodes. So, I've finished talking about Solonezhnoe. Now for life in Mikhailovka. Grandma was very kind, ran the house perfectly, was quite intelligent in her own way. While Grandpa was strict, very stingy, frugal. He didn't drink. He was well known in the village for his beekeeping. In the summer, he lived in the apiary. Well, okay, I was—how old was I—well, eight, already into my ninth year. I helped Grandpa with the farm work, I helped him harrow. And the boys and I rode bareback. We would jump on the horses, and off we'd go to the watering hole. Of course, we tried to gallop as fast as we could, and for this Grandpa would give us a licking. The horses needed to rest, and here we were having races. Well, when Serezha got a little bigger—he was the brother who was a year younger than me—Grandpa thrust me aside. Even though Serezha wasn't all that big, still he was a man, and Grandpa already thought of him as the master and loved him very much. Yes, that's what happened. So I was put into Grandma's hands. But I never learned to cook. Even now, I don't like to cook.

But didn't you say, Elena Trofimovna, that your parents were teachers? Your mama wasn't teaching at the time?

Mama began to teach just before she got married. She and Papa met as teachers in Solonezhnoe.

What did she teach?

The lower grades, in a rural [elementary school]. That's the way education there . . . By the way, Mama graduated from a diocesan school. You know what that is. For children of priests, girls. There was a diocesan school in Tomsk. It gave girls the right to teach in a rural school. It specifically prepared daughters of priests to teach in rural schools. My mama was one of three sisters, and all three graduated from this diocesan school.

Her father was a priest?

Yes, that's right. Our father was a sacristan, the man who assisted the priest during church services. He graduated from the seminary in Tomsk.

Do you remember what the civil war was like?

I'll tell you about it. There weren't any able-bodied men in the family [the grandfather was already old], but we had an interesting house. There was a kitchen, two-thirds of which was occupied by a Russian stove. This was the way things were in the village, because people—we did it, too—slept on the stove. There was also the *polati* [a large ledge, extending from the stove to the opposite wall, used for sleeping] in the kitchen, and there Grandmother held sway over the earthenware pot. The family was big, the cast-iron stew pot was big. We ate splendidly, everything was homegrown. Then there was the *gornitsa* [the room where guests were received]. It was such a clean room. And there was a room between the gornitsa and the kitchen, but it was more like a passageway. Incidentally, it was very cold; it wasn't heated. You could sleep there only in the summer. We slept on the stove, the shelf, or the floor. All the blankets were woven in a certain way. I've forgotten what it's called. We had real bedcovers[1]—they were part of Mama's dowry—stuffed with camel hair; the silk was a bright red. Of course, we didn't know anything about sheets, because everything was homespun; we made everything ourselves. Grandma was amazing. She could weave all sorts of designs. Mama would sew me a dress, and Grandma would add all

---

1. She meant that it was purchased rather than homemade. She spoke of such possessions with pride. Because virtually every item in everyday use was homemade, those few things that were purchased with money, like camel-hair bedcovers, acquired great social value.

sorts of designs on the border of the skirt and on the sleeves. We children were well-dressed, proud of our clothes, happy with them.

Now, our settlement was between two cossack[2] villages. Many centuries ago, the border was here. It was defended by the cossacks; their villages formed a chain. One cossack village was here and at the other end of the settlement there were also cossacks. Detachments of cossacks would dash by, run past, crying out. At the time, we didn't understand what was happening. It turned out that they, the Reds, were already somewhere in the vicinity.

The cossacks were Whites?

Whites, only Whites.

And how were the cossacks regarded?

I, for instance, I can only express my own feelings. Right now the cossacks are experiencing a revival. I'm very nervous about this because I remember that when the cossacks appeared, that is, the Whites ... Across the street from us was the church, the school, and the priest's home, and we could hear them flogging men on this very square.

The cossacks were doing the flogging?

And we, in the beginning, we referred to all the Whites as cossacks. As soon as the cossacks appeared, everyone would hide. We would simply hide. Since in our house the *gornitsa* was on one side and the middle room and the kitchen where the family lived were on the other, both the Reds and the Whites would put up their command at our place. I've never been able to forget what I'm about to tell you now. In that middle room there was a wide peasant bed, and from it a horsecloth, a kind of woven blanket—we called it a horsecloth—hung down to the floor. And I would hide under this horse blanket. And once, I, when the Reds stayed at our house ... The Reds ... We weren't afraid of the Reds ...

You weren't afraid of them?

That's right. Until this ... Because the Reds would appear, and they didn't carry out floggings. We never had to stop up our ears because of the screaming. Many died from these floggings or were crippled by them. That's why we were afraid. Well, I heard the tramping of feet, I crawled out from under this horsecloth. There was a chink in the wall, and I looked out. A woman was going past, and her braids were coming un-

---

2. Originally, cossacks were men who had fled to the periphery of Russia to escape taxation and serfdom. By the late eighteenth century, they had become servants of the Russian empire, defending its borderlands from attack. Cossacks lived in these borderlands and farmed when they were not fighting.

done, like this. It wasn't because she was a girl. She was a married woman; I knew her. Married women coiled their braids around their head and covered their heads with kerchiefs, and here her braids were coming undone.[3] But these were the Reds. Well, they took her there, someone cried out, but it wasn't her. It was men crying out; perhaps they were being interrogated. Then they took her away. When they took her away, I was afraid to crawl out for a long time. Even though these were the Reds, I was afraid. And then a few days later, I saw this . . . It must have been October, and we kids were playing tag. I, as I already said, was so long-legged, I could run like the wind. Of course, I got to the base first, before anyone else. To win, you had to touch the door, touch the door and shout "Keep away!" And I pushed the door so hard that it came open, it opened into the granary, where the grain was stored. The communal grain was kept there. And there were corpses lying there, and there was that woman, half hunched over. It must have been the way they had thrown her in, and her braids, well, her hair was frozen stiff. Either they had poured water on her, or it was blood, or something else. I shrank back. Since then, I have always been afraid of dead people.

You mean the Reds tortured her to death?

Yes, yes, oh yes.

But why? What for?

I didn't ask myself that question. Most likely, she . . . In the village some sided with the Reds and some with the Whites, some were for the Reds, some for the Whites. Perhaps she was a traitor or a scout.

Did she live in the village?

Yes, yes. She lived somewhere at the other end of the village. I would meet her, see her on the street.

And what age was she?

She was young.

Most likely she had children?

Well, there wasn't a soul around to ask. When either the Reds or the Whites were staying in our house, our family tried not to stick their noses out of the kitchen, and we kids were especially warned not to . . . I went back to the granary secretly, several times.

---

3. By custom, Russian peasant women braided their hair and covered their heads with a kerchief. Single women wore their hair in a single braid, which could hang down outside the kerchief; during the wedding ritual, the hair was combed out and braided into two braids, which would then be bound around the woman's head—completely concealed by her kerchief.

Elena Trofimovna, about the granary where all the corpses were piled up: Were they both those the Reds had killed and those the Whites had killed?

You know, I'm not even sure. I was afraid to ask.

Elena Trofimovna, did your family lean toward the Reds or the Whites?

I remember only one thing, that we were afraid of the cossacks. That's what I remember. Somehow the Reds didn't bother anyone. Most important, they didn't carry out floggings, and this was the first act of cruelty that . . . well, that I actually witnessed.

Well, that was the second period in my life. Now, for the third. Mama had two sisters. As I already told you, they also graduated from the diocesan school, and they, too, were teachers. And Mama's younger sister came to Solonezhnoe where we lived, and there she got married. She also married a teacher. He, too, was the son of a peasant, from the peasant intelligentsia. He, too, had graduated from the seminary and had got a job teaching in a three-grade village school. Well, they got married, and when they had a son—that was in 1920, I remember it well—they persuaded Mama to let me go live with them in Biisk, and there I started school. Biisk was an old, wealthy merchant city. A highway ran through it that went all the way to the Mongolian border. Now, to me Biisk seemed like a city right out of a fairy tale. It was there that I saw electricity for the very first time. Then my aunt took us to the theater, and this, too, seemed like something out of a fairy tale! Walking home from the theater in the dark with the moon shining, the electric lights high on the poles, snowflakes falling—that picture has remained with me all my life. And it was in Biisk that I completed nine grades of school. And then this aunt and uncle adopted me.

Why did they adopt you?

Because my brothers and sisters remained illiterate, they could literally neither read nor write.

Why was that? Because of their social origin?

No, it was simply because they had no opportunity to go to school.

Why? Was it because they remained in Mikhailovka to do the farm work. Is that it?

Yes. Because there was no way for them. That's all.

And thanks to the fact that you went to live with your aunt and her husband, you were able after all to receive an education?

Yes, only because of them. So I called her "Mama," "Auntie-Mama."

And how did your own mama react to this, to the fact that they adopted you?

Why, she was happy that at least one of her children was settled and could receive an education.

Is it because you were so poor? Is that it?

No, we were "rich." We must have been rich. After all, we were "kulaks." My grandpa was labeled a kulak and dispossessed.

Well, you'll have to talk about that in more detail. That's very important. Were you singled out and given to your aunt and uncle because you were the most gifted and liked to read more than anything else?

It was because I was the oldest and because I fit the needs of my aunt's family. But they really loved me.

Did you help with the baby?

Yes, I helped with the baby.

[Dolgikh's adopted family took her to Tashkent, and she spent her final school year in Tashkent, then returned to Biisk by herself to continue her studies.]

So you returned to Biisk alone?

Yes, I returned there alone. They didn't come, but sent along with me letters addressed to the teachers' college in Biisk, and I was accepted there. [The year] 1926 came and went, and then 1927. While I was a student at the college, I was editor of the wall newspaper. At that time, there were such wall newspapers. They were put out by the yard. Yes, I served for three years straight as editor. Then suddenly, a letter came to the college, to the Komsomol organization, demanding to know just why a kulak girl was studying there.

Did this letter come from the village, from . . . ?

From Mikhailovka. "What's more, she's receiving a scholarship." It was the first year that I was getting the scholarship, so I had bought myself a cheap fur coat and something to wear on my feet. I had very little money, so I also had to economize on food. Well, they called a special meeting of the Komsomol to discuss the matter. The director, who was a communist, came to my defense, saying that I was one of the best, one of the most progressive students, and so on. I really hadn't been trying to promote myself, to gain recognition; it was simply that I liked being entrusted with responsibility. They didn't expel me from the college, nothing like that. [She was relieved of her duties as editor but permitted to remain in school.] But there were some who wished me ill. Suddenly, a man came from the district

Komsomol committee and chewed out the Komsomol members for being apolitical and so on and so forth. "Look," he said, "here's a document that proves that this one is from a family of dispossessed kulaks." Only then did I realize . . .

So you didn't know at the time that your family had been labeled kulaks and dispossessed?

That's right, if there hadn't been this . . . , this special . . . But the director ignored it all and helped me compose a letter to the village soviet, saying that I was giving up my rights to the parcel of land that would be mine, and so on.

And you were also forced to renounce your family at that point, right?

Yes, that . . . , I was no longer a member of this family, that I hadn't lived with them for many years. But in fact, I went there every summer to help them with the farm work.[4] And—I only found out about this later—it turned out there was all this gossip going around about me.

So the director helped you, the director of the school?

He felt sorry . . .

And then there was some kind of gossip going around?

Yes, that too. Such dirty thoughts never even occurred to me. It was as if I was living in the clouds. But from that side . . . [Rumors circulated that the director of the school helped her because they were lovers.] True, I was in love, I loved a fellow classmate, if you can call it love. It was strictly platonic. And suddenly our names were being linked [that is, her name and the director's]. He was the noblest, the kindest, the most cultured man. Well, that period came to an end.

And as a result of the fact that he helped you, you weren't victimized, you weren't expelled from the school?

I was expelled.

Just the same, they expelled you?

They expelled me. So immediately I wrote a letter to my family, that is to my aunt and uncle. At the time, they were living in Krasnoiarsk. They telegraphed back: "Await your arrival." So I went there. What's more, the director had already written to the director of the teachers' college in Krasnoiarsk [to help her gain entry to the school and complete her studies]. When I arrived there, I received a warm welcome. Everything went as it

---

4. While it was evidently painful for her to say so directly, it is clear that she was forced to renounce her "kulak" family in order to continue her studies. Such painful choices were not at all uncommon.

should. The school year was already coming to an end, the students were already beginning to receive work assignments, and I was assigned to be a teacher of language and literature in a school for young workers in the district center of Shalo in the Krasnoiarsk territory. All at once, I was summoned to the NKVD. I went there, and they said to me, Tell us about your family. So I told them: . . . Serezha,[5] well he's so many years old, and so on . . . They thanked me and let me go. And in Shalo there was a man who had fallen in love with me. His name was Pavel, and he was a party worker from Irkutsk. He was doing on-the-job training in Shalo. He said to me, "Here's why they called you in: Out of the blue, an armed band appeared in the woods near Shalo, and it was headed by Petr Grebenkin." Well, my maiden name was Grebenkina. "But when they found out that your brother is still a boy, that's why they let you go in peace."

That was when collectivization began, right?

In our area collectivization began in '27.[6] That's when people were labeled kulaks and dispossessed in Mikhailovka. And here's what happened: First of all, they drove the kulaks from their homes. Well, they gave away our horse and the rest—cups, spoons, ladles—all of it they started to sell to people who had not been labeled kulaks. And there were people who were willing to buy these cups, spoons, and ladles. And all of our family was deported to the mountains, to some valley there. So they began to dig shelters. They weren't allowed to take anything with them—only the clothes on their backs. Everything was sold, all that "kulak" wealth. Of course, they confiscated the apiary. This happened toward winter, and that very first winter they let the bees freeze to death. When Granddaddy learned of this, he was struck dead, his heart ruptured, as they said later, because he loved the apiary, he loved the bees. There were melon fields, and everything was ruined. He and Kostia[7] went to some village—I don't remember the name of it—where Grandma's sister lived in the mountains. They went on foot and asked for alms. Some gave, some didn't.

And during this period of collectivization you were in Shalo?

Yes. And in Shalo, too, there were anti-kulak campaigns. I can remember that when I would hear some old woman howling at sunrise, I knew they were evicting someone. Tears, all the time tears. At the time, I had no idea

---

5. She was referring to her younger brother, who had remained behind in the village, with her birth mother.

6. In 1928, before the collectivization drive was officially launched, "emergency measures" were adopted to deal with the shortfall in grain, with Siberia the main target. Blaming the shortfall on "kulak hoarding," local officials imprisoned alleged kulaks and confiscated their property.

7. Kostia was her second brother, the son of her birth mother, and younger than she.

what had happened to my family. Now, just what did happen to my brother Serezha? He was fifteen, and at some point they rounded up all the young fellows from those shelters, all those young fellows, and drove them on foot 150 kilometers, drove them into Tomsk. Then from there they began to assign them to different sites. Serezha and his comrades were sent to Kemerovo in the Kuznetsk Basin. That's what happened. And it was there, in this very Kuzbas, that he worked on the construction of the coal and metallurgical complex for several years.[8] In the winter they had to dig ditches, foundation pits, and they were only released when the project was completed, when the first blast furnace was ready to be started up. He and the others had to wear sacks used to store salt; at best, they slept in barracks. They had no bedding, nothing. They kept dying off, and their bodies were hauled away somewhere. It's a good thing Serezha was strong in spirit and hardworking. He withstood it all. They were young, and no matter how tired they were, they liked going to the club to watch movies. They would be admitted but told ... By this time they had real pants, but before that they had to cut out holes for their head, their arms. Even hearing about it is awful. I only found out about all this recently, about five years ago, when I began to write my memoirs. I asked Serezha to answer questions, to write about this and that. His response was written in ungrammatical Russian, but it revealed what was most important. And then, when the dancing began—what was it they called them [the involuntary laborers], something very offensive—they would make an official announcement from the stage: "Those ... must get out." "Well," he would say, "We are getting out." And he had already taken a liking to one girl there.

And at the time of the anti-kulak campaign, what happened to your mama and sister? Were they also deported somewhere?

Yes, into the mountains to dig shelters, that's where Mama and the children were taken. Grandma passed away before this happened. And I'm so glad that she didn't live to see the day people were labeled kulaks and dispossessed.

Elena Trofimovna, many found a way out, escaped one way or another, by being adopted, changing their last name, getting married. ...

Well, I, for example, I've already told you about Pavlik, about the man I fell in love with, who said to me that if the NKVD had arrested me, he would have gone, too. I believed that this was true love. But to continue about myself. Just imagine: I lost my job in Shalo as well! What happened was this:

---

8. Involuntary laborers, alleged kulaks foremost among them, contributed significantly to many of the construction projects completed during the Soviet industrialization drive. The more unattractive and inhospitable the setting, the higher the proportion of involuntary (slave) laborers among the working population.

Mama, Galia, and Kostia came to stay with me for a while. Kostia was the youngest; he and Galia were still in school. And the history teacher said: "I find it hard to believe that these people are your relatives; they're so ignorant, they're illiterate." Well, okay, I'm not one to cry. When sorrow strikes, I turn to stone, but I don't cry. That's my misfortune; I don't know how to cry. And it's rare that I get angry, but here it was all I could do to restrain myself, to keep from telling her why they were that way. And then, not very long afterward, something suddenly appeared about me in the Krasnoiarsk newspaper. I didn't read it, I didn't even know about it, but my cousin was studying in medical school right there in Krasnoiarsk. She wrote me about it and said, "I became frightened that something might also happen to me."

Well, what did it say in the newspaper?

That in Shalo there was a teacher of Russian language, so and so, and that the upbringing, the education of Soviet youth had been entrusted to her, and so on and so forth in the same vein.[9] [This, of course, was about Dolgikh.]

They implied that you didn't come from a proletarian background, was that it?

That's right, that's right, that I was from a kulak family and so forth. And so this history teacher said spitefully, gloating at her own perspicacity: "I sensed immediately that something wasn't right here, and it turns out that enemies of the people were creeping about." That's the sort of thing she said. So of course, they fired me. But the director didn't make a big fuss about it. Although I hardly knew him, he tried to do it in such a way that I received all the money due me. He gave me a horse and wagon to use to get to the train station. First, I sent off Mama and the children to my "new" parents. And after that, Mama went . . . I think she went to her younger sister's. My new parents gave her money for the ticket. Again we were all scattered. We only got to spend a little time in Shalo together. My landlord and his family were such good people. They gave me three liters of milk, bread, and something else for the journey. All in all, they gave me such a warm send-off. And Pavlik had already proposed to me, and everyone referred to him as my fiance. He was a man of principle. He gave me the address of his Irkutsk apartment, of his friends, and told me to go there.

Do you remember what year that was?

That was in 1930.

---

9. Someone had informed on Dolgikh by writing to the newspaper about her kulak background. Her connection with a kulak family was problematic because as a teacher, she was responsible for the ideological purity of her students. Thus, Dolgikh was not secure even in the small, remote village, and she lost her position as a teacher.

So you were twenty years old?

Yes. Life, you see, had already worn me out. The first gray hairs had appeared on my head; I began early to turn gray. I didn't get to marry Pavlik; they separated us. The secretary of the raikom in Shalo turned out to be from Irkutsk. He had already returned there, and he happened to meet us when we were out walking. I had applied for work at the regional office of the board of education. Well, he found out that we were planning to get married. And later he said to Pavlik, "It's either the party or her." He said it that bluntly. Well, Pavlik said to me: "Nothing will come between us; we'll bear it, we'll find the strength." I was assigned to work in a village near the Taivet railroad station. Later, after several years, I learned . . . It turned out the postman had been intercepting Pavlik's letters to me, and only one letter reached me: "Why don't you write? What's happened?"

And he stayed in Irkutsk?

He stayed in Irkutsk. It turned out they were keeping track of us. And I know that when I went to the post office and asked for letters, I could feel somehow—what should I call it . . . the malice wasn't obvious—that someone was writing to me but I wasn't receiving the letters. They even seemed to take pride in the fact that they were doing this.

They were fulfilling their duty.

Yes, yes, yes. It could be this same Razhevskii had an influence, gave orders, the former Shalo secretary. I realized that only later. And a team of geologists was doing a survey in the village to which I was assigned. The team included a student from the Polytechnic Institute in Tomsk—he still had two years to go before he graduated from the Institute. And what happened was that his boss sort of played the role of matchmaker to get me to marry him. We got married. He was so kind, such a fine man, but later, all the same, he left me with our children, with three children. It's true that his coworkers really took him to task, but he fell in love with someone else. And once he fell in love . . . I never really loved him. I'm telling you the truth about it, and I've told my children, too. My children only learned about all this recently.

When did you have your first baby?

In 1932. And here's what the situation was: My husband and I had just arrived in Tomsk. And then his parents arrived. They had also been labeled kulaks and dispossessed, and they had been living with him while he was working on the geological survey. So when I had my first baby, they helped out. And then my mama came. Mama spent most of her life living with me. She would go visit one sister and then the other, but most of the time she lived with me.

At that time you were working, right?

Of course! And you know what the life of a teacher was like then—meetings, conferences, homework to correct, and the wages were really low, hardly more than a cleaning woman got. At least a cleaning woman could work several jobs at once, but just try to to teach at more than one school at a time! And my husband, he had to study for two more years before he finished the institute. Then he began to receive a decent wage, and most important, when a family is united, when people care about one another . . . We couldn't afford to dress well or have nice shoes or boots. You'd want one thing, and you'd have to wear something else. In general, I've lived all my life in need, all my life. Only during the war, when I began working at a defense plant, did my family finally have enough to eat. Then I wasn't restricted to the teacher's ration of 400 grams of bread per adult and 200 per child even when the child was growing rapidly. At the plant I received 800 grams of bread; I had a worker's ration card. And they gave me groats for the children and some other stuff. Before that, we went hungry all the time. What good are a teacher's wages? What's more, I've already said this, it's as if all my life I lived under the sword of Damocles. Why did I have such a feeling? I wasn't in a hurry to get into the party. So how did I find myself there? Well, the head of the district office of education and many of the teachers started urging me to join. God forbid! I was afraid. I had all sorts of excuses—the children, and so on. Well, okay, but why was it necessary? Because I had become an inspector; suddenly they had appointed me inspector of our district, of our urban . . .

They had made you a school inspector?

Yes, a school inspector for the lower grades. And you know how it was: In order to hold such a position, you absolutely had to be a communist.

That means as things stood you couldn't keep such a position?

No, I couldn't. And I wanted so much to keep the work. Look, I'd already been appointed an inspector! The head of the district office of education knew me in this job and valued me, and so I had to become a party member. At the meeting where they accepted me as a candidate for party membership, I was so happy, it was as if I had wings. They said so many complimentary things about me at that meeting!

Was this before the war?

No, after the war. In the raikom I was approved as a candidate for party membership, and that was it. I was also approved as an inspector, and the work began. And then suddenly, the party secretary of the raikom in our district was removed. Why? Because he had some uncle living abroad! Here my blood turned cold: He had some uncle he didn't even know, what's

Dolgikh in the mid-1950s

more, living somewhere abroad, and because of that they removed a wonderful man! That was the first thing, and then suddenly the chairman of the Kirov raiispolkom was removed. In his case, it had something to do with his parents. Well, at this point, I, to be frank, I got scared. I was really frightened: If they had already removed such big shots, what would happen to me, just a small fry? Yes, it was terrifying, and because of my children, too. It could leave a stain on their record.

Were you afraid that somebody might inform on you or that suddenly, somehow, it would come out that . . . ?

Yes, yes, yes.

Was that fear always with you?

Yes. It became clear that the business of political "cleansing"[10] hadn't stopped. People were not trusted, their contributions were not valued. Somewhere, some uncle, whom you'd never seen even once in your life . . . Now do you understand my fear? And it was with me all the time: at any moment, at any moment . . . And therefore I was happy when I was able to

---

10. The party periodically "cleansed," or purged its ranks of individuals found unsuitable for membership. In most cases, the consequence was simply loss of party membership, but in the second half of the 1930s and again on the eve of Stalin's death, party members with questionable backgrounds or connections might also be labeled "enemies of the people," arrested, and exiled—perhaps even shot. The "cleansings" to which she was referring here were apparently routine ones in which no one was repressed. Nevertheless, expulsion from the party likely would have damaged not only Dolgikh's prospects but also those of her children.

retire [in 1965]. Only then did I breathe easy. That's how it was. It was a pleasure, a joy to retire. And I took plenty of awards with me. For example, there's the medal for Valiant Labor, and I got it. They really honored me when I retired.

Elena Trofimovna, I'd like to ask you this: Did you join the party out of conviction or simply because you had to do so in order to hold onto your job?

They kept urging me to join. I would have held out, but then I wouldn't have been allowed to remain an inspector, because you couldn't hold that job if you weren't a party member.

So otherwise you wouldn't have joined?

No, no, I wouldn't have. I didn't have strong convictions like those people who march around now with red flags,[11] who continue to call themselves communists. I was, well, simply indifferent; it was all the same to me. I was totally absorbed in my work as a teacher. I gave it my all. I was a party member simply because I had to be. [The conversation then turned to family matters, childbirth, childrearing, and questions of women's health.]

You know, some women I've talked to say that the ban on abortion between 1936 and 1956 made things terribly difficult. Did that affect your life?

I experienced this firsthand when I lived with my husband. We spent ten years together. I had to have four abortions. One abortion was so terrible, it could have finished me off, because that woman [the one who did the abortion] shoved something into me. Suddenly half of my body went numb.

Did this happen during the operation?

Yes, yes. She herself got frightened. Then I rested up, and everything was okay.

But this woman wasn't a professional, right?

That's right. She performed abortions on herself and also on others. She said, "I'll do one for you too."

Did you pay for it? Or did you give her some kind of gift?

No, she wouldn't take anything from me because she got frightened.

And this happened during the period when abortions were banned, right?

Yes.

---

11. She was referring to the massive antireform demonstrations that occurred in 1994, during which demonstrators demanded a return to communism.

And people simply knew about these women [those who performed abortions] somehow? The information was passed on by word of mouth?

How could it have been otherwise? Someone told me about her. After that abortion I went to see a doctor. She said, "I could refuse to scrape your uterus, because it's possible infection has set in." [The doctor feared fatal complications.] So. Anyway, it was my last abortion. It's so stupid. So when I got divorced, I felt relieved in that sense, because men, they don't understand this, and they don't even want to understand. I had three children, that's enough. I paid my debt to nature. And that's it.

Did you have a maternity leave when your first baby was born?

At the time, I wasn't working, because I was with my husband on the geological survey. I began to work in '33. Alik was born in '32. From '33 on, I worked in a school that was right next door. Mama brought up the children. She fed them, while I went to meetings and prepared lessons and sat up late into the night correcting homework. That's how it was.

Elena Trofimovna, do you remember what there was to eat? Your children were small, it was the '30s.

As the wife of a student, I would go to the student cafeteria with a small pot, and they would fill it for me. We had very little to eat because in the '30s, collectivization was going on, everything had been ruined, everything was very expensive. And here we had three small mouths to feed. Because of this we never celebrated any birthdays; we had too many worries. On the whole, we had very little to eat.

What was the most difficult period in your life?

The period of collectivization. When everything in the whole country was wrecked. Now you can buy something for your money, although I almost faint when I see prices in the thousands.[12] I simply can't get used to it. When I first got my pension [in 1965], it was 36 rubles, 84 kopecks. And then suddenly my pension began to grow and grow, and now it's more than 80,000 rubles. This sounds like an enormous sum of money. Young people laugh at me.

And how many years of service did you have?

I had thirty-five. All my life I've felt the government was to blame for the pitiful existence teachers and doctors led.

---

12. In 1994, when this interview took place, inflation had increased prices by over 1,000 percent within a brief period of time. As a result, Dolgikh could purchase almost nothing with her pension of 88,000 rubles.

You said that you and your husband got a divorce. Was it difficult to obtain the divorce?

No, it was very simple.[13] He applied for it, I went, and they gave me what I needed, a document so I could receive alimony. That was all. I didn't contest it. Most likely because I was, and am, still in love with that man I told you about [Pavel]. When I went to the editorial office of the local newspaper in Irkutsk [to ask after him], they no longer remembered him there. This was in the '70s. And then they sent for the stoker; he had worked there for a long time. He said: "Well, how should I put it? They swept all of them away." It was all clear, even without any explanations. And it's possible he got in trouble on account of me, if only because . . .

Which is to say, he disappeared like many others?

Yes. Well, that phrase "swept away" alone conveys a lot. So I have no respect for communists nowadays. They've forgotten a great deal, a great deal.

Still, I would like to read to you from my memoirs.[14] You're already used to the way I speak. "My generation was hardly out of swaddling clothes when it experienced World War I." That's true, I was still in swaddling clothes. [She reads on.] "My generation experienced the October revolution and the civil war. In youth it got to know firsthand NEP, collectivization, industrialization. In adulthood, the Great Patriotic War, with all the burdens of wartime. The thaw under Khrushchev, stagnation under Brezhnev, and the apogee of Stalinist repression. In old age, Gorbachev's perestroika, with all its consequences. The thorny path of true democracy, advancing toward private property, toward a market economy, advancing to do battle with the military-industrial complex . . . "

---

13. Dolgikh was divorced in the late 1930s. Divorce had already become more difficult than in the 1920s and early 1930s, when a spouse could obtain a divorce regardless of whether the other partner agreed to it. The process grew even more complex after 1944. See Dubova's interview, beginning on p. 17.

14. These memoirs consist of several very large volumes, each running to hundreds of pages.

Four Years as a Frontline Physician

VERA IVANOVNA MALAKHOVA

Posadskaya first heard about Vera Ivanovna Malakhova from our other narrator from Tomsk, Elena Ponomarenko. Ponomarenko mentioned her as someone who had served as a physician at the front for the duration of World War II. Unfortunately, it turned out that Malakhova was born in 1919, two years after the revolution, so she was too young to fit the parameters of our book. But then other people Posadskaya knew in Tomsk also recommended Malakhova highly. So Posadskaya decided to visit Malakhova, after all. Malakhova was living in a small, one-room apartment on the top floor of a five-story building without an elevator. Her apartment had a tiny entryway and a minuscule kitchen. In a small room overflowing with objects, a beautiful piano made of dark brown wood stood out. On the piano were old photographs of her parents, a photograph of her son, and a photograph of Vera Malakhova herself in uniform. The piano itself seemed a relic from its owner's past.

Vera Malakhova was very beautiful. She had extraordinarily radiant, dark gray eyes. How young she is, Posadskaya thought when she first saw her. Malakhova met Posadskaya in the courtyard of her building, and if she had not walked with a cane and breathed heavily as they climbed the stairs, Posadskaya would have found it difficult to believe that Malakhova was a woman who had lived through the war, had been wounded twice, and had recently undergone a serious operation. "I only seem young, but in fact I'm really sick," she said. "At the front, every year was considered the equivalent of three. So you have to add another eight years to my age!" And that is how it happened that Vera Malakhova became one of our narrators, despite the fact that she was born after the October 1917 revolution.

We feel compelled to include in this introduction things about which Malakhova herself would never speak but that Posadskaya saw with her own eyes. Malakhova was poor, practically destitute. She was not getting enough

Malakhova in 1994

to eat and lived on bread and "tea" made of nothing but hot water. When Posadskaya asked why she did not call someone to fix the broken toilet (war veterans are supposed to receive such services for free), Posadskaya learned that Malakhova simply feared drawing attention to herself—she had not paid her rent in six months. Posadskaya, who was raised to revere war veterans and to believe that society has a responsibility for the old and infirm, and who took a great liking to Malakhova, felt guilty about the way Malakhova had to live—alone, in ill health, and practically forgotten. But Malakhova herself did not complain. Instead, she was eager to talk about the past, particularly about her experiences at the front during World War II.

Malakhova was born in 1919 to a workers' family in the Siberian city of Tomsk. Just as their "bad" origins closed off opportunities for several of our narrators, Malakhova's "good" one, as the child of a working-class household, opened doors for her, and it remains a source of pride. She became the beneficiary of Soviet efforts to advance people of her class and gender in the decades following the Bolshevik revolution. She received a small stipend while attending a rabfak, which helped her family to survive after her father became ill with tuberculosis. In 1936, after completing her studies at the rabfak, Malakhova entered medical school. To maintain the health and productivity of the population, the first Five-Year Plan had called for an enormous increase in the number of physicians. Admissions to medical schools dramatically expanded, while the qualifications for applicants were lowered and the training period was reduced to four years, much of it on the job. Malakhova became one of tens of thousands of young people, mostly female, who studied medicine under the new system. She graduated in four years, in June 1941, on the eve of the Nazi invasion. Three months later, she left Tomsk for the front.

Like all physicians, Malakhova and the other new graduates were required to serve in the war effort, and most of them were more than eager to do so. The most terrible enemy had invaded their homeland, and to defend the land was an almost sacred responsibility: "What was there to talk about? We had graduated, they had given us our diplomas. Naturally, it was our duty to go to the front." Malakhova served four years there. Her responsibility as a physician was to run a mobile field hospital that served soldiers in the infantry. This meant that she and her aides marched alongside the troops and did their work wherever and whenever there was combat. They would put up their tent, lay out their instruments, and deal with the carnage. Like all field physicians, they were constantly in physical danger, and their mortality rate was high: Only the troops themselves suffered greater casualties than women physicians who served with rifle battalions, as did Malakhova. She participated in the battle of Stalingrad, an epic struggle that raged from September 1942 until early February 1943. Fought street by street and house by house, the Battle of Stalingrad took over a million lives. It ended in a Soviet victory that halted the German advance eastward and turned the tide of the war. During her military service, Malakhova was wounded twice. She was decorated many times for courage under fire and received the Red Star, the second most prestigious medal for military service that the Soviet government awarded.

In Malakhova's memory, the four years she served in World War II overshadowed virtually everything else. She began to speak of her wartime experiences very early in her interview. Every topic, whatever it was, led almost inexorably to the war. Finally, about an hour into the interview, Posadskaya stopped trying to stem the tide, and let Malakhova's memories of the war take over the narrative. The interview comes to about four hours of tape and more than 120 double-spaced pages of transcription. When Malakhova talked about the war, her narrative followed no particular temporal sequence: She began in the very thick of things and only much later, because she was asked, did she tell Posadskaya where she was when the war broke out and why it was that she went to the front. The narrative consists of a series of vivid stories, each one relating to some aspect of her wartime experience. Many of these stories are vivid and dramatic: For example, Malakhova described what it was like to come under bombardment, to escape from German encirclement, and to suffer almost unbearable physical deprivation.

But Malakhova's account also served to expose some of the failings of the Soviet war effort. Until a few years earlier, the government-controlled press and media had treated the Soviet record in World War II as flawless. The war was used to legitimate the Soviet system. In this official version of history, the heroic Soviet people, whether inspired by the party or in Stalin's name (depending on the politics of the time), fought fascism in defense of the socialist motherland, and thereby proved that their system was superior. War stories became part of this authorized history, and only authorized versions could be told, while the terrible human costs of victory—some of them easily avoidable, some of them directly due to government policy— were kept from the record. But in recent years, the situation has changed and the sanitized cult of World War II has come under attack, so much so that young people sometimes deface war memorials. Malakhova was deeply offended by popular denigration of the war experience, complaining that "Now they spit on us, on all the veterans"; but at the same time, she was enabled by the new freedom to speak of the hitherto unspeakable. During her interview, Malakhova debunked the myth that soldiers invariably entered battle with Stalin's name on their lips and that Komsomol and Communist party members were invariably honorable and brave. She discussed shameful episodes that had been hidden until recently—for example, the practice of abandoning wounded during retreats from German attack, or the treatment of Soviet citizens who fell into German hands as spies and traitors. She referred with contempt to the conduct of Special Services officers, assigned to the front to oversee the former political prisoners who had volunteered to fight. Malakhova was at her most vehement when she spoke about abuses of power. She portrayed some high-ranking party and military men as sexual predators and referred to sexual harassment about half a dozen times. The first time, she observed that "This is something about which no one has ever said anything," and she was right. Fifty years after the events she described, her sense of outrage was still strong.

Voluntary unions and romantic love were a different matter to her. Malakhova was a romantic, and love also figured as a prominent theme in her narrative. "Love—there has to be love," Malakhova declared. "This is the finest, the loftiest feeling a person can experience! . . . You can move mountains, when you really love a person." She herself loved in this way, and this love was one of her most treasured memories. Her lover was another physician, a senior officer who at one point saved her life by helping her to escape from German encirclement. Later, as she lay in the hospital recovering from shell-shock at the battle of Stalingrad, he risked his life to swim across the Volga with a birthday present, a package of raisins—a scarce delicacy that he had saved for her. Not long after, he was mortally wounded and died in her arms, uttering as his last words, "How will you live without me?" Although she subsequently married, bore a son, separated from her husband, and took a lover, the memory of her wartime lover was still fresh.

Romances such as hers were often misinterpreted by her contemporaries. In the prudish Soviet social culture, the existence of love relationships at the front damaged the reputations of the women who served there. Despite women's extraordinary achievements, their collections of medals and awards for bravery and heroic action under fire, after the war ended, popular opinion in the Soviet Union insisted on stereotyping women who served at the front as sexually "loose." Posadskaya, born in the late 1950s, remembers that women who had been at the front continued to have an unsavory reputation when she was young. Such attitudes were so widespread that some women veterans became fearful of wearing their uniforms and medals in public. "I didn't like to show myself [with medals]," Malakhova remembered, "because many people thought I was some kind of frontline 'W' [whore]." Relating her experiences of World War II enabled Malakhova to set the record straight and to demonstrate at length that she "fought honorably," to use her words, as did most other women who served with her.

Malakhova and Posadskaya met five times. Malakhova talked about her life in great detail and from time to time exclaimed: "No one ever asked me about that!" Because of her war record, she is interviewed often, especially on Victory Day, but generally the newspapers print only a few phrases about where she fought and what medals she received. She was immediately taken by the idea of our project—to preserve stories of women's lives in the socialist period, told in their own words. Her own story provides a unique, woman's perspective on one of the defining events of the Soviet era.

❖   ❖   ❖

Vera Ivanovna Malakhova: I was born in Tomsk, in that faraway Siberian city—faraway, that is, if you live in Moscow. I was born there in 1919.

I went to school, and when I was in school, they had a strange system of instruction based on a so-called five-day week. We went to school for four days, people also worked for four days, and on the fifth day everybody rested. Then, suddenly, there was a six-day week: We went to school for five days, workers worked for five days, and on the sixth day everybody rested.[1] At that time, Sunday simply lost its meaning. What's Sunday— nothing but a church holiday! But then they went back to the normal calendar. Well, I was a good student, although I didn't get straight As.

---

1. In an effort to increase productivity during the industrialization drive of the early 1930s, the government first changed the week to five days, with one day off, and then to six days. This meant that Sunday was no longer free for religious observance.

Anastasia Posadskaya-Vanderbeck: Vera Ivanovna, what sort of people were your mama and papa?

My mama and papa were ordinary people. Papa was a metal worker. At that time he was very well known because he was the best in Tomsk at making different machine parts, even the most difficult and complicated ones. Mama was only a housewife, but Mama was . . . I, too, am proud of my genealogy, because Mama was the daughter of a famous master wood-worker.

How many children did your parents have?

I was their only child because Mama had me, understand, at such a difficult time. It was 1919; there was typhus here and other infectious diseases too—I don't recall which ones. Kolchak was here and with him the Kolchakovshchina.[2] And the revolution had come to Tomsk, and then there were armed bands roaming about. In short, nothing was heated anywhere, it was bitterly cold, and Mama got terribly sick after she gave birth to me. All my life—it started when I was small—I begged Mama for a brother or a sister. Well, what could Mama say? How could she explain why I was an only child? When I got older, I understood that Mama had had peritonitis, and after that she couldn't have any more children. Grandma used to tell us that when she came for Mama at the hospital, Mama was unconscious, and so they took her home in that condition. Grandma said that there were lice crawling everywhere on the hospital walls.

Vera Ivanovna, what sort of house did you live in?

We lived in a basement, but since I got sick a lot and Papa also got sick, we had to move out of that basement. Papa wore himself out scraping together enough money to buy a house. This was in the 1930s. We lived on Lermontov Street. All the houses there were small, but they had large plots of land. People even kept cows. Then in 1937 and 1938, they began to take everybody away. The Black Maria[3] would come in the night; only at night did they take people away! And you could hear everything, because at that time there were no buses. You would hear them stop at somebody's house, and then in the morning you would learn that that man had been put in prison. Then they would come again, and another homeowner would be put in prison. Papa was sure it would be his turn next, so he said to Mama: "Lena, pack me some dried bread, two changes of underwear, and everything else I'll need." And we waited, and every night we expected the

---

2. This is a reference to the civil war between the Bolsheviks (Reds) and counterrevolutionary armies (Whites).

3. "Black Maria" is what people called the cars in which members of the NKVD, the secret police, arrived to arrest "enemies of the people." They were the size of ordinary vans, usually painted a military-style khaki color.

worst. I remember that so well; the terror I felt as a child. We lived in constant fear that they would suddenly take Papa away. And my school friends were all from families of the intelligentsia, and all their fathers had been put in prison. Their fathers were all shot. This, of course, weighed upon us terribly.

Yes. But you said that your papa was a skilled worker. Yet despite his class origins,[4] you were afraid they would take him away?

God, yes! Absolutely certain they would take him away, even though ... True, they didn't take away any of his friends, any of those who were skilled workers, that is. There was one who was a tailor and sewed clothes when we lived in the basement. None of them were touched.[5] But it was another story when we moved to Lermontov Street and acquired our own house. On that street everybody owned his own house, and since they literally put every single person in prison who had a small house, it meant they put everybody who lived on the street in prison. I don't know what god was watching over Papa, but somehow he was never arrested. Perhaps he was passed over because he was already on workers' disability. We weren't touched, but they put all the other homeowners around us in prison. Papa escaped that fate.

After your papa began to ail, did your mama go to work?

No, she didn't go to work. Papa received a tiny pension. I had to quit school, just after I started the ninth grade. Rabfaks were being organized in Tomsk, and they even gave scholarships to those with very limited means. Mama said: "Vera, enroll there; otherwise, how will we manage?" By that time, Papa was very sick. And so I enrolled in the rabfak, and after studying there for a year, I completed secondary school, although God alone knows how we managed to learn a thing.[6] Be that as it may, in 1936, I passed all the entrance exams[7] for medical school.

Was your house equipped with any conveniences?

We had electricity, but no running water, no indoor plumbing. All my life I had to haul water, carrying two buckets on a yoke.

---

4. Workers were the most privileged class under Soviet rule, so presumably someone of worker origin such as her father would be less vulnerable to arrest.

5. Malakhova contradicted herself here. She insisted that workers were arrested regardless of their origin, but then she went on to say that none of the workers she knew were arrested.

6. She was referring here to the low level of instruction in the rabfak.

7. In 1932, after a period of preferential admission for working-class and poor peasant applicants, entry examinations for universities and other institutions of higher education were reintroduced.

Did you have a well?

There was a well, but we could use it only for watering the vegetables we grew. We lived on swampland, and because of this, the water was dirty.

Where did you get your drinking water?

There was a pump for drinking water two blocks from our house. At that time, there were special booths with pumps, and winter, summer, and fall Mama and I both had to haul water, carrying buckets on a yoke. It was especially hard when we had to haul water for washing clothes. And then for some reason, the water dried up in our well, so that, in addition, we had to haul water for the vegetables.

How did you celebrate the holidays?

You know, when I was in school, we were not even permitted to talk about Christmas! God forbid! They even banned Christmas trees, and they made us kids keep watch to see who was putting up trees. Understand? That's how it was.[8]

They told you to do that at school?

That's right. The teachers made us do that. And they were especially vigilant during Shrovetide. We had to be on the lookout to see who was preparing *bliny* [thin, flat pancakes like blintzes, typically folded around a filling, which were traditionally eaten during this Russian Orthodox holiday], and so on. Can you believe that?! But that's the way it was. And when they permitted people to put up Christmas trees again—this was around 1936—we were beside ourselves with joy. My grandfather, together with my uncle, made me a wonderful present. I had a favorite teddy bear. To this day I have him—although he's become all moth-eaten, I keep him in the cupboard. Well, for this teddy bear they made a wooden bed, a sideboard, a wardrobe with tiny hangers, and a table for six, with six tiny chairs. Grandfather did it all with his very own hands, together with my uncle, and they gave it to me for Christmas.

They forbade this, they forbade that, but it made no difference: We celebrated all the holidays, including Easter. I've celebrated Easter all my life. How could you ban the celebration of Easter! Why, it's the most beautiful holiday; the Easter table is so lovely!

Vera Ivanovna, were your papa and mama religious?

You know, Papa even took me to church. Papa sang beautifully. At that time, everyone knew the prayers and sang. I also adored singing, and I had a grandmother who was very religious. It was fine with Mama, too. We were

---

8. These trees, associated with Christian ritual, were prohibited in 1928. They were reintroduced in 1936 but renamed "New Year's" trees.

religious. See, I have icons. This is a consecrated icon. Grandma blessed me with it. I remember her words: "Dear child, while you are alive, never get rid of this icon." But at that time, one couldn't display icons anywhere, so it always lay hidden away in a chest of drawers. That's how it was.

Were you baptized?

I was baptized. I was born in 1919. Of course I was baptized![9] When my son was born, Mama said: "If you don't baptize him, I won't have anything to do with him." So I said to her: "Mama, have him baptized as many times as you want, only don't neglect him."

Vera Ivanovna, did your papa like to cook or . . . ?

No. The one thing Papa liked to do was to have all of us prepare Siberian *pelmeni* [small, usually meat-filled dumplings] together as a family. In general, it wasn't customary to prepare ham for Easter, but we prepared it just the same. But the thing we did that I liked best was to bake *kulich*es [traditional Easter breads, baked in tall, round tins], using kulich molds. Papa made special kulich molds for all of Mama's friends, and we had a big one for Papa, a medium-sized one for Mama, and a smaller one for me. And also for guests and for children. When you talk about kulich, again everyone had different tastes. Papa liked his kulich to be chocolate, Mama liked kulich with raisins and vanilla, and I adored kulich with walnuts. There were all these molds and different kinds of dough, and of course the smell was always such that you knew the holiday was coming. It was spectacular! We also prepared *paskha* [a traditional Easter dish, a kind of sweet cheese spread usually served with kulich]. Grandpa made Mama special wooden molds for paskha. On each little mold he carved the words, "Christ is risen," and decorated the mold with a tiny lamb or a baby chick or a flower. Mama always boiled the *paskha*. And again each of us had the same special flavor: For Papa there was chocolate paskha, for me paskha with walnuts, and Mama made herself paskha with raisins and vanilla. So there were three paskhas. And of course, we dyed Easter eggs, put them in pretty vases, and did all the other things. Well, what else was there? On the holiday, guests would come to call, and, if someone liked to drink, they would have a glass, wish their hosts a happy holiday, and depart. Often people dropped by just to offer their congratulations. It was special; it really felt like a holiday. For Pentecost I always got a new dress. Mama knew that was my favorite holiday.

Did your mama sew it herself?

She had a treadle sewing machine, and she sewed beautifully on it, but then Mama had taken courses. Mama had taken courses. When the subject

---

9. Two years after the revolution, when she was born, it was still relatively easy and safe to baptize a child.

came up . . . She always said that Soviet power was good in that . . . Actually, it wasn't good in a lot of ways; all our friends were thrown in prison, a lot of people we knew, and in fact, many people at that time suffered terrible fates. But in the 1930s Mama always said that thanks to Soviet power, you could study anywhere you wanted, that anyone who wanted to could study for free—as long as you weren't lazy. Whereas when she was a child, it was quite different: "I cried and got down on my knees. 'Papa, send me to apprentice, to learn to sew.' But he answered: 'You must go out and earn wages.'" Mama finished the parish school when she was twelve, and they sent her to be a nanny in a doctor's family. So at twelve she was already a wage earner. That's how it was.

Vera Ivanovna, please tell me, what were relations like between your father and your mother?

On the whole, I think things in our family were good. I would even say that our family was rather old-fashioned; we kept all the Russian holidays, all the Russian traditions. Papa, however, tended to be somewhat jealous, and I was witness to several scenes when he let go and uttered very harsh words. I was still small at the time, but I remember, and I remember that it made me cry a lot. How could Papa get angry at Mama and be so rude to her, I wondered. Deep down inside, I already sensed that one shouldn't speak to a woman like that. Yes. But evidently I kept my feelings to myself. Then by the time I had begun to study in the upper grades, Papa was seriously ill, and all our energies were directed at making him well again. To be frank, we lived from hand to mouth. These were the prewar years, and everything was rationed. But, as I've already mentioned, our vegetable garden saved us. And I entered the rabfak, and they gave me a very small scholarship. But all the food, everything went to Papa. He had an advanced case of tuberculosis, and they instructed us to feed him well—to give him fat and everything—and somehow we managed to obtain expensive medicines for him. But none of this helped. It made no difference because his tuberculosis was so advanced. And right before the war started, in May, we lost him, and we buried him.

Your mama didn't remarry?

No, she never remarried. They were already living together in a so-called "free union" before the revolution. Even then, churches . . . And then there were upheavals, and they didn't have a church wedding, nor did they have a civil ceremony. It was only when they enrolled me in school that they went to register their marriage. For some reason, they needed my birth certificate.

Were you brought up to think that you and your future husband should register your marriage, no matter what?

In this regard, Papa was extremely strict. In general, I was brought up very strictly, very strictly. For example, I played the piano well, and I always accompanied all the singers and all the dancers at school. They would have parties at school in the evening, and I had to be home at ten o'clock sharp. God forbid that I should be late. Once, a party at school went on until eleven, and the entire class had to accompany me home so they could explain to Papa that the school director had kept me at the party.

Vera Ivanovna, how did they prepare girls to be women?

My mama even put off preparing me for the changes that happen to girls. What happened was this: I went off to visit my godmother in the country. That was mama's younger sister. She went off to harvest potatoes so they could store them for the winter, and I was left alone. Then I went to cut a supply of firewood for the winter, and I had to do it with this young man. We had to saw down trees. He would saw a big tree trunk, it would fall, and then we would take it and put it on the cart. Once, I didn't get out of the way in time, and a tree trunk fell on my stomach. The blow was very, very hard: It was impossible to breathe, it was so painful. Well, we started back on that same cart, sitting on those felled tree trunks, and he held me up by the waist. I kept moving away; I was just fourteen years old, after all. I would back away and think: What am I doing, sitting that close to a young man. Well, we made it back safely, but in the evening my body began to undergo a physiological change. It was normal, but it happened prematurely because the tree trunk hit me so hard. Mama had never explained anything to me. And what do you suppose I concluded? When I noticed that I had some strange sort of discharge, I thought: Good God, I sat right next to him, and he embraced me. Undoubtedly I've gotten pregnant! How can I go home now? For three nights I cried and didn't know how to deal with the physiological, so to say, workings of my body.

So you started to menstruate?

Yes, I had started to menstruate. And I was in a terrible state. I didn't understand anything. That shows the way we were brought up.

This wasn't your first period?

Yes, it was my first, my very first! And Mama didn't warn me beforehand about anything! I, you see ... When my godmother returned, she said: "Well, now we'll make some buckwheat pancakes. I've managed to get some flour." But I replied: "No, no, no. I'm going home." And that very evening I left. I was in tears. She didn't understand a thing: "It looks like all these household chores have worn you out." I arrived home with a tear-stained face. Mama began to suspect something, and she said to me: "Let's go into the bedroom. Vera, you know girls undergo changes in their bodies as they mature. Don't be afraid. I've sewn you some special napkins just for that purpose." That was it. Then I sighed with relief and burst into tears. [She laughs.] So you see how unprepared I was.

Was it usual for girls to get married at an early age?

Well, there was one case in high school, where a girl we knew graduated and got married. This was such an extraordinary event for us all! It was incredible! We were shocked. We had been brought up to think—and this was reinforced by life itself, because 1937 and 1938 had taken their toll—that until you got on your feet, received your diploma, and were able to earn something, you shouldn't get married, because heads of families were all sitting in prison; there were no grown men around. It was a different matter for young fellows, but for a girl—until you had your diploma, a profession, and regular wages coming in, there was no use even thinking about getting married. It was completely out of the question! No wedding bells until you graduated from university. And by the time we did that, the war had started. That's how it was.

Did your mama want you to get a university education?

Of course, of course. You know how highly people regard doctors! In general, ordinary families like my family—after all, my papa was a worker—really looked up to teachers and doctors. And then I had the chance to become a doctor! Papa especially wanted this! When I said that all the girls had decided to major in chemistry and enrolled in the chemistry department—almost all, a lot of them, at least half had gone to the chemistry department—he said: "No chemists in our family; absolutely not! Only a doctor for us." Papa's word was law. Mama was for it, too.

If a family had such limited means, then why didn't the parents say, Better you go to work, then you'll immediately bring home earnings?

You know, perhaps that was true in many cases, but all my girlfriends—almost all of them had lost their fathers—my girlfriends all came from highly cultured, highly educated families. And I must tell you that they all had a hard time getting into the university, they had to overcome a lot of obstacles. They were not admitted to the Komsomol, while people kept trying to convince me to join it because my parents were [from the working class]. I don't know what to say. . . . With me it was just the opposite: I was invited to join the Komsomol. At one time I wanted to join, but then Mama said: "Papa is so sick! If you join, you'll have to go to meetings all the time, and who will help me?" I said: "You're right, Mama. I'm an A student; I don't have to join." And so I didn't join. And during the war, when I went to the front, I was neither a komsomolka nor a member of the party, but I don't think I fought any worse than many party members. Take for example the slogan: "Forward, for party, for Stalin!" Although I was only under attack twice during all the time I served at the front, I never heard anyone shout: "For the motherland, for Stalin, for communism, forward!" No! Perhaps someone did shout or say it, but I didn't hear it. I'm being honest with you, telling you what I myself experienced. And did I really fight any worse than communists and members of the Komsomol? I don't think so. In our regiment there were some Komsomol members who behaved dishonorably. They tried to escape to the rear, several of them did. They tried somehow to get assigned to support services in the rear, outside the line of fire—even officers did it. But this was just a few. So I wouldn't say that rank-and-file communists ... You know, some commissars behaved very dishonorably.[10] We had a commissar who was absolutely *disgusting*! Nobody ever talks about this, but I'll tell you. Once he summoned me without warning in the middle of the night and said: "Sit down, we need to talk." I replied: "Aye, aye, comrade major." I didn't sit down. He spread out his greatcoat—it was chilly—and said: "Sit down on the coat." I replied: "I will stand." "No, no, no, you sit down." Well, I didn't have the right to disobey. At that time I was still in the lower ranks, and he was already a major. I sat down on the edge of the coat. He began to move toward me. He moved closer and closer; and suddenly—bang! He put his hand under my skirt. I jumped away and said: "Ah, so that's the kind of conversation you had in mind!" You know, it made me so indignant. I remember, I began to shake. Under ordinary circumstances I would simply have slapped his face. But that was impossible in this situation; I couldn't slap the face of a man who outranked me. He didn't lose his composure. "I just wanted to test you," he said. I replied: "You know what, you can test your own wife and check up on her. But you have no reason to do that to me!" Later, he really got back at me! That sort of thing happened to me twice. Then I also had it happen with the commander of a regiment. I also cut him off, so to speak. But I was forewarned that this commander always sent for women who were newcomers to the regiment. Now, I wanted very much to stay in our division but in an artillery regiment rather than an infantry regiment, because sometimes you got a ride on a vehicle rather than having to walk. Yes. I often got to ride on vehicles carrying shells. So a medical orderly came to our regiment, and the commander sent for her in the middle of the night. And she said: "Vera Ivanovna, I'm not like you; I will simply curse him out." She had such a foul mouth! I said: "Lida, don't." She was young. She smoked and rolled her own cigarettes. He summoned her. Later she came back, terribly agitated and white as a sheet, and she said: "I cursed him out. He had the nerve to propose we live together." Yes, there were commanders like that. Party members, too. Therefore, I took it all with a grain of salt. I think that I fulfilled my duty as a soldier honestly, my duty as a medical soldier, so to speak. Even the commanding officer of the division[11] used to commend me because my oper-

---

10. Commissars were party workers who served in the Soviet army and were responsible for ideological work among officers and soldiers.

11. This means he was head of the division and held a rank superior to that of the man who sexually harassed her.

ating table at the RFS was in better order than in all the other regiments. It
was neater than all the others.

What does RFS stand for?

Regimental first-aid station. When we were withdrawn to get cleaned up,
so to speak, to rest up a little, we were referred to as a medical company.
But when we were with the regiment and the regiment was in combat, we
would set up the RFS or first-aid station. It could be set up quickly, and we
had everything there: stretchers and all kinds of bandages. I even made the
operating tables semi-sterile, so to speak; that is, I protected the sterilized
instruments with a white sheet, because often everything would collapse.
The ceiling would cave in, dirt would be everywhere, and it would fall on
these ... And there I had everything I needed: sterile syringes with needles
ready at hand. And this was called the RFS, the regimental first-aid station.
We had a small field tent that we used. You'd arrive: There would be no village left, everything was burned to the ground. So you would put up this
tent; medical orderlies would get things ready quickly. We did all our work
in tents. In the beginning, we would hang a large white flag with a red cross
on the tent. But then the Germans took to bombing us, using those crosses
as markers, and immediately an order went out: no red crosses, no hanging
out flags with red on them. So we began to make small wooden boards
with a wooden arrow on them, pointing the way to the medical station of
so and so, and to mark them with a small red cross. From the air you
couldn't make out at all where the RFS was, but the soldiers knew. Once
they spotted the arrow and the small red cross, they knew the RFS was
somewhere nearby.

In the beginning, the commander of our regiment, the forty-seventh, was
Mitilev; then after him there were others. The commanding officer of the
division was Baichuk. A very well-known man. He died in Ukraine, when
he was serving as our divisional commander. And he didn't die of war
wounds, either. He died because ... There was very heavy fighting going
on, and three times a village passed from one side to the other. And he ...
They had given us raw recruits, high-school students—by the way, they
were from somewhere near Moscow—and they were completely untrained.
They didn't even know how to hold a rifle, whereas I—I, for example, already knew how to fire a carbine, a TT pistol, and had learned to ride a
horse. And in their very first battle they all perished, every single one. Absolutely none of them survived! It was a massacre. Baichuk took it very
hard. He set out, and on the road his heart ruptured, and he died. He
couldn't bear it. Actually, he had a massive heart attack, although then they
simply said the heart ruptured. And they buried him.

Vera Ivanovna, let's back up a little. What were you doing when the war began?

I don't know—perhaps at that time I didn't understand politics very well—I didn't know that the war was about to begin. We didn't know anything! And suddenly, at four o'clock, they announced on the radio that Kiev had been bombed, and other cities as well, and that we were at war. Well, we all—you know, it was such a sunny day—without even talking to each other about it, we all ran to the medical school. And a meeting was already going on there—everybody came, and it spilled over into the courtyard. And, of course, it was mainly Komsomol and party members who were giving the speeches, volunteering us all as one to go to the front. What was there to talk about? We had graduated, they had given us our diplomas. Naturally, it was our duty to go to the front. But just the same, we wanted to hear the speeches; there was such an outburst of emotion!

Tell me, was it possible for women to get out of going to the front?

It was. Just imagine, it was. I'll tell you about the group that graduated with me. In our class there was a certain Tonia. She tried to get pregnant, either by getting married or living with some guy—I'm not sure which. And that was it. And while our division was being organized to go to the front—that took three months—she presented an official document attesting to the fact that she was three months, or whatever, pregnant. Well, obviously, somehow she had managed to charm someone, because they would have sent her to the front anyway, even if she were three months pregnant. But they didn't send her. So you could get out of it that way.

Only that way?

Only that way, yes. How else? Well, if you were some sort of invalid, a cripple . . . [you could get out of it].

That means that all those who graduated with you . . . [went to the front]?

Yes, of course. We were all physicians; we were physicians.

Vera Ivanovna, how many men and how many women graduated with you from medical school?

In my class there were mainly women, of course. Very few men. And when the war began, they were worth their weight in gold. Those who survived combat duty at the front rose to very high ranks. I was amazed: They became lieutenant colonels, majors, colonels—in the medical service, of course. Yes.

So they were promoted?

They received promotions because for the most part they went into administrative work. We had a certain Kostia, for example. And by the end of the war, this Kostia had already risen to the rank of lieutenant colonel. See. In the beginning, he was the commander of a medical battalion. Well, he saw a lot of combat; no doubt he was decorated. And of course, he was a communist. Even at the front, communists were more likely to receive promotions, of course. And since I was not a party member, I wasn't singled out for prestigious awards. Look, you've seen what I have; are these really important medals?

Vera Ivanovna, can you list the medals you received?

Well, I was awarded the Order of the Great Patriotic War, First and Second Class—there're only two classes—and I was awarded the Order of the Red Star.[12] And then I was decorated for the taking of cities, and that includes the medal I prize most! When people ask me which medal I value the most, I reply, the medal for Stalingrad. In my opinion there was nothing more terrible than Stalingrad.

The battle for Stalingrad was hell, literally. I was already seasoned by that time. I had already been wounded and nursed back to health in the medical battalion, and it was after that that I found myself in the battle for Stalingrad. Even so, it was absolute hell! I'll tell you how one girl, a nurse named Nadenka, perished. She was so obliging, she did so much for the wounded; when things needed to be done, she did them. Well, she and the quartermaster went to get their usual dinner. They brought it to them in thermoses. The only thing they fed us, you know, was millet gruel. We even called it PMS—perpetual millet soup. Yes. Well, they took this soup, this watery gruel, and they went and sat down to eat in a dugout. And they had just begun to eat, when there was an air raid. Every other hour, the Germans were bombing us. You could check your watch by the bombings; they were terrible pedants. They swooped down terrifyingly, dived, and dropped anything, you name it: not only bombs, but rails, tractor wheels, tractor parts of all sorts. Everything made a noise, shrieked to the howling of sirens. In the beginning, we didn't know just what was flying, what kind of strange monsters, and then it turned out these monsters were actually metal tractor parts. And the rails, the rails were especially dangerous: They pierced the ground because they were dropped from a great height. And that time, the entire dugout caved in, and all the soldiers who were in it died instantly. They were crushed. And when they dug them out, they didn't find any survivors. That's how Nadenka perished.

---

12. This order is a very high honor, second only to the Gold Star of the Hero of the Soviet Union, the most prestigious order of all.

[In response to one of Anastasia's questions, Malakhova began to talk about love.]

Love—there has to be love! This is the finest, the loftiest feeling a person can experience! Yes, there's no telling what incredible feats people can accomplish in the name of love! You can move mountains, when you really love a person; that's the first thing. And then there is . . . If they are suited for each other as man and woman, it is good, of course—good when there is physiological compatibility, so to speak. Everyone has sexual desires, everyone! But this compatibility isn't always present, and not all women can experience it. Women often seek me out as a doctor. I have often spoken with them, and I know that some of them experience nothing before the birth of their first child. It is only after the birth of their second child that they say, "Something felt good, and before that, I felt nothing at all." Some say that if a woman doesn't have an orgasm, she will never get pregnant. That's nonsense! Utter nonsense! Because many have never even experienced it, and yet they have no trouble giving birth or getting pregnant. And they love breast-feeding their baby, what pleasure they discover in breast-feeding! I, too, breast-fed, and I know that this is truly a great . . . You are released . . . , when the milk comes in, your breasts hurt so! There's such pressure from the milk! And when the baby sucks this milk, you feel that you are giving life to a living being, giving it your energy! In my opinion, there is no greater joy than this: to breast-feed a baby, to give it your very own milk. And the baby is so gentle, so helpless; he sniffs about. Then he sucks and sucks. In my opinion, a woman experiences no greater feeling than this. It seems to me that it is a heavenly sensation, a heavenly feeling to be a mother. I don't know, perhaps my views are old-fashioned.

And I think that love . . . Real love existed at the front, too. You see this portrait of Georgii Antonovich? It was such a wonderful, good feeling. By the way, I knew he was from the Caucasus. But I didn't know what his nationality was. Well, after the encirclement, in Stalingrad, he died of peritonitis in my arms. He had been badly wounded, they had put a hole in his intestines, and we couldn't save him. And when he was dying—with peritonitis, they were always conscious to the end. Enough said—so many of them died in my arms! Oh! I don't even know how many. And you know, his last words . . . He lived another two days, and I could see him grow thinner and thinner before my very eyes, his skin darkened, and his nose became incredibly pointed! They didn't give him anything to drink, because they thought . . . , but why not give him something to drink, all the same he's going to die. And he, his last words were: "Well, how will you get along without me?" He had brought me out of the encirclement. "How will you live without me?" And he really loved me and thought that when the war was over we would be together, we would get married, and the rest.

Did you love him too?

Well, you know, I did like him. For starters, he was two years older than me; and then, he was tall, he was serious, he kept order among the men. All the soldiers in the medical company loved him because he was a just man and brave.

What was his position?

He was the regiment's senior physician. At that time, there were four doctors; later, there were only two for each regiment. There weren't any more doctors available; all the rest had been killed. There was the regiment's senior physician; there was the commander of the medical company; there was an epidemiologist, who was the sanitation inspector; and there was the junior doctor, the one who treated patients—that was me. Although all three of them were graduates of the academy, they said very openly, Vera, we haven't the faintest idea how to use a stethoscope, how to diagnose a sick person, and so on, only you can do that.

All three of them were men, weren't they?

Yes, all three were men. And when we were encircled . . . Kostia Galkin, the sanitation inspector, the epidemiologist, was such a wonderful man! He loved to laugh; he was so happy-go-lucky. And, oh, the jokes he told! And you know, once when German tanks had started straight at us—they simply crushed people and fired rounds of shells—he went crazy and headed straight for the German tanks. There was a wheat field, the tanks were coming across it, and we looked and saw Kostia headed right for those tanks. We cried out, "Kostia! Kostia!" We liked him so much. "Come back!" But he did nothing of the sort.

Here's how Georgii Antonovich Khukhlaev led me out of the encirclement. He was an excellent horseman. He had an orderly, and this orderly had a horse. For two days, we had gone without water; we became completely dried out! It was June and very hot! The Germans were bombing us, they were shelling us, their tanks were coming at us. In short, everyone was completely exhausted, and the wounded were crying out, water, water, a drink of water! . . . But there was no water, not even a drop! It was the second day. And Georgii Antonovich said to his orderly, "Unsaddle the horse, take a bucket, and find me water, whatever it takes." Suddenly, tanks were coming at us. There was a small woods, Kostia went into this thicket. Georgii Antonovich said to me, "Get on the horse!" But before that, he said, "Take off your dress!" I thought, Good God! He must have lost his mind too. Why should I . . . ? At that time, we were issued these dresses like uniforms. Well okay, he dragged out his bag—he was so tall—and gave me his second pair of pants and said, "Put on these pants!" Well, I thought, he's really crazy. I couldn't disobey him; he was the regiment's senior physician! So I pulled on the pants, and somehow he hitched them up for me. "Get on the horse!" He took me—I was small, and of course, thin, not the way I am now—and he put me on this horse, which had no bridle, no saddle, no—you know, those things you put your feet in, I can't remember what they're called—stirrups! No stirrups, nothing. He sat me on the horse, twisted the mane around my hands, and said, "If you don't want to fall into the hands of the Germans, hang on tight to the horse, dig in." Now, we had straps that we used to drag the wounded off the battlefield with. Once I had to do that. And from those straps he made me stirrups, loops, and he put me on the croup of the horse, and put my feet into those loops, in boots, and he wound the mane around my hands. And he said: "Press against the horse, grab him around the neck, dig into him. I'll do the rest." He called to his own horse, and my horse galloped after him, and that's how he rescued me from the encirclement. We dashed across the field. We escaped the tanks, but the shooting continued, shells were exploding, the horse kept rearing. How in the world did I manage to stay on? I had never ridden before, never even been close to a horse. Well, I'd seen them at the front, but I never thought I would get on a horse. It was my terrible baptism by fire!

Then we got lost and wandered into some ravine.

What year was this?

It was the summer of 1942, the beginning of July. And when we wandered into this ravine, we found several soldiers already hiding there. Georgii Antonovich told me to get down, but he couldn't get me off the horse because I was so frightened, I had dug my nails into its neck and was holding onto it for dear life. Slowly, soldiers began to gather in the ravine; twelve or fourteen of us must have gathered there. And Georgii Antonovich said: "Vera Ivanovna is the highest ranking among you. She's a senior lieutenant. Obey her." And he whispered in my ear: "I won't abandon you. I'm going to find out where the division is and how we can get out of the encirclement." We already knew that we had been encircled by the Germans. I thought, Good God! . . .

And where was this?

This was near Kastornaia, the Kastornaia station. It was an important railroad junction. Well, I thought, he'll soon be gone. I said, "What if you're wounded?" He replied, "I won't be." That's just how he said it: with confidence. And so he rode off on this same horse. And the ravine was quite deep. He left, and, as soon as he left, we heard the sound of a motor. *Zhi-zhi* . . . A *rama* was flying overhead. Now, a rama was a German plane with two fuselages, a double tail, and a single motor. [This plane flew very low, for reconnaissance.] All the frontline soldiers knew just what it was. And this rama began to descend; it descended and landed on the very field where the tanks were—quite a distance from us. I said: "Guys, we're done for. What have you got for weapons?" It turned out one person had a carbine, some had automatics—but not everyone had them yet, not everyone had a rifle, even. And Natasha, who was in charge of medication, was there, too—I don't know how she got there—and Andrei, the medical orderly, crept up. And there were also signalmen, ordinary soldiers. "Yes," I said, "That's it. They're about to get us. They'll get out of the rama." Now, ramas could "see" everything. They had amazing sighting devices. I thought, that's it: They've spotted us; now they'll finish us off. At that moment, Andrei said to Natasha—Natasha was a member of the Komsomol— "Natashka, here, take this German leaflet. Let's crawl out of here."[13] We all wanted water to drink something awful! We hadn't had anything to drink for two whole days. Way off in the distance, I noticed a crane standing in a village; it was a well. "Let's crawl over there and get a drink," said Andrei. "Don't you dare," I said. "I'm senior to you in rank; don't you dare." He crawled off and so did Natasha; neither of them returned. Later, after we had gotten out of the encirclement, we were told that everyone in the village had been lined up and questioned: Who is a Communist? Who is a Komsomol? Who is a Jew? And she was a komsomolka; she had her Komsomol card with her. Well, by all accounts, they were among those who were shot. The Germans finished everyone off: all the communists, all the Jews! There were a lot of Jews in our medical battalion, and they were all shot—every last one of them. They shot all the communists and Komsomol members, too. June of '42. That's when the most horrible battles took place, that's when we retreated.

Toward evening, late in the day, Georgii Antonovich suddenly appeared. He had found out where the rest of the unit was, and he led those of us who were left, out of the encirclement. We managed to join up with the unit, but we had to fight our way out. We were right with the soldiers, under attack. It was awful. And since we had had absolutely nothing to drink, our lips were cracked and bleeding. And my dress—I had taken off his pants—was all crumpled, all dirty, all spattered with mud. While we were fighting our way out, you know, the villagers . . . We kept going from one village to the next: That village was occupied by Germans, this village was occupied by Germans. . . . Then we ended up in another village and found "ours" there. "The Germans were here, but now they've left." "Give us some water, some water!" And when we passed by, erect, with all our automatics and carbines at the ready, you know, they poured water on us, and whoever got even a drop was so happy. They simply poured water over us. But we couldn't afford to stop; we had to break through! And that's how I got out of the encirclement.

---

13. He was promising that if she carried a German leaflet, the Germans would not harm her.

When did Georgii Antonovich die?

He died in Stalingrad—either in August or September. He came to wish me a happy birthday, so he was still alive at the end of September. I had suffered shell shock and was recuperating in the medical battalion. I couldn't hear a thing. He swam across the Volga to see me on my birthday [he risked his life to do this, as the Germans could easily have shot him], and he brought me a present: a handful of raisins mixed with sugar. There was no sugar to be had, and then for some reason they gave them these raisins, and he saved them and saved them, so he could bring them to me for my birthday. I don't remember exactly when he died.

Later, [in the 1960s] when I came back to Stalingrad as an honored guest of the city,[14] I went to the spot where our support services had been, where the medical battalion had been, to look for the cemetery. And what do you think I found: The whole cemetery had been destroyed, and on that spot they had built houses. There wasn't one single grave left! I couldn't even recognize the spot. Quite by accident, I spotted an old school. There had been a small school there during the war—one story, of course. I went into the school. All the children were in a single classroom. I was wearing the blouse of my uniform. And the teacher said: "Oh, just look who has come to see us. Such an important guest!" All the children rose to greet me. I said: "Please excuse me. I'm looking for the cemetery. I can't find it." The teacher said: "There's a certain woman here who will know," and she told one of the children to go fetch her. The woman, whose name was Malanevna, appeared. We set out, and I said to her: "Do you remember an incident during the battle for Stalingrad, when they bombed our support services terribly? The medical battalion for all our divisions, and the cemetery for our entire army was right here." "What do you mean! It's all been destroyed," she retorted. "Well, hasn't anything remained, not even one soldier's grave?" She took me to a sort of park where there was some kind of wooden booth or box—I don't know how to describe it. And can you imagine! They had put up only a little star, and on one side was written: "Here lie the soldiers of the sixty-second army." They didn't even indicate which divisions. I burst out crying. I was so insulted. So many soldiers had been laid to rest in Stalingrad! And they didn't even have the decency to make a soldiers' grave for them. How could they have done that! Soldiers had . . . We had managed to make a cemetery. Each soldier had had his own grave, and it was marked—by a piece of wood, by some kind of metal object, by whatever we could lay our hands on—and on each were painted the words: Here lies so and so.[15] Now there was nothing! Everything

---

14. In 1967, a grandiose monument was erected at Stalingrad. As a veteran of the battle of Stalingrad, Malakhova was probably invited to the unveiling of that monument.

15. The modest memorial created by comrades and friends under the most difficult circumstances had been destroyed and replaced. Thus, Malakhova suffered another loss, in addition to the original loss of her lover. Thanks to her efforts, the names of her two friends and her lover were included in the listing of those who died in the Battle of Stalingrad.

had been destroyed! [Malakhova remembered other events of the war years, and in response to a question from Posadskaya, began to talk about her first experiences as a physician at the front.]

Vera Ivanovna, tell me about the laundresses at the front, who did all the washing for the troops.

The laundresses at the front . . . Once, when we were in the second echelon, that is, when we were not fighting on the front lines but were getting rid of the lice—we washed ourselves as best we could and with whatever we could find—I was walking along in one village, and suddenly, what did I see: near every hut there was a washtub—one of our washtubs, a Russian washtub, a wooden one to boot! I went inside. Good God! How many girls there were! Wearing shabby, faded military shirts. Their hands—I can't describe them! Their hands were in terrible shape from all the lye they used and from the soap, although soap was very hard to get. And they were doing the laundry for the entire army. They were washing shirts covered with pus, and shirts stained with blood, and all the sheets of the medical battalion. You see, we had hospitals, and the wounded lay on those sheets. Everything was stained with pus, with blood, and they were washing everything. God, you know, I was so upset! And I felt so bad for these girls, felt so bad that . . . Only girls were doing this work. Some man was in charge, giving orders. Perhaps he had been wounded at the front and was a former soldier. And they were doing all the washing by themselves. I don't know what they got to eat. They all seemed to me—this was my only experience, I only encountered this once—but they all seemed faded. Honest to God. Just like their military shirts, they seemed faded, discolored. You know what a military shirt is like when you have to spend the summer in it and have nothing else to wear. You sweat, and everything gets covered with sweat, with salt, with blood, you name it. That's how it was for those girls. My heart ached for them, honest to God. So they treated women unjustly at the front in a great many ways, a great many ways. And I have never read a single word about those women anywhere!

And did anyone ever question you about them?

No, never. You're the first person I've told about this, and it's my own personal experience. Signalwomen also had a very hard job to do at the front. They had to lay—signalers, understand this, I'm not talking about hauling a portable radio transmitter behind someone's back—that's also hard work. These people had to lay cable, wire, along the front lines. And one of them who was with us—her name was Valechka—she must have lived with somebody, probably with the head of communications, because even here in the infantry battalion she got pregnant. And they wouldn't let women in her condition leave the front until they were seven months pregnant! She had to stay and do that work until she was seven months pregnant! Her belly was already so big it looked like—it's hard to describe—a drum, and the poor thing, she had to carry 10 kilos, if not more, 10 kilos of wire wound on a spool with an iron base, and she not only had to carry it but she had to lay it, dragging it from company to company in the battalion! How in the world could she do that, pregnant? We had three cases of pregnancy: Zina Belousova—she was my right hand; she was married. She and her husband had gotten married at the front. Then there was Anna Georgievna. She was a FCW, but such a modest . . .

FCW means?

Field campaign wife. But she didn't let on; she was extremely self-effacing! She was so industrious; and she was completely humpbacked. The commander of the regiment—our commander was Mikhailov—was a splendid man!

So he was her field husband?

Yes. And she used to come right out and say to me: "Vera Ivanovna, I'm a freak. Who am I? At least I will live for my baby." And she also had to stay in the regiment until she was seven months pregnant. No one had the authority to send her to the rear.

Vera Ivanovna, did people at the front treat women who got married differently from women who had a relationship without marrying?

Well, you see, this Anna Georgievna did such a good job of concealing everything, that many didn't even suspect, didn't know a thing. But when she became pregnant . . . Good heavens, how could such a . . . !

Well, what about those who didn't conceal it, who were very open about the fact that they were FCWs?

Those who were open about it? Well, it seems to me a few even flaunted it. We didn't like them. We were upright, we behaved honorably, we didn't like the FCWs. They got special privileges. We were all in the infantry. We would have to march 35 to 40 kilometers at night, while they were transported on horses. Each regimental commander had his own horses and carriage, later even his own vehicles. Whereas we in the rank and file, we had to march on foot.

So wives got to ride?

Yes. By the way, Batiuk was an excellent man, but he had an FCW whose name was Anka Moskova. I must admit, she was an excellent surgical nurse, excellent! But if he summoned her, she would drop everything, and others had to do her work. While she would go do all his washing and all his ironing; she would care for all his needs, so to speak. And everyone knew this. And when he died, she immediately began living with the head of the "special section" [army secret police]. And everybody began to hate her! You already had a liaison. Well, okay, it was with the commander of the division. Since Batiuk was a good commander, we overlooked it. But what sort of person are you? You were in love, you were in love, but then what? The body hadn't even had time to grow cold, and she was already living with someone else!?

Vera Ivanovna, remember you talked about how women often suffered from amenorrhea. Right?

Yes, some did. And some had normal periods. On the other hand, I suffered a great deal.

Your periods were heavy, right?

Oh!

So it got even worse during the war?

Absolutely. From fright. There was nothing I could do. Under normal circumstances, after menstruation the uterus should close and the blood vessels constrict, and then everything should return to normal. But this didn't happen, so the blood would flow and flow and gush and gush. Later, Tamara—she was the regiment's senior physician, she already knew about my problem, and she would simply leave me alone, not take me on the march, for three or four days. By the way, I was very good with a map. I was an A student in military preparedness, back in medical school. I was very good at reading topographical maps, and they would give me a map. The men, the officers in the regimental headquarters, always gave me a map. I always had a map folded up in this map case, so when I was left alone I could find my way right to our troops. I knew the direction. I already knew who our army neighbors were, so to speak. I knew all the army corps. There were three corps, and in each corps three divisions. I knew them all.

So you would catch up with your regiment?

Yes, I was able to catch up with it. They trusted me, and I think most likely they knew what the problem was. Some secret! And nobody said anything to me about it. What could they do, since they had sent us girls to the front lines? What could they do!? In general, of course, women shouldn't be in the infantry! They shouldn't! Weren't there enough men? How many of them took it easy in the rear! How many?! It was scandalous! While we, young girls—I was only twenty-one when I graduated from medical school—we were at the very front lines! Of course, there was nothing more dreadful than being a doctor in the infantry and running the regimental first-aid station! Nothing was more dreadful than that! Even the tank units, even they were never as close to the enemy. And then, our men who belonged to the tank crew—when we were near Kastornaia, when we hadn't yet gone into battle but were still moving toward the front lines—the guys in the tank stood up and said, Girls, girls, come over here. Well, we kept on walking; we weren't giving in so easily! We were full of ourselves: If you want to, you come over here. One of them began to tease us: "Girls, come over here. We'll give you a lift; we'll dress you up." And I remember how they gave us those ribbons—remember, I told you how they used them to drag away the wounded—they gave us blue and red ribbons. And from those ribbons—they were made of jersey—we sewed ourselves stockings. They never gave us any stockings! We walked around in men's drawers and in men's shirts. There were no bras. We sewed ourselves bras from those green triangular scarves that were used for bandages. The senior physicians chewed us out, but what were we supposed to do?

Were the senior physicians men?

Yes. The senior physicians were almost always men.

So then it seemed to them that no one needed bras?

Well, I don't know what they thought. Our needs were not their concern. On the sly, we sewed ourselves undershorts and bras.

So there was no women's underwear?

Nope.

And was there any underwear for men?

Sure, there were drawers and shirts with strings right here.

So everyone wore the same underwear?

Yes. Well, if I'm going to tell you everything, then I'll have to tell you about the bathhouse in Stalingrad, where we washed together with the men. Together with the men! We used one side of the room, and they used the other. There was a common bathtank. For the water, hot or cold, there were two enormous tanks. Do you think that anybody laughed? We were all too bashful. When the men went to get water, they covered themselves with their basins. When we went, we covered ourselves with basins, too. And the men turned their backs, so we could fill our basins with water and go off into our corner. They were in another corner. That's the way it was. No, it was all very chaste, and by the way, the soldiers, the sergeants were better in that respect than the officers. The officers felt superior. They could "persuade" women to have intimate relations with them. That's what I think, but I don't know for sure. I don't know of any situation where some man was brazen, forced his attentions on a woman, no. I've already told you how the regimental commander summoned me and then Lida, and how Lida cursed him out good.

Well, in general, of course, life was hard. There were those physiological needs that had to be taken care of, when we had to . . . It was very hard,

very hard, because . . . We'd be marching along, and there would be men
everywhere you looked. We marched at night; the infantry moved at night.
The troops had to be moved, but they couldn't be moved in the daytime
because the Germans would have bombed us. They were always on the
lookout. The rama was always flying overhead. So it was impossible to
move in the daytime; we could only move at night. You'd be marching
along, exhausted, worn out beyond belief. Suddenly you'd have the urge to
go, but how could you? And then they "saved" us. At the time, it seemed
to us that they were old. The older ones were perhaps fifty, and to us they
seemed like old men. Usually they were in transport carts, and what did
they do?

These were men?

Yes, men. It was dangerous to go off somewhere, because sometimes there
were mines. So the three of them would stand up, turn their backs to us,
open their greatcoats wide, and say: "Dear daughters, go ahead, don't be
bashful. We can see that you can't march any further." So we would squat
and then pee, sometimes we would . . . But otherwise, you had to hold it in,
and of course, your bowels suffered and all the rest. If you could manage to
find some bushes, then you could . . . Your stomach would hurt, your blad-
der would be bursting, you simply couldn't march another step. That's the
way it was.

And men could simply . . . ?

Those men didn't even watch us. It was easier for men: They just turned
their backs, and that was it. And when we finished marching, toward
morning, they would give the command, Dig latrines, dig latrines! So that
we would only go in one spot and later there would be no infection. And
when we left, they tried to fill those latrines at least with dirt. And that's the
way it was. Of course, it was very hard, very hard, when we were on the
march. All in all, I think that they really looked after us. I don't have anything bad to say about ordinary soldiers.

   How those soldiers fed me in Odessa! How we ate. That was the second
time I went into combat shoulder to shoulder with the soldiers. That happened to me only twice: Once when we were coming out of the encirclement and once near Odessa. I was hungry, exhausted. It was awful!
There were terrible meteorological conditions: The weather was really unusual. Later, the citizens of Odessa said that they hadn't seen such weather
for a hundred years. It rained, and then immediately everything on us
turned to ice, everything was covered with a sheet of ice. Our waterproof
capes were like that. They puffed out so they looked like icy scales. It was
beastly cold! And in the next division, more than thirty men froze! They
lost their strength, sat down, and literally froze to death. But they kept dri-

ving us onward.[16] And then we marched through reed-covered flats. It was marshland, and some soldiers drowned in the icy water. That's the way we marched toward Odessa. Yes. And when we approached the city—we approached it from the steppe side—we were hungry and exhausted. We were absolutely starving. We had already gotten through, repulsed the attack, broken their lines. We were fighting against Romanian troops. [Romania was a German ally.] And I looked and saw a field kitchen near the road—it was not from our division—and they were pouring soup out onto the ground. And our soldiers were shouting: "Don't throw anything out! What have you got there? Is it bean soup? Give us some!" "In what?" Well, there was nothing to put it in. So a soldier said: "Look, over there, see that stuff?" So they went and found a basin. It was April 10, the roads were bad, and the basin was filthy. The soldiers wiped the basin with a greatcoat and got a full basin of bean soup. It was brown, a dark brown. They all sat down by the side of the road around this basin, got their spoons out of their boots, and proceeded to eat. I walked past. Ah! My mouth started to water. For two whole days I hadn't had anything to eat. Boy, was I hungry! One old man said: "What is it, sister? Lads, move over; let little sister have something to eat." I came up to them. "Well, why don't you eat?" "I don't have a spoon," I answered. "What sort of blankety-blank are you? Just what sort of soldier are you? Why don't you have a spoon?" Then he said: "Well, let me finish eating." He finished, wiped the spoon with his dirty greatcoat [she laughs], wiped it off, and gave it to me: "Eat!" He stood near me. I said, "I'll eat fast." "That's okay. Keep the spoon as a souvenir." And I still have that spoon.

[After discussing current affairs, Malakhova returned to her memories of the war, and then began to speak about the role of the army secret police.]

We had a "special section" known as SmerSh. Then we also had a "special section," the OO.[17] I couldn't stand either of them. Usually, they would occupy the best house in the village. Once I had such an argument with them, a terrible one, because the special section had occupied one house, and in another house, can you imagine, they put the spies they had uncovered. And once . . . As I told you, I always marched with the reconnaissance

---

16. Malakhova was referring to a characteristic of "Stalin strikes." Troops were ordered to move out and occupy designated points within a particular period of time, "at any price." In practice, this meant a very high casualty rate and great suffering for the soldiers.

17. The acronym SmerSh meant "Death to Spies" and referred to units whose role was to uncover people spying for foreign powers. The "Special Section" (Osobyi Otdel) was a division of the secret police entrusted with uncovering and crushing "internal enemies." Secret police were especially numerous in the infantry, the most dangerous branch of service and the one that contained the greatest number of men who were in prison for "political crimes" before being released to fight the Germans.

party. The scouts would go ahead, and I would follow in their footsteps, so as not to step on a mine.

Why did you go on reconnaissance missions?

I didn't actually go on them, but we . . . The regiment would be relocated. I would go first, behind the reconnaissance party. I needed to get to the village so I could take the best house for the regimental first-aid station. A battle would take place the next day, and we had to get ready. I arrived in the village. What the hell: the best house, the biggest one . . . [had already been taken]. Sometimes there would be lots of wounded soldiers. I was already seasoned; I understood that we might be flooded with wounded. And here was an enormous house, with two wings. A soldier stood guarding it with an automatic. I said, "What are you doing here?" "I'm standing guard," he said. "What do you mean 'standing guard'? Get out of here. I'm going to set up the first-aid station here." "No, this house is occupied by the special section." I said: "What do you mean, 'special section'?" I simply brushed him aside. He barred my way with his automatic: "Don't take another step." And people said to me: "Vera, don't mess with them. They're 'spooks' [secret police]. What can you expect from them?" In general, nobody liked them. I'll be blunt: They were *detested*! And just what sort of spies did they think they would catch in our infantry? I never saw a one of them, not a one. But the way they behaved . . . It was I who needed a large house, not one that had been bombed out. There would be a flood of wounded soldiers! And, see, the special section got to stay there. They took an enormous house, the largest house in the village. Oh, I don't know what to say. I didn't like them, I really didn't.

Were they really so privileged?

How can you ask! We're talking about the special section. They were NKVD [members of the secret police]. Everyone understood what had happened in 1937 and 1938. Many had fathers who had been killed, shot, and now the sons had been "freed."[18] You see, they were no longer considered enemies of the people, once the enemy had invaded the motherland. And the sons demonstrated courage at the front, all of them, despite the fact that their parents had been executed. So you can understand the way many viewed the special section. Although nobody in my family suffered, I didn't like them, and I never had anything to do with them. Never!

---

18. In the 1930s, the child of someone identified as "an enemy of the people" in many cases was persecuted. During the war, "sons" were offered the opportunity to "demonstrate their loyalty," by spilling their blood. The special forces exercised particular surveillance over such "sons," regarding them as potential traitors who might take vengeance for what had been done to their parents.

So, Vera Ivanovna, you were in the medical company?

I was the attending physician in the medical company. There was such a position—attending physician. The regiment had a senior physician, who was essentially an administrator. He oversaw the wounded. The first wave of wounded came to us, to the regimental first-aid station. And when we had bandaged someone, somehow stopped the flow of blood, applied a tourniquet, noted that the tourniquet had been applied at such and such a time and that the wounded soldier should be evacuated immediately . . . We were always being bombed, we were always under artillery fire, and sometimes the Germans would be coming right at us. That is why the wounded, if the soldiers were already seasoned, tried to get to the rear. They only wanted us to fill out "wounded in action" cards for them. "Oh, write me out . . . " Without that card, they wouldn't even take care of wounded soldiers.

So this was a legal document?

Yes, a legal document! You had to make out one for each wounded soldier at the first-aid station. "Oh, hurry up, little sister." They called all of us "little sister."[19] It didn't make any difference whether you were a doctor, a doctor's assistant, or a medical orderly. To them, we were all "little sister." "Little sister, hurry up and give me a 'wounded in action' card." [The card served as proof that the soldier had actually been wounded at the front.] So we would make out the card, and if the wounded soldier could still walk, if, for example, his arm was wounded, or his neck, or his head—but it wasn't a "penetrating" wound, as we said—he left on his own. Because those who couldn't walk, many of them, perished if they weren't evacuated in time. The Germans would start bombing, and that was it. They would target both us and the wounded.

Where did they run—to the medical battalion?

Yes, each soldier knew just where our medical battalion was located.

And where was the medical battalion located in relationship to the front?

Our medical company and the regimental first-aid station were located three kilometers from the front lines. All the time we were being bombed, we were under artillery fire, and mines were going off—both long-range and short-range ones. While the medical battalion was located at least seven to ten kilometers from the front lines, sometimes further, and everything was aimed from afar: the bombs, the artillery fire. So our unit was right in the line of fire, right in it! Frequently under machine-gun fire and

---

19. The Russian term of endearment used here (a diminutive form of the word *sestra,* or sister) can be understood as meaning both little sister and nurse. We chose the first variant in our translation because it better conveys the warmth, informality, and asexuality of relations between ordinary soldiers and female medical personnel at the front.

quite often under direct German attack. Sometimes we had to—no one has ever admitted to this—but sometimes we had to abandon the wounded, because we simply couldn't carry all of them away on our backs, and they themselves would say: "Girls, run, the Germans [are coming]. They're already coming down the street." They had their weapons cocked, and they would shoot. We would throw away our medical smocks, jump out the windows, and bring up the rear of those running, behind those who had brought in the wounded. That's the way it was at the front. And nobody ever writes about this, either: We would leave the wounded, and then if they were unlucky enough to be captured by the Germans, how unjustly the Soviets treated them later![20] "How could you fall into the hands of the Germans? Why didn't you commit suicide?"

Our side treated them that way?

Yes. Our side, the special section. How could that be? All the time we were told, If you are captured by the Germans, it's your duty to kill yourself. Only traitors to the motherland fall into the hands of the Germans!

Who taught you that?

Political workers and the special section. It was our duty to destroy ourselves. Well, how could you do that?![21]

[After discussing some cases where people were captured, and other events from her life at the front, Malakhova recalled a case of extreme sexual harassment.]

We had just reached Stalingrad, and Krasnov, the commander of the medical company, did such a repulsive thing, played such a dirty trick. He was very handsome, but he was so mean that nobody could stand him. Here's what he did in Stalingrad: He had learned that the girls planned to wash, and he took a bunch of grenades. Everybody had dug into the bank, afraid to lift their heads because of the bombing. Everybody, meaning the advanced group of our medical battalion. He took a bunch of grenades, he knew that the girls were washing. Well, and how could they wash in a dugout? They had to use basins—at least they could get rid of the lice. Well, you yourself understand, perhaps they could wash themselves, at least wash their private parts. He threw the grenades near the door to the dugout and yelled: "Air raid!" Everyone knew that by each dugout there were trenches to take shelter in. The girls jumped out stark naked, because they were

---

20. Malakhova speaks here of the military policy of "standing firm until the end," of "dying, but not yielding." The result of this policy was that anyone serving in the Soviet military who remained alive to be captured by the Germans was regarded as a "traitor to the motherland." Any captive who returned to the Soviet Union suffered harsh punishment.

21. Malakhova was particularly outraged because suicide is a sin according to the Russian Orthodox faith.

washing. Word of what he did reached the political section[22] of the division. Now, we had an amazing commissar; he was an amazing person. In fact, he was the only political worker I ever respected. This business was reported to him, and Krasnov was sent off to a punishment battalion. And the battalion[23]—well, that was certain death.

You said that the Germans shot all the communists, Komsomol members, and Jews. Were there many Jews at the front?

As I told you, when we were near Kastornaia, the Germans shot all the communists, Komsomol members, and Jews. Oh, how they hated . . . Our entire medical battalion was wiped out near Kastornaia; it was almost entirely Jewish. Every single one of them was shot. After Kastornaia . . . very few were left in our battalion. I'm not sure there were any left. Well, there was Sonia Iasorepskaia. She was a marvelous surgeon, an excellent surgeon, a very clever woman, and she loved to sing and dance; that was the fashion. We sang songs together, Sonia and me, even in Stalingrad, because I also loved to sing. And we had Serezhka Senshin, who was an excellent accordion player. We even put on amateur talent shows.

Then there's the Christmas tree—there just isn't time to tell you everything—but I put up a Christmas tree in my unit, which the entire division came to see! The entire division. Actually, it wasn't a fir tree but a small oak. Fir trees were nowhere to be had in Stalingrad, so one of the doctor's assistants—oh no! I mean a driver—brought me a small oak tree. And we painted its dry leaves green with "zelenka" [a disinfecting agent, colored a poisonous green]. And we made all sorts of ornaments, me and my friends—we made them as a surprise—and we tied them to the tree, so that there would be sparkling things on it. We even took the tubes from enemas—nobody suffered from constipation, and we had all those enemas and glass tubes that . . . They were clean. And we hung them, as well, tied on threads. All in all, we had an amazing Christmas tree! But when the commander of the medical battalion came, he reprimanded me. It was my first and only . . . [reprimand].

But why?

He reprimanded me because I hadn't gone to the New Year's party at the officers' club. You see, the officers had a large dugout, but I chose to stay with my own platoon. And my right hand, Tasia Levishina, my assistant—she was

---

22. The ideological sector of the Soviet army, responsible for conducting the work of the party. (See also footnote 10.)

23. Punishment battalions were special infantry battalions in which people who had gotten into trouble for one reason or another got the chance to "expiate their guilt with blood." They took part in the most dangerous operations, operations from which it was virtually impossible to emerge alive.

also a junior officer—and she didn't go, either. And all my nurses, the medical orderlies, and all the orderlies who were already up in years also didn't go. That's why they all adored me, because I didn't abandon them on such an important holiday, didn't go to celebrate with those officers. I hadn't gone, and neither had Tasia. "Just why are Malakhova and her assistant absent?" You see, I was a singer. So everybody came from the party to me, to my dugout, and when they got there, they saw the Christmas tree! The Christmas tree! At first, they were overjoyed. Now, the commander of our medical battalion was almost as blind as a bat. He came up to me, wiped his glasses, and said: "Oh, a Christmas tree with ornaments on it." And then: "But what is that?" On the tree we had tied thermometers and other glass objects. "What is that? It's insubordination! Take them off!" He began to yell at me: "Take them off immediately! You're to report to the New Year's party in the officers' dugout on the double!" That was it. He spoiled our entire celebration.

And what a celebration it was. In place of a table the orderlies had driven in pegs and put stretchers, and they were covered with a clean white sheet. In helmets . . . where had they gotten them? Somewhere the soldiers, the orderlies who were already up in years had gotten tangerines. Where could they have gotten hold of them? No one supplied us with tangerines, since we weren't yet *gvardeitsi*.[24] And in another helmet there was candy—for us, for the girls, and, of course, there was vodka for us. Everybody got 100 grams of vodka, even if they weren't *gvardeitsi*. On holidays they would give all of us vodka. And we had this vodka in our canteens. We all drank some vodka and had something to eat. And the cook prepared the kasha a little bit better than usual, a little thicker. Yes. And so we celebrated, and they even brought us a phonograph with the one and only record. And we wound it up and sang and danced. We were so happy! Even though I was already an officer, I didn't go to the officers' party, didn't trade them for the officers. So what did the officers do? They forced us—we didn't have the right to refuse—they subjected us to military discipline. Tasia and I went almost with tears in our eyes. At that time the chief surgeon was courting me, and he obviously had designs. And he was . . . With his enormous paw, he seized hold of me and sat me down on his knees, put my hands like this behind my back. By this time, all the officers were very drunk. "Penalize her!" I struggled and struggled, but they simply poured some vodka in my mouth. In order not to choke, I gulped it down and immediately became drunk. And so I got poisoned, for two whole days I threw up, and he had to keep watch over me for those two days to be sure I didn't die. That's how it went.

---

24. *Gvardeitsi* was the name given to regiments that had earned special distinction in a military campaign, for example, by taking a major city. Such regiments were supplied somewhat better than their ordinary counterparts, receiving larger rations of sugar, vodka, and dried food.

What was the most frightening aspect of daily life at the front? What did you fear the most?

I was wounded, twice I was wounded and suffered shell shock. Bombs directly hit the building I was in. I was absolutely terrified of bombings. I feared artillery fire, too, but somehow not with such . . . You know, I was so afraid.

When you say bombings, you mean bombs dropped by airplanes?

Yes . . . I was even called the regimental "ear." There were installations, bell-shaped ones, that detected sounds. My nerves were so affected that when airplanes were flying overhead, even though I couldn't tell where, I could pick up the sounds and distinguish our airplanes from the sound of the German army. This was true also when we were in Stalingrad. Then in Ukraine, both the Italians and the Romanians bombed us, and I could identify the airplanes perfectly by the sounds they made. It was terrifying—I never hid my fright—I was absolutely terrified of the bombings. It was awful! And especially after I was shell-shocked at Stalingrad. When I got shell-shocked . . .

Vera Ivanovna, tell about the times you were wounded.

Well, I was wounded for the first time after Kastornaia, in Krasnaia Poliana, where I was processing the wounded. We were in this Krasnaia Poliana—the house is fixed in my mind: It was a brick house, a good house, but for some reason it had a thatched roof. And stupidly we designated that house the first-aid station. Remember, I told you that we had to hang out a white flag with a red cross. And the only thing I remember is that there was no artillery fire; everything was quiet, peaceful. We processed all the wounded, and then Georgii Antonovich said: "Let's clean the TT pistols." Since I was an officer, I had a pistol, and so the two of us sat at the table, took apart the pistols, and cleaned them. I already knew how to shoot; I'd learned how. Suddenly—let's say he was sitting here, and I was sitting here, facing the window. And right here was the wall, and there . . . In the village on the doors there were usually some kind of curtains with roses, with giant roses—I remember them well—and here, as always in villages, there was a large wall—it was so enormous—and on it were small photos behind glass and a ticking clock. And suddenly there was a crash, and the ceiling caved in, and, worse still, the entire wall collapsed! The entire wall; it was not very far away, just a short distance. And he instantly grabbed me—he sized up the situation immediately—and, bang, put me under the table. You can't possibly imagine what it was like! Bricks, beams, dirt, the whole wall with the clock still ticking somewhere nearby, and then: "Are you alive?" I answered, "I'm alive." Once a bomber pilot had flown over, we knew he would return to bomb again. As a rule, they made three runs. The pilot would return and again swoop down and bomb. Near the house they had already dug those trenches—they always did that—so we could take cover from the bombs and from artillery fire. "Everybody into the chinks"—that's what they called the trenches—"everybody into the chinks." We all ran out, and our only medical orderly was wounded in the lung. Georgii Antonovich gave the order, "Dress his wound!" I raised my hand and looked and said, "Georgii, you're wounded. You're all covered with blood!" But at that point we couldn't do anything about it. We jumped into the chink. I was all covered with blood, and I couldn't figure out where it was coming from. It turned out that it was my hand that was wounded and the blood vessels had been cut. It was I who was all bloody, and I had smeared my blood on him. When we got into the chink, he said: "I'm not wounded. You're the one who's wounded!" And so this Krasnov—that's the only time he was ever considerate of me—he bandaged my hand. He pulled out his *ind-paket* [first-aid kit], took out a cotton-gauze bandage, twisted it, quickly applied a tourniquet, and somehow . . . The airplane flew over a second time. I remember so well the face of that German pilot. He swooped down and saw that we were in the chink like sitting ducks, and he began to shoot at us with his machine gun: t-t-t-t. And those bullets—they kicked up such streams of dust and dirt—but none of us were wounded. And just as soon as they had flown away—we knew that within a few minutes they would be back for a third attack—Georgii Antonovich gave the command: "Everybody, hurry, out of the chink! Get out of the village!" And he took me by the hand and started running. And I didn't even feel the pain, just imagine! I was so frightened, I was in such a state of shock, that I didn't feel any pain. And after we had run away, the Germans bombed again, and killed the fourteen-year-old daughter of the peasant woman with whom we were quartered.

Vera Ivanovna, was each soldier given a first-aid kit?

Absolutely. And before we got to the front, they also issued all of us small black medallions.

What were they?

They were little containers that screwed open and shut, and inside was this long, long piece of paper with a list of things: your surname, first name and patronymic; your date of birth; your education; your rank or title and profession; who your parents were and where your parents lived. All this information was rolled up tightly and put in this little metal container that screwed tightly shut, and men kept them right here on their chests in tiny pouches. This was to ensure that, if someone was badly wounded or died, later they could get that medallion and identify who it was.[25] We women

---

25. If a soldier perished on the battlefield and this could be documented, the death was considered "honorable" and his or her family obtained the right to special rations and a number of benefits, including privileged access to scarce housing or a reduction in rent.

carried ours in the pockets of our military shirts. I don't know what became of mine. After Kastornaia it disappeared somewhere. And nobody gave us another.

I see that you have kept your mama's amulet with a prayer in it. Right?[26]

Yes, I've kept it. The amulet is a very old one; it belonged to my grandmother. I think that even the prayer was . . . my grandmother got that prayer somewhere. She gave the amulet to Mama, and Mama gave it to me, and so I went off to the front with it. At that time, Grandmother was still alive.

And this is a stethoscope, right?

Yes, it's a stethoscope. I've kept it disassembled, like this, in a small pouch. Once a bit of shrapnel came at me and damaged it, but perhaps it saved me. Yes.

So you had this amulet in place of a party card, right?[27]

[Laughing] Yes, that's right, in place of a party card. I didn't have a Komsomol card or a party card. If they had found out that I had an amulet, very likely I would have been . . . But who would have made fun of me? The soldiers would never have done that, never!

What sort of things did you eat at the front?

Once, we actually ate *propastina* [that is the meat of a dead horse—a horse that died for some reason, not one that had been killed for food]. Imagine, I okayed it, gave permission to eat it! In April of '42, when we found ourselves in the active army—we were in the second echelon—we were starving. We were literally swollen from hunger![28] Well, we got to one village— the support services had lagged behind, the horses were dying, there was nothing to eat—and they gave me the following order: "Go inspect. The soldiers have cut up the carcasses of three horses." The intestines of one had come out, and it had rotted. The other two were in better condition. The old-timers had skinned one and found meat here—I no longer remember what that part is called—near the back, and they had cut it off and put it in a kettle to cook and sprinkled it with salt. At that time, there was absolutely no salt. Salt was worth its weight in gold. They boiled this dead horse. They boiled it and boiled it, and I kept saying, Cook it longer. I

---

26. She had been showing Posadskaya her souvenirs of the war.

27. In the Soviet army it was considered morally and politically correct to carry your party or Komsomol card in your breast pocket, an indication of your devotion to the homeland. Museums devoted to the war contain vast numbers of bullet-pocked, bloody party cards, which belonged to fighters who perished on the field of battle.

28. It is worth noting here that soldiers did not always live well, despite Pavlova's belief that they did. See interview beginning on p. 47.

didn't really know a thing about . . . Well, finally I figured it was done. Okay, now someone had to try it to see if it was fit to eat. Everyone was in such a hurry to eat. It was the responsibility of a doctor to try it. I no longer remember all the details, why I was the one who had to sample it. Nobody else wanted to do it. What if you got poisoned? Nobody knew whether it was safe to eat propastina.

So propastina is . . . ?

The meat of a dead horse. This horse had died and was lying somewhere in a stream. It was April, not all the snow had melted yet. The meat smelled like it was tasty, but there was no salt, no bread. We had even eaten up all the dried crusts, which were the emergency rations. These dried crusts they gave us were so hard, they were like stone! But there was nothing left! What were we to do? Well, they poured some in my mess tin. At that time, I still had my spoon; later I lost it. In Odessa I had nothing to eat with. Okay, I tried it. It tasted sweet! Possibly it was an old mare or a stallion; perhaps it was young. Who the heck knows? The meat tasted sweet. There was no salt, no bread, nothing at all! But just the same, I tried it. They said, What's going to happen to you? Everyone stood there waiting: Would I kick the bucket, would the meat do me in, or . . . [she laughs].

Did you have to wait a long time?

Did we have to wait a long time? I—to tell you the truth, I had no idea. We had a professor who lectured on hygiene, the hygiene of nutrition, personal hygiene, whatever. So I said to them: "The professor didn't tell us, so I haven't the faintest notion how long we have to wait." "Well," they asked me, "Give us an idea. How long does food . . . how long does food hang out in your stomach?" I said: "Well, it depends. Some people digest things in forty-five minutes; others take a whole hour." So, okay, we waited twenty minutes. But it smelled so good. Thirty minutes—all the guys were "dying." "Let's eat!" [She laughs.] I'll never forget it! They divided up the meat and put some in each soldier's mess tin. But I made them boil it a very long time. So, the meat of that dead horse had been thoroughly cooked, and we stuffed ourselves. We stuffed ourselves, and nobody seemed to be dying. And after all that, we heard the creak of wheels. The support services were approaching, and they had brought us food supplies captured from the Germans. Good heavens! They had brought Astrakhan roach [a fish from the Caspian sea] and butter! True, it was rancid, but just the same it was real butter. There was tobacco for the officers and *makhorka* [strong Russian tobacco] for the soldiers. They had also brought bread—true, it was stale and hard as a rock, but they'd brought it. And those who hadn't eaten any of the dead horse meat roared with laughter: "Ha-ha-ha! You gorged yourselves on a dead beast! Look what we're going to eat!" Well, so what; none of us died. Besides, we knew it was okay to eat meat from freshly killed horses. We ate it all the time. But this one had been dragged out of the stream, and who knew what came with it. So that's the permission I once gave to eat dead horse meat. That's how it was.

Vera Ivanovna, did you want to say anything more about Stalingrad?

Before the battle of Stalingrad, before they took us across the Volga to the right bank of the river—we came from the left bank, we came on foot from Sredniaia Akhtuba. They lined us up in the middle of the night, the entire regiment, and that commissar—the one I already told you about, the one who wanted to "test" me once—he lined us up and urged us to join the party. Many filled out the application forms, resting the papers on each other's backs. I don't know what they could possibly have written in the dark. And he kept saying: "Join the party, so you can die a party member."[29] And we—that is, I and the other girls in the regiment—were trying to guess the future: If we made it out of Stalingrad alive—by this time there was heavy fighting going on in the city—if we made it out of Stalingrad alive, then we would all undoubtedly live to see victory! We made this wish. But of all of us . . . There must have been about eighty women from Tomsk. We had different kinds of jobs: Some were signalwomen, others were mail carriers, what else—still others were cooks. And out of that number only about five lived to see the end of the war. And that was that.

And after Stalingrad?

And after Stalingrad, we found ourselves way, way back in the rear: When the Don front joined us, we were 340 kilometers from the front lines! Straight away it was quiet. Not one bomb fell; there wasn't a single shot. You know, it was weird! We all went deaf from the silence, strange as it may seem. We all walked around like lost souls. There was no need to duck, nothing to be afraid of.

Vera Ivanovna, let's go back a little. You didn't join the party at that time?

No, no, God forbid! It was that same commissar, who had "tested" me, who was urging us to join the party. He had already "tested" me before Stalingrad. Remember, I told you about it, how he had crawled under my skirt, and I said: "Check up on your own wife, but you have no reason to do that to me!" Yes. And I simply loathed him.

---

29. At the front, the party tried to induct as many new members as possible, especially on the eve of major battles. It was considered especially honorable to join the party under these circumstances, evidence of a person's limitless devotion to the homeland and willingness to "fight till the end, to the last drop of blood."

If you had joined the party, would you have gotten more promotions, do you think?

Absolutely. You know, after the war I worked as a physical therapist in a clinic, and they summoned me and said—one of our doctors had gone off somewhere else—and they said: "Vera Ivanovna, become a candidate for party membership." I was completely taken aback and said: "But why?" "You know, we want to make you head physician." I immediately blew up! I said: "Ah, so that's how it is. If I don't have a red cover, it means I can't be head physician? It means that my brain won't work?! And if I become a candidate for party membership, then I can become head physician?!" "Well then, so much for that." And right there, the conversation ended.

If you had been a man, do you think you would have advanced?

That I don't know. Perhaps then I would have joined the party, but not so I could have made a career for myself. I don't think I would have done it for that reason. We were brought up differently then, after all, and I looked at things differently. I really thought like a woman, and as a woman, I was really upset that men treated women that way. Although I lived . . . I'll tell you straight out: I'm not a communist. Even now many are surprised: "Is it really true you never joined the party?" And I answer: "I never did." "Vera Ivanovna, you're such an activist, you're always organizing things. Why do you live so poorly? Don't all the communists live well?" I respond: "No one has ever given me a thing. I had to trade my parents' house for this wretched room."

You mean the government didn't just give you an apartment?[30]

No, I didn't qualify for it. I was on a list for one. In the beginning, there were a thousand people ahead of me, then a hundred. Then, suddenly, I was number nineteen, and then I went back up to number ninety. And I understood that nobody was going to give me anything! Absolutely no one. Despite the fact that I was a veteran who had served at the front.

Vera Ivanovna, how did you meet your husband?

My husband and I met after the war was over. I had a lot of suitors; I received a lot of formal proposals. Matchmakers even came to see me. The suitors came, wearing their war decorations; they looked very important. But I had pretensions. I wanted someone who was bold—and not a coward. I wanted someone who appeared to be cultured, educated, so to speak.

---

30. In the postwar period, the government introduced various privileges for veterans, most important among them the right to move to the top of the waiting list for a free, government-owned apartment. Malakhova felt insulted because she never received such an apartment, despite her service at the front. She believed, probably for good reason, that it was because she never became a party member.

Malakhova in 1945

I didn't really consider myself a member of the intelligentsia, and I wanted a husband who had more education than I did, a better upbringing—that was important to me—so that I could learn from him. Well, the matchmakers kept coming, and I kept refusing.

But later I really regretted . . . when I got myself involved with this blockhead, this drunk. Well, what could I do? And he's the one who turned out to be the father of Herman, my son.

It was some kind of holiday, and they invited me, too. By this time, officers' clubs had appeared in those German towns,[31] and after all, I was a good dancer. Well, the war had ended; I had come out of it alive. Now there were dances to go to; the division had its own brass band! Lord! It was all so splendid. I was young, after all. I loved to dance! I came to the party, and I was introduced to the chief of staff, a captain. He danced with me several times there, at the officers' club. And then he said: "Vera, I'll seat you here at this table." It was somewhere off in a corner, as if I was a total nonentity, and I felt insulted. But I didn't let on that it bothered me. I was still wearing waterproof boots. Meanwhile, all the girls who had worked back at head-

---

31. At this point, Malakhova was in Germany, Soviet troops having pursued their enemy onto its home territory.

quarters were really well dressed, whereas I had on an old, worn-out military shirt, recently laundered, to be sure. Then they served ice cream to everyone, but they didn't bring any to me. After that, the chief of staff came up to me: "Why didn't they serve you any?" Now, at the party, there was one . . . She was such a preposterous creature. She even boasted that she went with the scouts on reconnaissance missions. Well, to make a long story short, they served her ice cream twice. When the chief came up to me, I pushed him away and said: "Get out of here. I don't even want to talk to you." I stood up and walked off. At that moment, the band began to play, and this man, my future husband, saw it all. He was the adjutant to the chief of staff, to this captain. Now the chief was indignant that I had pushed his hand away. He was even holding something in his hand, and it fell. I don't remember right now what it was. Perhaps it was a glass of tea, perhaps something else. And this man, my future husband, immediately invited me to dance, to cover things up, so that nobody would notice. We began to dance. He was very tall, and he was a good dancer. Well, and then I said: "Oh, take me home; see me home." I knew that he was this captain's adjutant. He said: "It isn't proper, Vera Ivanovna. After all, the captain invited you." I said: "It suits me. Take me." So he took me. He had a car; he was the chief's driver. So he drove me home. And he began to court me. He courted me, and he courted me, and he courted me.

What was his name?

Oh, Lord, I've forgotten what his name was . . . Evgenii. [She laughs.] It got to the point where I couldn't stand the sight of him. He made me so sick I even forgot his name. Well, to make a long story short, he began to drive me all the time, take me here, take me there, and he won me over. It was: "Verochka, Verochka, Verochka." Yes, that's how he did it. He didn't make a formal proposal. I simply—I don't know why—I myself moved in with him. I can't explain it. And right away I got pregnant. Right away! And then I realized that he had begun to drink. I already realized it then, there in Germany. He began to drink and really hit the bottle. And I said: "Why do you drink so much, Zhenia?" "Well, we've just won the war, and everything." What was he talking about? The victory celebration was over. Then I sensed that I'd missed my period for the second time. I wasn't menstruating. So I went to see this old man, this gynecologist who had taught me. He said: "Congratulations, Vera Ivanovna, you're three months pregnant. Are you happy?" I told him—he was like a father to me, he was already up in years—I told him everything, told him that it could have been different. I had so many suitors! Now this had happened, and I didn't want to live with him. The old doctor said: "If you have an abortion, you will be a cripple for the rest of your life." So I stayed with him. We traveled around all the towns, and I ordered a coat and a knitted dress, and this, and that, and shoes. He didn't bring any of the things home. Instead he brought home four empty suitcases. He'd spent all the money on drink. And then, when we went to live in Tomsk, Mama used to say, "Vera, what kind of husband have you found for yourself?" But a son was born. He needed a father. I thought he would come to his senses. But he . . .

Your son was born in '46?

Yes, he was born in '46. But you know, since my husband arrived in Tomsk after me, and I didn't even want to show my face in public with him, many people thought that I too had been a "W" [whore]—that's the way they referred to women who had been at the front. Unfortunately, many people thought that. And once my husband and I went to a May Day parade. And he said: "Ver, put on your military decorations." I said, "I won't put them on." "Put them on. You're going with me, you earned them. I know everything there is to know about you, and you earned them honorably. Put them on!" Well, I had the Order of the Red Star, the Order of the Great Patriotic War, and various other medals. I didn't put on my medals; I only put on my decorations. And what do you think happened: We were coming back from the demonstration, and my husband lagged behind. And I ran into some man who said, "Ah, here comes a frontline W." My husband went up to him and punched him right in the face! And the sidewalk was next to a ravine, and this man fell right into the ravine. "You, creep, don't you ever insult a woman again!" That's the only thing that was good about him. And I lived with him for four years, and Mama used to say, "Either get rid of him or get out of my sight." I tried to leave Tomsk with him, but nothing came of it. He continued to carry on the same way. We left for Central Asia, and I got pregnant a second time. I had nothing to prevent it. I thought: This is terrible! When I gave birth to my son, I had had to have an operation under anesthesia, and I barely survived it. I had gone through such an ordeal giving birth to my son. I thought: and now . . . that's it. I'll die. I said: "Take me home, take me." "I won't take you." I said: "That's it. Tomorrow I'll go and hang myself on the first post. You know me!" So he was forced to take me. And I went back to Mama, and here in Tomsk I had an abortion.

Did you have to have an illegal abortion?

Yes. To begin with, I summoned a midwife to teach me how to use a soap solution. I knew someone who was a very good midwife. She made me douche with a soap solution. Then the contractions began, and I started to bleed. As soon as I began to bleed, we could call an ambulance—now it wouldn't be considered an abortion. Once the bleeding started, who knew what had caused it. Of course, I lied and said that I had lifted something very heavy.[32]

---

32. She engaged in this dangerous procedure in order to evade the regulations outlawing abortion.

Malakhova at a Victory Day celebration in 1974

Where did you give birth to your son?

I had my son here in Tomsk in a clinic. And when my husband came for me, he practically had to carry me home in his arms. With one arm he held the baby, and with the other he held me by the waist, because I couldn't even walk. I had had a terrible operation. They gave me an overdose of anesthesia, and I turned a lemony-yellow color. How I survived, I don't know! In the first place, everything ripped! I had to have a lot of stitches! They put in eighteen stitches: on the perineum, on the vagina, on the cervix. Everything was torn!

Was the baby very large?

Well, I had an "operation" where they used large metal forceps, like these, so they could pull the baby out by the head. They did it all with these forceps! There was a Jewish woman doctor[33] there; they sent for her in the middle of the night. I had already been in labor for several days, and I could no longer do anything. I was completely exhausted, and apparently I

---

33. Malakhova often identified people by their ethnicity—far more than this chapter would suggest, because many of these ethnic references occurred in sections that we omitted. Unlike this reference, most of these were positive: a "wonderful Jewish doctor"; a "beautiful gypsy woman," and so on. At the very least, this custom indicates that even kind and open-minded Russians may perceive non-Russian national identity as an important characteristic of the people they encountered.

Malakhova at a Victory Day celebration in 1996

was beginning to lose consciousness. They summoned her in the middle of the night, and she got angry! At first they gave me just a little anesthesia, and in a state of agitation I broke all the straps, tore them apart. So she said, "Give her the whole bottle."

Why were there straps?

Well, they used straps to tie your hands and feet to the operating table.[34] And this doctor said, "Give her the entire bottle!" I was still conscious for that. And they gave me too much and overdosed me.

And what was in the bottle?

They used ether then, ether. An awful anesthesia! Well, that's how I gave birth to my son. It was such an ordeal! And after that, to have more children . . .

Vera Ivanovna, you never got married again?

No, I never did. For some reason I took it very hard that I never found the equal of the man who died in my arms in Stalingrad, this Georgii Antonovich Khukhlaev. All in all, things never worked out for me.

---

34. Birth without painkillers was the norm in the Soviet Union at that time. To keep women in pain from resisting physicians' efforts to assist at childbirth, the women were sometimes strapped down.

Vera Ivanovna, what would you wish for yourself today?

Only for good health. I want to accomplish so much, I want to do more for my division. After the war, I did all I could to bring glory to my division. Now they spit on us veterans in every way they can. Still, I would fight . . . especially on behalf of women. Because we are dying, because it's not right that they labeled women who were at the front—excuse me, but I'll come right out and say it—whores. They don't deserve to be called that, they weren't like that. There were very few FCWs, and most of those lived with one man, with just one person. There weren't very many who were really dissolute. There were some, but they were exceptions. We women lived honorably and fought honorably.

It's too bad there isn't more time. I could tell you so much more! But no one's interested. Journalists always latched onto one thing. "That's all, Vera Ivanovna, that's all."[35] They always wrote some tiny article. Wham, bang, and that was it. Nobody is interested. Absolutely nobody is interested now. And we are dying out. Most of us are gone. We are the last. And that's that.

---

35. Every year, Soviet newspapers and journals published articles to commemorate the anniversary of victory over the Germans in World War II. Journalists often interviewed veterans, but they inquired only about a relatively narrow range of topics that conformed to official representations of the war effort.

◈ Afterword: Evaluating the Soviet Experience

The narratives presented on the preceding pages reflect the diverse lives and experiences of ordinary Soviet people; but despite their variety, they have in common the fact that they are *women's* narratives. The events of the Soviet era sometimes affected women differently than men. In addition, the government intentionally undertook policies relating to women, the family, and children that affected women directly.

In our introduction, we emphasized the negative aspects of the stories told in these pages, which seemed to us unavoidable: The carnage of the civil war, the expropriation and persecution of kulaks, and the terror of the 1930s were real-life events, and not one of our narrators escaped their impact. How can one ignore the terrible personal price that was paid for the public achievements of the Soviet era? Yet taken as a group these interviews paint a more complex and even contradictory picture, at least from the viewpoint of women who did not themselves suffer imprisonment or exile and who had survived to a ripe, albeit in some cases impoverished, old age. For some, suffering and repression remained at the heart of their story; others apparently learned to find their way in the system and came to embrace its values, even when this required that they efface aspects of their own pasts. Antonina Berezhnaia, who lost her noble status and was evicted from her father's estate, became a heroine of production and came to identify almost exclusively with her role in the workplace. Sofia Pavlova, the most successful of our narrators, mentioned almost in passing the loss of her beloved second husband during the late 1930s. Although Elena Ponomarenko's accession to the demands of her superiors brought the death of her beloved mother, it did not shake her faith in the Soviet system. In their interviews, these women chose to emphasize what the system offered them and to take pride in what they achieved rather than to dwell on the sacrifices they made.

The women's responses make it impossible to assess their narratives solely within the framework of Western feminism or their lives simply in terms of "advances" or "equality." In the introduction to this book, we emphasized increased opportunities for women to play a public role, their continued secondary status in the workplace, and the personal price exacted for public progress; but some of these women would no doubt argue with our emphasis on personal cost, and most would object to an interpretation that stresses women's secondary status. They certainly did when Anastasia Posadskaya interviewed them. Armed with questions we devised beforehand that were rooted in our feminist perspective, Posadskaya frequently encountered incomprehension and outright resistance in her subjects. They had difficulty thinking about their lives in the terms she presented to them. Perhaps the many years of Soviet propaganda insisting that men and women were perfectly equal and that women enjoyed all the rights that men did made it difficult for them to adopt a different perspective; or perhaps they had learned to accept the rigid gender stereotyping that reemerged in Soviet society during the 1930s. Even as they spoke of themselves as exceptional, the women embraced those very gender distinctions that make the care of home and family almost exclusively a woman's responsibility: "You mustn't forget that a woman has a family, that in the final analysis she is the source of the family," Pavlova explained. In response to Anastasia's question about how being a woman affected her life, Pavlova said that people did not always treat her like a woman: "They demanded from me the same things that they demanded from a man," she insisted. In reply to a similar question, Elena Ponomarenko answered that she should have been born a man, that she had often dressed like a man, wore a hat like a man, and had calloused hands like a man's. With the exception of Malakhova and Berezhnaia, however, the women were reluctant to consider that being a woman might have had negative effects on their professional life. Even when evidence of their inequitable treatment in the workplace emerged in the course of their interviews, most denied that gender was a contributing factor to such inequities. They were more likely to use their gender to beg off social responsibilities than to see it as an obstacle to their social advancement.

At the same time, most of the women embraced a key element of Soviet ideology—that contributing to production and working for the public good were of utmost importance—and they apparently derived genuine satisfaction from their participation in public life. Almost all viewed work as intrinsically valuable and as a source of their own self-realization. They were also gratified by the support and recognition of their peers in the workplace. Fleisher, for one, rejected outright her husband's belief that women's place should be in the family, and she refused to leave her job: "And it seems to me my children didn't lose out because I worked all my life," she said. "After all, they saw that I was not only a mama, that I bore not only the cares of the family. They saw that despite these obligations I had made something of myself, that people respected me, took me seriously, and for them, you know, that meant a great deal." Whatever limitations these women experienced, the Soviet period in fact opened doors for most of them. Rather than dwelling on how much farther they might have gone, they were instead glad of the gains they had made. Most of our respondents expressed pride in their public achievements. In general, Soviet women participated in public life to a much greater degree than did women of the same generation in the West. A few of the women found work a creative outlet: Dubova took pleasure in decorating cakes; Berezhnaia became an inventor; Fleisher wrote textbooks for the minority peoples she taught. The others found similar ways to express themselves creatively outside the workplace. Dolgikh collected and published a book of folk riddles and Malakhova wrote poetry, as did others whose stories have not been included here.

Despite the generalizations we have made about women's experiences, the narratives themselves make clear that one cannot speak or write of "Soviet women" or even of "Russian women in the Soviet period" as if they all held identical expectations or lived identical lives. Although our selection of narrators was more or less random and their stories do not directly reflect important negative dimensions of Soviet experience, such as internment in the camps or the persecution of minority groups, their lives are nevertheless enormously varied. They demonstrate the variable effects of state policy and the importance of individual character as well as of gender and family and social situation in shaping a person's life course, even in Soviet society, where life was intensively regimented and personal choice narrowly circumscribed. For all the commonalities engendered by their womanhood and motherhood, each of these women experienced a revolution that was uniquely her own.

✸ On Choices,
Methods,
and Silences

The eight narrators whose stories compose this book were located and interviewed by Anastasia Posadskaya-Vanderbeck. She received vital assistance in this effort from women in Tomsk, Ekaterinburg, and Novozybkov, who are part of a network connected to the Moscow Center for Gender Studies, which Posadskaya directed until a few years ago. Informed of Posadskaya's search for "ordinary" women who had lived through the entire Soviet period, these contacts identified women who might be willing to speak with her. They also arranged for Posadskaya's lodging in their towns and helped her to gain access to the homes of potential narrators, in itself a difficult matter, as nowadays people do not readily open their doors to strangers for fear of being assaulted. Because we wanted to learn about women's family life as well as their public experience, we sought as narrators women who had married and borne children. We also hoped to include a range of educational, occupational, and social backgrounds, including at least one worker, one peasant, one physician, and one teacher, medicine and education generally being considered the most feminized of Soviet professions. We planned to avoid the narratives of "heroines" because we feared they would be too close to conventional, Soviet-style biography, and we did not actively seek out stories either of success or of suffering. Instead, within the limitations inherent in any network of contacts, our operating principle was to identify as wide a range of experiences as we could for ethnic Russian women born before 1917.

The realities we encountered proved much less straightforward than we had envisioned. Posadskaya's initial appeal for assistance yielded many potential interviewees, but when we approached them, the majority refused an interview outright. Others, after initially agreeing, changed their minds when Posadskaya tried to arrange a meeting. This pattern strikingly contrasts with that observed by Alison Owings, who interviewed German women about their experiences of the Nazi period and found every one eager to speak, including a woman who had once served as concentration camp guard. However, the Nazi period lasted twelve years and ended in

1945, whereas the Soviet experience continued for many decades and formally ended only recently, in 1991. The reasons for these women's refusals are no doubt rooted in the particular nature of Soviet history, in which the official version of the past has been the only acceptable one, and alternative versions have been persecuted at least since the 1920s, making the very act of remembering dangerous. People were sometimes suspicious of Posadskaya's motives: Why was she asking these questions? Could she possibly be an agent of the KGB, the secret police? In addition to fear, they often showed pain and trauma at remembering. Women sometimes would be so overcome by emotion that they could not speak. The most dramatic instance of this occurred when Posadskaya showed up to interview a World War II veteran living in a retirement home. The woman greeted her with apparent eagerness, having gotten herself all dressed up for the occasion and pinned on all her medals; but when the interview began, the woman lapsed into silence, tears streaming down her cheeks, her lips trembling as she struggled to catch her breath. Posadskaya waited quite awhile, but the woman never regained sufficient composure to participate in the interview, and Posadskaya eventually had to leave without it. Even women who proved both willing and able to share their stories often became very agitated as they confronted their painful pasts, and many wept during their interviews.

While some dealt with their pain or fear by remaining completely silent, others practiced the art of silence selectively. This was often the case with peasant women who had lived all their lives in the village, where people for centuries have been suspicious of the motives of outsiders. Posadskaya interviewed about a dozen peasant women, all but one of whom never lowered their guard. Instead of rejecting an interview outright, they would agree to it and then reveal absolutely nothing about themselves. They would give very brief answers to questions, often in a tone of surprise, as if they wondered why Posadskaya even asked such a question, or as if the answer went without saying. For example, when she would ask, Were you born in this village, they would answer, Yes, of course, or Of course not, with an interrogative intonation, as if Posadskaya should somehow have known this already. Or they would choose a safe subject, such as their relations with a family member or a story they had heard from someone else, and stick with it. Irina Kniazeva, who tells her story in these pages in exceedingly condensed and unadorned language, was the most eloquent of these peasant respondents.

Silence, however, is an important component of all these interviews. Some narrators refused to speak of painful events or mentioned them only elliptically and then changed the subject. Others provided external details but no indication of what the experience felt like. Sometimes we learned about key events only at the very end of the interview, when the narrator had become more comfortable; at other times, painful events remained outside the framework of the narrative. Dealing with these silences and omissions has been one of our most challenging tasks in assembling this book. We wanted at all costs to avoid putting words into our narrators' mouths. On the other hand, we did not want to mislead the reader by ignoring contradictions in an interview or sections where a narrator skipped over a well-known event or misrepresented something in the past. We have resolved this dilemma in part by adding footnotes, which we have used to point the reader's attention to silences, contradictions, or what seem to be deliberate misinterpretations of questions or events. We also have used footnotes to explain or amplify a particular point or to comment on the narrator's language, on the forms of her speech and thought.

Like other matters, the question of Russian ethnicity turned out to be more complex than we had anticipated. Some of the women who tell their stories in these pages are Russians only in the broader sense of the tsarist adjective *Rossiiskie*, which included all of the various populations that made up the prerevolutionary empire—a "Russianness" that is probably as common today as the more narrowly ethnic one. Thus, Pavlova is of Polish extraction, Ponomarenko of Ukrainian, and Malakhova of Belorussian. All spoke Russian as their native language. We decided against using an interview with a Tatar woman because she had some trouble speaking Russian and because her experience reflected particularities of her culture that we would have had trouble contextualizing. We also excluded an interview with a woman of German extraction who had suffered exile and penal servitude during the war years, because as we read over the transcript, it became clear to us that the woman had agreed to the interview unwillingly and only as a result of lingering fears of those in authority, one of whom Posadskaya appeared to be. It seemed unethical to use an interview conducted under duress. Finally, although we had sought an interview with a Jewish woman, we decided not to use the one we obtained because the woman, a physician, resisted identifying herself as Jewish, and her narrative proved disappointing in other respects, lacking the depth and substance of other interviews.

Anastasia Posadskaya conducted interviews in four locations—Moscow, Tomsk, Ekaterinburg, and Novozybkov—and in villages nearby. Apart from Moscow, Russia's largest city, she chose those sites because they were in some sense "typical," because her women's network provided access there to potential narrators, and because our financial resources did not permit extensive travel. Tomsk is an old Russian city in the middle of Siberia, a place of exile both before the revolution and in Soviet times. It is surrounded by former camps and current correctional facilities. Before the revolution, relatively well-to-do peasants also lived in the area. With four university-level institutions, Tomsk has long been one of the main educational centers in Siberia, a place to which young people came to take ad-

vantage of the new opportunities for education that the revolution introduced. Ekaterinburg, called Sverdlovsk in Soviet times, is a huge industrial
city in the Ural mountains. It is a region rich in natural resources and was a
center of industrial production both before and after the revolution. It
seemed an excellent place to explore women's participation in the industrial
labor force. Posadskaya also interviewed people in the surrounding region,
in the town of Zarechnyi and in three villages. Novozybkov is a small town
in southwestern Russia, close to the Belarus border. Before the revolution,
the town was within the boundaries of the pale of settlement to which most
Jews were restricted. Posadskaya hoped to learn something about Jewish
life in these interviews and also about women's experiences of occupation,
because the town was occupied by the Germans during World War II.
Moreover, Novozybkov is very different from the other towns she selected:
It is semirural, with only a two-year pedagogical college and no institutions
of higher education, and it has no real industry, apart from a single, small
factory outside of town. Posadskaya conducted twelve interviews in this
area, but none of the interviewees were forthcoming about their lives, so we
have included none of their narratives in this book.

We worked together closely in selecting, editing, and annotating the interviews. Each of us separately read through all of the transcripts and listened to the tapes of all twenty-five narratives. We agreed at once that
many were too fragmentary or superficial to meet our standards, and we
quickly narrowed the choice to twelve possibilities. We then sat down side
by side and went through each of the twelve transcripts together, reading
each sentence aloud in Russian, then probing its meaning and significance
to the narrative as a whole. If we were already fairly certain that an interview would be included, we made preliminary cuts at this time, discarding
sections that did not add substantially to the narrative. We also began editing and noting places where footnotes were needed. In the process of making sense of a difficult section for the purpose of assisting the translator, we
sometimes uncovered silences or complex meanings that we had overlooked when we had read the transcript by ourselves. Exploring these difficult passages led us into rich and wide-ranging discussions that contributed
vitally to this book's introductory chapter, the brief introductions to the interviews, the afterword, and the footnotes. We worked through all twelve
transcripts in this fashion. The process led us to eliminate four interviews,
three of them (of a Tatar, a Jew, and a German) for the reasons noted
above. The fourth, the narrative of another physician, we eliminated because we thought it added nothing to the picture provided by the other narrators we had selected. After this preliminary reading and editing, we carefully reread the eight interviews we had chosen and fine-tuned the editing,
in some cases making further cuts, in others restoring material, and in addition, ensuring that our cuts did not deprive the narrative of coherence.
Once again, our close reading yielded insights into the text and stimulated

illuminating conversations. The process of selection and editing lasted about two and a half months. When we completed work on each narrative, we sent it to Sona Hoisington, our translator. We began to receive completed translations from her about three months after we commenced our work. These translations were excellent on the whole, but because Hoisington did not have Posadskaya's insider's feel for the nuances and subtexts of the spoken language, we decided to edit the translations as well. Each chapter went through a painstaking review in which Posadskaya would read aloud the original Russian, Engel would read the English translation, and together we would decide whether the translation captured the meaning. In most cases it had; but when it missed the mark, we would explore the original Russian until we arrived at a more satisfactory variant. This process unexpectedly unearthed further hidden meanings, which likewise contributed to our framing of the narratives. We then sent the corrections to Sona Hoisington, who either incorporated them or offered a superior alternative, drawing not only on her considerable skill as a translator but also on her impressive knowledge of Russian and Soviet culture and society.

Of the twenty-five successful interviews, we chose the eight that appear in this book because they were the most diverse, offering the broadest variety of perspectives on key issues of Soviet history and women's experiences. We included Irina Kniazeva's interview because we felt it was crucial to have an interview with at least one peasant woman. Not only did peasants represent a key sector of the population in terms of their numbers, but the very success of the revolution depended to a significant extent on the government's ability to transform peasants' outlook and way of life. Illiterate all her life and lacking access to radio and television until just a few years ago when she moved to a city, Kniazeva remained largely outside the Soviet value system, retaining a peasant consciousness. We selected the narrative of Sofia Pavlova because hers was so clearly one of the "success stories" of the revolution, that of a bright, energetic, working-class girl who benefited immensely from the government's efforts to advance women. Likewise, the narrative of Elena Ponomarenko appears in the book because it, too, demonstrates the opportunities the revolution made available to women and men of humble origins: A peasant by birth, Ponomarenko became a journalist, with only seven years of education. The life of Vera Malakhova, a working-class girl who became a physician, might also be said to reflect the new opportunities for lower-class women. But we chose her narrative for other reasons, too. By contrast with Pavlova and Ponomarenko, who remain loyal communists to this day, Malakhova has adopted an ambivalent, often critical attitude toward the Soviet period. Moreover, she spent four years at the front during World War II, and her narrative sheds fascinating light on women's frontline experiences. We included the four remaining narratives because each illustrates the consequences of the Soviet government's persecution of individuals on the basis of their social origins as well as the variety of strategies that women adopted to cope. Anna Dubova, the daughter of a deeply religious and comparatively well-off peasant family, fled the assault against the kulaks, married to conceal her origins, and became a factory worker, as did millions of other uprooted peasants during the 1930s. Elena Dolgikh was less successful. Persecution on account of her alleged kulak background poisoned her personal life and almost kept her from practicing the profession of schoolteacher. Vera Fleisher, the daughter of a Russian Orthodox priest, belonged to another persecuted group, the clergy, but she also married a well-paid physician who served in the army, and her narrative provides glimpses into the way of life and attitudes of the Soviet middle class. Finally, Antonina Berezhnaia, the daughter of a nobleman whose family lost everything in the revolution, managed to transform herself into an exemplary worker and a stalwart supporter of the government. Her interview is the only one to mention the widespread hostility women encountered when they entered male-dominated professions.

Our desire to present a broad variety of perspectives on Soviet history and women's experiences also guided our decisions as to which parts of the interviews to retain and which to cut. We chose to maintain a question-and-answer format in order to make clear when the interviewee was following her own line of reasoning and when she was prompted to speak of something in response to our agenda; however, where questions were raised to clarify a point or where Posadskaya's comments were merely responding to the narrative, we omitted her part of the dialogue. In some cases, we also greatly abbreviated Posadskaya's questions in order to avoid drawing attention away from the narrator. In consequence, Posadskaya's artful questioning, which sometimes prompted our narrators to speak of difficult or painful things, has been unintentionally obscured. For example, Posadskaya succeeded in eliciting some of the women's testimony about underground abortion only after talking at considerable length about her own and other women's experiences.

The desire to preserve and enhance the variety of the narratives also led us to eliminate repetition among the stories in the form of similar references to contemporary circumstances, and to omit many lengthy discussions of the lives and fates of relatives and friends. Thus, for instance, we cut descriptions of the origins and social roles of ancestors, the occupations and personal relations of brothers and sisters, and in Malakhova's case, the personalities of many women and men with whom she worked at the front. We eliminated this material because we wanted to include all eight interviews and we feared that too long a book might not find a publisher. We therefore deliberately chose to focus primarily on the events that our subjects themselves experienced. This decision, however, had the unavoidable consequences of exaggerating the apparent self-involvement of our subjects and of overemphasizing the "I-ness" of their narratives at the expense of their "we-ness."

In all our editing and cutting, we have tried to preserve the flow of the narrator's thought as much as possible. In a few cases, we have moved material around to enhance cohesiveness or to provide a transition; in a few others, we have shifted a statement to the end of an interview because it seemed to provide a perfect conclusion.

In order to make the text more readable, we have omitted the customary bracketed ellipses that would have indicated cuts. This book contains only a portion of each interview: We cut approximately two-thirds of the Dubova interview, half of Pavlova's, half of Fleisher's, one-third of Berezhnaia's, half of Kniazeva's, four-fifths of Ponomarenko's, half of Dolgikh's, and two-thirds of Malakhova's. The complete, unedited Russian transcripts of these eight interviews as well as of the four we elected not to use are available at the Hoover Institution in Palo Alto, California, as are the tapes of all twenty-five interviews.

Selected Bibliography

Atkinson, Dorothy, Alexander Dallin, and Gail Warshofsky Lapidus, eds. *Women in Russia*. Stanford, 1977.

Attwood, Lynn. *The New Soviet Man and Woman: Sex-Role Socialization in the USSR*. Bloomington, Ind., 1990.

Barber, John and Mark Harrison. *The Soviet Home Front, 1941–1945*. London and New York, 1991.

Boym, Svetlana. *Common Places: Mythologies of Everyday Life in Russia*. Cambridge, Mass., 1994.

Bridger, Susan. *Women in the Soviet Countryside: Women's Roles in Rural Development in the Soviet Union*. Cambridge, England, 1987.

Buckley, Mary. *Women and Ideology in the Soviet Union*. Ann Arbor, Mich., 1989.

Clements, Barbara Evans. *Bolshevik Women*. New York and Cambridge, England, 1997.

Clements, Barbara Evans, Barbara Alpern Engel, and Christine Worobec, eds. *Russia's Women: Accommodation, Resistance, Transformation*. Berkeley and Los Angeles, 1991.

Conquest, Robert. *Harvest of Sorrow: Soviet Collectivization and the Terror-Famine*. New York and Oxford, 1986.

Dodge, Norton. *Women in the Soviet Economy: Their Role in the Economic, Scientific, and Technical Development*. Baltimore, 1966.

Dunham, Vera. *In Stalin's Time: Middle-class Values in Soviet Fiction*. Durham, N.C. and London, 1990.

Fitzpatrick, Sheila. *The Russian Revolution: 1917–1932*. New York and Oxford, 1994.

———. *Stalin's Peasants: Resistance and Survival in the Russian Village After Collectivization*. New York and Oxford, 1994.

Garros, Veronique, Natalia Korenevskaya, and Thomas Lahusen, eds. *Intimacy and Terror: Soviet Diaries of the 1930s*. New York, 1995.

Getty, J. Arch, and Roberta T. Manning. *Stalinist Terror: New Perspectives*. New York and Cambridge, 1993.

Ginzburg, Eugenia Semyonovna. *Journey into the Whirlwind*. New York and London, 1967.

Goldman, Wendy Ziva. *Women, the State, and Revolution: Soviet Family Policy and Social Life, 1917–1936*. New York and Cambridge, 1993.

Goscilo, Helena, and Beth Holmgren, eds. *Russia, Women, Culture*. Bloomington, Ind., 1996.

Hansson, Carola, and Karin Liden. *Moscow Women*. New York, 1983.

Holland, Barbara, ed. *Soviet Sisterhood*. Bloomington, Ind., 1996.

Hosking, Geoffrey. *The First Socialist Society: A History of the Soviet Union from Within*. Cambridge, Mass., 1985.

Kollontai, Alexandra. *Selected Writings.* Translated and with an introduction by Alix Holt. Westport, Conn., 1978.

Lapidus, Gail Warshofsky. *Women in Soviet Society: Equality, Development, and Social Change.* Berkeley and Los Angeles, 1985.

Sacks, Michael. *Women's Work in Soviet Russia: Continuity in the Midst of Change.* New York, 1976.

Schlesinger, Rudolph, ed. *The Family in the USSR: Documents and Readings.* London, 1949.

Stites, Richard. *The Women's Liberation Movement in Russia: Feminism, Nihilism, and Bolshevism, 1860–1930.* Princeton, 1978.

Index